DO YOU KNOW WHERE YOUR CHILDREN ARE?

"Do you know what people are thinking every time these teenage terrorists appear on the television screen being led from courthouse to jail? They think, 'But these girls look so normal.'

"There is the one whose hair could have been painted by Botticelli, whose wardrobe is the sort compiled only through serious mall time. We're repelled by the horrible crime, and then we're confused by the young and immaculate murderess. And that name—not even a bad novelist would call a heartless villain Melinda Loveless."

—Jim Adams, columnist, *Louisville Courier-Journal*

"Who am I, you may wonder. I am someone you know well. Yourself."

—convicted teenage killer Laurie Tackett

LITTLE LOST ANGEL

MICHAEL QUINLAN

POCKET BOOKS

New York   London   Toronto   Sydney   Tokyo   Singapore

An *Original* Publication of POCKET BOOKS

POCKET BOOKS, a division of Simon & Schuster Inc.
1230 Avenue of the Americas, New York, NY 10020

ISBN: 0-671-88468-9

First Pocket Books printing February 1995

10 9 8 7 6 5 4 3 2

POCKET and colophon are registered trademarks of Simon & Schuster Inc.

Cover photos: background photo, "The Witches' Castle," by Paul Schuhmann from the *Courier-Journal;* inset photo by Interstate Studio

Printed in the U.S.A.

For Jacque and Steve
and in memory of
Shanda

ACKNOWLEDGMENTS

Many people deserve my thanks but none more than Detective Steve Henry and Prosecutor Guy Townsend. Their graciousness never wavered during my lengthy interviews and my dozens of phone calls to their homes and offices.

My appreciation to Judge Ted Todd and his staff, especially Jenny Redwine. Thanks to Sheriff Buck Shipley, Sgt. Curtis Wells, Deputy Randy Spry, *Madison Courier* reporter Wayne Engle, photographer Joe Trotter, and attorneys Russ Johnson, Wil Goering, and Bob Donald. Also thanks to Donn Foley, Marc Botts, and everyone else who helped me gather the facts, and to Eileen and Mike for their computer help.

At the *Louisville Courier-Journal*, thanks to editors Hunt Helm and Karen Merk, reporters Pam Runquist and David Goetz, and the photo and library staffs.

Thanks to my literary agent, Ann Rittenberg, and my editors at Pocket Books, Claire Zion and Amy Einhorn, for guiding me through uncharted waters.

And thanks to my family for their love and support.

Most of all, thanks to Jacque and Steve and the rest of Shanda's family for sharing their memories and friendship.

AUTHOR'S NOTE

This is a true story. In order to tell it in narrative form I re-created some dialogue and descriptive details from my interviews with one or more of the people involved or from police reports, depositions, and court testimonies.

All of the names, places, dates, and events in this book are real.

Jealousy is cruel as the grave; the coals thereof are coals for fire, which hath a most vehement flame.

—Song of Solomon 8:6, Old Testament

Prologue

Under cover of darkness, the blood-stained sedan moved slowly along the narrow, winding roads of the southern Indiana countryside. With each turn the car's headlights threw a momentary flash of illumination through a black forest of pines, hickories, and elms. The silence of the cold winter night was marred by the constant growl of the sedan's broken tailpipe.

As a pair of headlights approached from the other direction, the driver let up on the gas, easing the tailpipe's rumble. It might be a police car, and they couldn't take the chance of being stopped for a noisy muffler. A nosy cop might notice the scarlet handprints on the trunk or find the bloody tire iron lying under the seat. Holding their breath, the driver and front-seat passenger watched the car pass them by. The driver's steely eyes shifted to the rear-view mirror, following the car's tail lights until they disappeared over a hill.

The sedan picked up speed as it passed through a small town with the biblical name of Canaan, then entered the woods again and drove deeper into the darkness. They drove for hours, searching the edges of the road for a place to dump the body of the twelve-year-old girl locked in the trunk.

Tired of arguing, they traveled now in silence. The driver, a hard-edged blonde, had wanted to throw the body off a bridge into a creek. But the passenger, a slim brunette, had called the driver a fool. "Don't you know she'll float."

They were far from Canaan, in a stretch of deep woods, when they heard a noise barely audible over the tailpipe's roar, a soft thumping coming from the trunk.

The blonde stopped the car in the middle of the road and left the engine idling. She pulled the trunk key from the key chain and reached under the seat for the tire iron, then stepped out into the cold air. She instructed the brunette to slide over behind the steering wheel. "Rev it," she said, "in case she screams again."

The blonde walked stiffly, purposefully, to the rear of the car and opened the trunk where Shanda Sharer lay imprisoned, still clinging to life.

1

Shanda Sharer's normally neat bedroom was in disarray. The closet door hung open, and skirts, blouses, and jeans were strewn about. A cassette tape of Mariah Carey blared in the background as the twelve-year-old primped in front of her mirror, studying her latest outfit from every angle. After three years of drab Catholic school uniforms, she was in a tizzy deciding what to wear the next day—her first day at Hazelwood Junior High.

"Ta-da!" Shanda announced as she slowly descended the stairway, mimicking the elegant style of a Paris fashion model.

Jacque Ott turned her attention from the television and smiled in appreciation at her daughter, something she'd done a dozen times that night. "That's it. I like that one best," she said with a hint of finality, hoping her daughter would get the point. The modeling had dragged on for hours, and Jacque was eager for Shanda to go to bed.

"Me too," Shanda said with a sigh, relieved to have finally settled on the perfect ensemble for her debut into Hazelwood society.

Putting things away wasn't nearly as much fun as getting

them out. Exhausted, Shanda flopped onto her bed and reached for her diary.

"Well, this year I'm going to a different school," she wrote. "I'm sort of scared I won't fit in because I heard that there were hoods, pretty girls, and 'all-that' guys. I wish my mom would understand that I don't want to be twelve. I want to be thirteen. I wish I could tell everyone at Hazelwood I'm thirteen but I know my mom won't go along with it."

Shanda could easily have pulled off such a charade. She'd just celebrated her twelfth birthday that June and was already losing the awkwardness of adolescence. She had a trim, athletic figure, long blond hair, dark eyebrows, wide hazel eyes, and a dimpled smile. These pleasant attributes had not gone unnoticed by the boys at her previous school, St. Paul Catholic. They'd flirted with all their young charms and she'd enjoyed the attention, often giggling about the young Romeos with her girlfriends.

But that seemed so long ago now. She and her mother had moved across the Ohio River from Louisville, Kentucky, to the small town of New Albany, Indiana, and tomorrow she would walk into an unfamiliar school filled with unfamiliar faces. Through her uncertainty, Shanda clung to the thought that her life would be so much easier if she were only a little older.

"I love my mom very much but she doesn't understand how much I want to be thirteen and have people spend the night on school nights," Shanda wrote. "I can't talk on the phone past ten. At everybody else's house I can but not here. I love my mom but sometimes she doesn't understand. But I still love her!!!!!!"

Shanda had slipped the diary under her bed and was snuggled beneath the covers when Jacque entered the room and sat down beside her. For what must have been the tenth time that day, Shanda lamented, "I don't know anybody at Hazelwood." Then she asked the usual follow-up question: "Mom, do you think everybody will like me?"

Shanda was exaggerating a bit when she said she wouldn't know anyone. Her cousin Amanda Edrington went to Hazelwood, and just the day before Shanda had met a girl in the neighborhood, Kristie Farnsley, who was also starting the seventh grade there.

"You'll meet friends just like you did at St. Paul," Jacque assured her. "You've never had any problem making friends. You know that."

The comforting words seemed to ease Shanda's worries. Jacque didn't let on that she too had reservations about Hazelwood Junior High.

Shanda had thrived at St. Paul, where she'd made good grades, had many friends, and participated in cheerleading, volleyball, gymnastics, 4H, and Girl Scouts. But Jacque worried that Shanda would be lost in the crowd at Hazelwood, which had twice as many students in just the seventh and eighth grades than St. Paul had in the entire school. She'd wanted to enroll Shanda at Our Lady of Perpetual Help in New Albany, but the tuition was more than she could afford. She'd just gotten divorced—for the third time—and money was scarce.

Jacque's first marriage had been to her high-school sweetheart, Mike Boardman. Their marriage had lasted only two years after their daughter, Paije, was born. Her second marriage had been to Shanda's father, Steve Sharer, and she still thought of her early years with Steve as the best times of her life. But that marriage too had ended in failure.

Shanda was seven when Jacque had married Ronnie Ott, who, at forty-one, was ten years older than Jacque and offered the financial security that she felt she and her two daughters needed. That marriage had fallen apart after four years, and now Jacque, an attractive thirty-six-year-old blonde, was once again a single mother. Paije, now nineteen, lived with Jacque's sister, Debbie, in an apartment across the street from Jacque's townhouse. Despite the differences that had led to their divorce, Jacque remained on friendly terms with Steve Sharer, who had remarried and now lived with his wife, Sharon, and her two children in nearby Jeffersonville. They saw each other at Shanda's school activities. Shanda's home life was as stable as could be expected for a child with divorced parents. She enjoyed her visits to her father's house and was pleased that she and her mother now lived so close to Paije.

"Shanda was thrilled about her and I having our own place," Jacque said. "She used to say that we were roommates. I think it made her feel grown up."

Hazelwood Junior High School sat behind New Albany High School in a neighborhood of older, well-kept, wood-frame houses. A military cemetery was just south of the school. From the third-floor windows of the main classroom building, students could see the hundreds of identical white gravestones, arranged in neat rows, that marked the resting places of New Albany's war dead from the Civil War through Vietnam.

One of three public junior highs in the city of 30,000, Hazelwood drew many of its eight hundred students from blue-collar areas on the east side of town. The parents of most students worked in Louisville or in the stores and light industry of New Albany or its two sister cities, Clarksville and Jeffersonville. The three cities, nestled together on the Indiana side of the Ohio River, shared common boundaries and were so alike in size and character that visitors from Louisville often confused one with the other.

Their joint chamber of commerce referred to the three as the "Sunny Side" of Louisville. But actually there was a sense of living in Louisville's shadow. The interstates that flowed through all three towns brought fast-food restaurants and motels, but southern Indiana residents turned to Louisville for its television and radio stations, concerts, plays, and fine dining.

Many New Albany residents felt as if they had the best of both worlds. They could buy a house in a nice tree-lined neighborhood for half what it would cost in Louisville. If they wanted culture they could cross the river to see a touring company performing *Phantom of the Opera* at Louisville's Center for the Arts. But more likely they'd spend their weekend nights at the local high school, watching their own or a neighbor's son play basketball in front of five thousand cheering fans.

Unlike the rougher areas of Louisville, they could walk any street in New Albany at any hour without fear of muggers. There was an ease to life here. At lunchtime on weekdays, downtown office workers nodded to each other as they crossed paths on their way to cafeterias and delis. An old-fashioned wooden Indian stood guard outside the only tobacco shop in town—a shop that sold as many baseball cards as it did cigars.

New Albany, Indiana, was a slice of small-town America. A town that went to sleep early, woke up early, and yawned frequently. A town seemingly immune to the violence that filled bigger cities. A town in which people took life as it came and raised their children without fear.

When Shanda came home after her first day of school she was brimming with good news. She loved Hazelwood. Her teachers were nice, and she had already met some friendly boys and girls.

"Shanda was just glowing," Jacque said later. "She seemed so happy. I thought, Well, I sure wasted a lot of time worrying about nothing."

But it was just two days later that Jacque received a call at work from Hazelwood's assistant principal. The news was startling. Shanda had been in a fight with another girl. Jacque couldn't believe it. Like most children her age, Shanda had been in arguments before, but none had ever gone beyond name-calling. Jacque knew her daughter had a mischievous nature and liked to play the class clown, but she'd never been punished for anything more serious than talking in class.

When Jacque got home she found Shanda in tears. Her daughter had a cut on her face and a bump on the back of her head.

Jacque sat in stunned silence as Shanda explained what had happened. It had started when a girl in Shanda's class told her that she wanted to break up with her boyfriend but was too scared to give him back his ring. "I'll do it for you," Shanda offered, eager to prove her friendship. "Just point him out to me after class."

7

The girl's boyfriend was leaning against a locker on the second floor of the school when Shanda boldly walked up and handed him the ring.

"What's this?" the boy asked.

When Shanda told him that his girlfriend wanted to break up, the boy became angry. "Then why doesn't *she* give it to me?" he asked. "Who are you?"

"Look, just take it back, okay," Shanda said, determined not to let her classmate down.

A crowd of students began to gather, adding to the boy's embarrassment. "Hey, I don't even know you, girl," he said. "Why don't you just butt out?"

At that moment a wiry girl stepped out from the crowd and moved between Shanda and the boy. "What's your problem?" the girl asked, eyeing Shanda up and down, taking her measure.

"I don't think this is any of your business," Shanda replied shakily.

"That's my cousin Nathan you're talking to," the girl said, stepping closer to Shanda. They were now only inches apart.

Shanda's pulse was racing. The strange girl exuded toughness. Her short brown hair was cut in a boy's style. She stood with her shoulders squared, the sleeves of her sweatshirt pushed up and her fists clenched.

"I don't want any trouble," Shanda said. "I'm just trying to—"

She never finished. The girl bumped her chest into Shanda, pushing her back into a locker, and wrestled her to the floor. The girl was on top of her in a flash, her fists flying. Shanda tried to defend herself but the girl was too quick, too strong. The girl hit Shanda in the face, driving her head backward to the hard floor. The crowd of students had formed a circle around the fight, some shouting encouragement to the girl on top—"Get her, Amanda!"—but none offering a hand to stop the attack.

Finally a teacher pushed through the students and pulled the girl off Shanda. Down to the dean's office marched the three of them: the angry teacher, the still cocky Amanda, and the dazed Shanda. One week of in-school detention was the punishment dealt to both girls. Amanda smiled smugly at her sentence, while Shanda asked, "What's in-school detention?" She was told that she and Amanda would spend the next five school days in a special classroom for students who didn't follow the rules. Shanda glanced at the cool, pugnacious face of her assailant and shivered.

"Shanda told me that the other girl thought the whole thing was funny," Jacque said. "I told Shanda that I didn't like this school, but she kept saying that everything would be okay. I felt sorry for her but she still got grounded for a week. I told her it was her responsibility to stay out of fights."

The fight with Shanda wasn't the first for fourteen-year-old Amanda Heavrin, who lived with her father and older sister in a small, weather-beaten house in one of New Albany's poorer neighborhoods. Amanda's mother had left home years earlier and her father, Jerry Heavrin, had custody of the children.

Amanda struggled with her schoolwork. Although slightly built, she was a good athlete and played on the Hazelwood basketball team. While she tended to be quiet and polite around adults, she walked the school's halls with the swaggering gait of a jock and was seldom seen wearing anything but her usual uniform: baggy jeans, sweatshirt, and a baseball cap. More than one Hazelwood student had mistaken the plain-faced, flat-chested Amanda for a boy.

While Amanda's boyish appearance discouraged male suitors, it had attracted the attention of eighth-grader Melinda Loveless.

Melinda had been held back a year in school and was approaching her sixteenth birthday. She had a graceful figure, ivory-smooth skin, a delicately beautiful face, and long black curly locks. Boys, some several years older, stayed on her heels, begging for dates, but Melinda was not interested in them anymore. For after several unsatisfying sexual experiences with boys, Melinda had decided to follow the example of her older sisters, both of whom were lesbians, and find herself a lover of the same sex.

Melinda was drawn to Amanda because she thought the

fourteen-year-old resembled her father, Larry Loveless. Although he'd beaten Melinda's mother and would later face charges that he'd abused his two older daughters, Michelle and Melissa, Larry and Melinda had been very close. He'd left home two years earlier, after a violent argument in which Melinda's mother stabbed him with a kitchen knife. Melinda had fallen into a deep depression after her father's departure, but in Amanda she'd found a substitute for her affection.

Melinda lived in a small, two-story home directly across from a cemetery along Charlestown Road, one of New Albany's busiest streets. Her mother, Margie, had divorced her father shortly after their violent fight, and although she held down a good job as a nurse at Floyd Memorial Hospital, she'd struggled to make the house payments. Within a year of her divorce, however, Margie had remarried. Her new husband, Mike Donahue, held down a job in Louisville, and between the two of them they provided well for the household, which included Melinda and Melissa (the oldest sister, Michelle, having moved out by this time). Melinda had her own room, her own stereo, and a closet full of fashionable clothes, but she was unhappy. She resented her new stepfather and resisted his attempts to become friends with her.

She spent more time than ever with Amanda, exploring their desires in the secrecy of their bedrooms. Earlier that year, Margie had questioned her youngest daughter about a hickey on her neck, and Melinda had admitted that she and Amanda were lovers. Margie had responded to the admission with anger and disappointment, unable to understand why all three of her daughters were lesbians. But after a while she'd learned to accept Melinda's sexual preferences.

Hazelwood students already knew about the two girls, who would often hug and kiss in the hallways. Some of the students harassed them, calling them "dykes" and "lesbos," but the two young lovers ignored the taunts. They had each other, and what others thought didn't make much difference.

On the afternoon of her fight with Shanda, "Amanda Poo" had bragged to Melinda that she'd given the new girl a sound beating and complained about having to spend a week in detention.

At first Melinda wasn't particularly concerned about Amanda's punishment, since they had both been in this kind of trouble before. It just meant that they would not be able to spend time together between classes. But after a few days Amanda's preoccupation with the girl she'd been in the fight with began to bother Melinda. Amanda said that she and the girl, named Shanda, had made up and that she really liked her. In fact, it seemed as though Shanda was all that Amanda ever talked about.

Worried about the effect Shanda was having on Amanda and determined to get to the bottom of their relationship, Melinda came in late one day so that she would be placed in detention with the two girls.

"Shanda was a very pretty little girl," Melinda would say later. "I was sitting on the right side and Shanda and Amanda were together on the left side. Shanda went up to the desk to get some homework. I guess that was how it all started. Amanda was just staring at her and I noticed it. Then they started passing notes in the same room that I was in."

Melinda did a slow burn as she watched Amanda and Shanda exchange smiles. From time to time Amanda would turn and smile at Melinda, and Melinda would smile back. But it was a false smile that hid an inner anger. The seed of jealousy had been planted in Melinda's mind.

When the teacher told the students they could leave, Melinda grabbed her books and waited for Amanda in the hallway. She wanted to talk to her—alone. But Amanda came out with Shanda at her side. The two girls were giggling playfully and nudging each other. Amanda walked up to Melinda and introduced Shanda.

"Amanda told me that they were friends now," the older girl recalled. "I could tell that Amanda liked her a lot."

That afternoon after school, as usual, Melinda brought Amanda up to her bedroom, the place where they'd last made love. But this afternoon Melinda had something else on her mind. Earlier she'd watched Amanda stuff some notes from Shanda into the top pocket of her suspenders.

11

Melinda was not going to put up with this and, once inside her bedroom, tried to snatch the letters out of Amanda's pocket. "Let me look at them!" she screamed.

"No," Amanda said, trying to push Melinda off her. "There's nothing in them. Just leave me alone."

"What are you hiding from me?" Melinda smacked Amanda across the face and wrestled the notes away from her.

"One from Shanda said she thought Amanda was cute," Melinda said later. "Stuff like that. I told Amanda to stay away from Shanda. I told her I didn't think that it was right, you know. I said, 'Just tell the little girl that we're together, we've been together two years, and just leave it at that.'"

But Amanda couldn't leave it at that. She was infatuated with Shanda and determined to win her over.

2

Shanda was in the kitchen helping her mother fix dinner when she broke the news that she'd become friends with the girl who'd attacked her.

"Shanda, I don't think it's a good idea," Jacque recalled telling Shanda.

"But, Mom, she said she was sorry about the fight," Shanda replied. "She apologized. She just wants to be my friend."

"She sounds like a rough type to me, Shanda," Jacque cautioned her daughter. "I don't want you running around with that kind of girl."

"Please, Mom," Shanda pleaded. "You always said you should give people a second chance. I don't have any close friends at Hazelwood, and Amanda wants to be my best friend."

In a decision she would come to regret, Jacque allowed Shanda to continue her budding friendship with Amanda. "I knew that she was trying to make some new friends at Hazelwood, so I decided to give Amanda a chance," Jacque recalled. "I thought, Well, maybe I'm misjudging her."

A few days later Jacque set eyes on Amanda for the first

13

time. She was returning home from work when she noticed someone sitting on the front porch with Shanda. That in itself was enough to irritate her, because she'd forbidden Shanda from sitting on the porch when she wasn't home. As soon as the two girls caught sight of Jacque's car, Amanda bolted from the porch and ran behind the townhouse.

"Who was that?" Jacque asked, getting out of the car.

"Do you promise not to get mad?" Shanda asked.

By now Jacque wasn't mad, but she was curious. "Yes, I promise."

"Come on out, Amanda," Shanda yelled.

Amanda walked shyly from her hiding place, and Jacque was stunned.

"I honestly couldn't tell she was a girl," Jacque said later. "She had on a ball cap, her hair was real short. She had on boys' clothes. But she had a pretty face. I tried real hard not to let her know how disturbed I was by her appearance. She acted real nice and said *yes ma'am* and *no ma'am*. I told her that I didn't care if she came over to the apartment but that she wasn't allowed there until I got home from work."

After Amanda had left, Jacque sat her daughter down for a talk. "Shanda," she began, "do you think there's anything odd about Amanda?"

"No, why?" Shanda asked.

"Well, why does she wear that boys' baseball cap?"

"Oh, she really hates her hair," Shanda replied. "She just got it cut and she thinks it looks terrible. She thinks it's ugly. She wears a hat to cover it up."

"Shanda, she really does look like a boy."

"I know," Shanda said. "I told her I wanted to fix her hair and put some makeup on her. I think she'll be a lot happier with herself when I do."

Shanda said she felt sorry for Amanda because she didn't have any nice clothes. She told Jacque that Amanda didn't have a good life at home, that she lived with her father and hardly ever saw her mother.

"I really felt that there was something not right here," Jacque said later. "But Shanda kept assuring me that everything was okay."

Shanda had been one of the first girls in her class at St.

Paul to have a boyfriend, which at that age meant nightly phone calls and holding hands at ball games. She had a flirtatious nature and would introduce herself to boys at the local skating rink or mall. Shanda was never shy.

"She could just walk up to people she didn't know and start a conversation," said Amanda Edrington, Shanda's cousin. "She had a sort of magnetism, particularly with boys."

"Shanda was boy-crazy," said Shelley Suell, a friend from St. Paul. "She used to have the biggest crush on the guard at the skating rink. We made a pact not to get mad at each other if he ended up liking one of us more than the other."

Another friend from St. Paul, Joyce Robertson, remembered the time she went to the movies with Shanda, not knowing she'd arranged for two boys to meet them. After kissing her date in the darkness of the theater, Shanda tapped Joyce on the shoulder and asked why she wasn't doing the same.

While Shanda's exploration of her sexuality was just beginning, her knowledge of homosexuality was extremely limited. Her parents had no openly gay friends. In fact, she'd never met anyone who professed to be homosexual. To Shanda the words *gay* and *lesbian* were simply punch lines to off-color jokes she sometimes overheard.

Amanda Heavrin had heard the jokes too. For two years at Hazelwood she'd been the butt of callous remarks from classmates who knew of her relationship with Melinda Loveless. And at home, Amanda's father had begun to question why she dressed like a boy and had even asked her if she was a lesbian. She'd denied it and began telling her father that she had a boyfriend so he wouldn't suspect the truth about her and Melinda.

Amanda enjoyed her sexual relationship with Melinda, but there were times when the older girl was too possessive. More than once Melinda had slapped her around for just looking at another girl. When Amanda felt herself attracted to Shanda, she began to take precautions to prevent Melinda from finding out.

Amanda had apologized to Shanda during their first day together in detention and Shanda had agreed to be her friend. But Amanda wasn't sure if she could convert this new friendship into something more. It would have to be a secret seduction, one that took place outside of Melinda's presence.

It started with handwritten notes. In the first, dated September 13 and addressed to "Shana," Amanda hinted at her homosexuality (in this and subsequent letters minor errors in punctuation and spelling have been corrected by this author):

If we wouldn't of fought this would never have happened. I don't want you to think I'm a bad person or anything. I don't like to fight. I hate fighting. It's just when I had you on the ground getting ready to hit you I couldn't because you looked so helpless down there. But you swung at me and missed so I started hitting. I want the truth. Do you even know how to fight? If not, don't feel bad. I will help you if you want me to.

I have a question to ask you. I know this may sound dumb, but do you like girls? Well, do you kinda in a way like girls? If so I think it's so cool because it's so different. Is that why you're so nice to me? Do you think I'm cute or something? Please tell me the truth. I won't laugh 'cause I think it's cool.

Your friend,
Amanda H.

In another note three days later, Amanda alluded to recent conversations she'd had with Shanda. The relationship had been moving forward at a quick pace: Amanda had already told Shanda about her lesbian relationship with Melinda and was beginning to pressure her into a similar friendship.

Shanda,
I was wondering. Do you still like me? If so I'm glad. I have a lot in store Friday or Saturday when I see you. Do you know what I mean? I'm just joking or do you want me not to joke? Do you want to happen what I got in store? If so, answer back yes.

Love,
Amanda

P.S. I think I'm starting to like someone. You know her.

Using a combination of flattery and suggestive promises of the pleasures of lesbian love, Amanda was daily weaving a web of enticement and Shanda was slowly being drawn in. In the following letter, written on September 26, about two weeks after their first meeting, Amanda was quite open in her intentions:

Shanda,
What was wrong with you yesterday? You sounded so sad on the phone. So what's on your mind? You wanta fuck? Na, just joking. Well, I don't know. Last night I meant everything I said to you about making love to you. Shanda, you're so beautiful, hot and sexy. I want you. I can't say it enough.

Love,
Amanda

The following weekend Amanda invited Shanda to spend the night with her, and Jacque, totally blind to what was going on, gave her approval. That night, in the seclusion of her bedroom, Amanda came through on her promises and made love to Shanda. Although the experience was a triumphant one for Amanda, a letter sent the following day indicates that it had been a traumatic night for Shanda:

Shanda,
I really had a great time with you last night and I'm looking forward to more. Please don't cry anymore, OK.

Love,
Amanda

If Amanda was worried that Shanda might let out their secret, she need not have been. By the next day Shanda had wiped away her tears and was ready to resume where they had left off. She was intrigued by the new feelings she was experiencing, and she told Amanda so in this note:

Amanda,
   I loved last night too. I want more too and always. I
want what we had last night. If you want.

Love,
Shanda

In less than three weeks, Amanda had succeeded in
enticing Shanda into a sexual relationship. Shanda, who had
always been boy-crazy, suddenly found herself involved
with another girl.

During early adolescence it's not uncommon for males
and females to experiment with homosexuality, says Judith
Matheny, a clinical social worker in Louisville who special-
izes in adolescent sexuality.

"It's a time of sexploration," Matheny says. "Same-sex
encounters at that age are usually a safe environment in
which to explore the new, intense feelings brought on by
puberty."

Most early sexual experiences, especially of this sort, are
hidden from others. "If people were honest in discussing
this," says Matheny, "you would probably be surprised how
many have had some sort of early experience with someone
of their own sex. We don't talk about this because we live in
a homophobic society."

This early experimentation, however, "in no way means
that someone is homosexual," Matheny stresses. "The
preteen and early teen years are ones in which boys and girls
are just beginning to gain a sense of their own selves and
their sexual identities, and it is something that will continue
to evolve."

Dr. Richard R. Troiden, in the book *Gay and Lesbian
Youth,* writes that, as a general rule, lesbians report awareness of their same-sex feelings at an average age of between
fourteen and sixteen, males a couple of years earlier. And in
most cases a few years will pass between the time someone
first perceives themselves as homosexual and when they
have their first same-sex experience.

* * *

Shanda was only twelve. Still a child. After being systematically drawn into a relationship unlike any she'd ever experienced, she was ashamed and confused. Isolated from her usual confidantes—her girlfriends at St. Paul—Shanda's emotions were in turmoil.

During her first days at Hazelwood, before Amanda had begun monopolizing her time, Shanda had made a few other friends. But when they saw her hanging around with Amanda, they kept their distance.

Kristie Farnsley was one of them. She had met Shanda the day before school started and they'd ridden the bus home together a few times. The two girls seemed to be hitting it off, but before they could get very close, Kristie's brother warned her to stay away from Shanda because her friend Amanda ran with a rough crowd.

"I didn't really talk to Shanda too much after that," Kristie said.

Shanda's cousin Amanda Edrington, who also went to Hazelwood, knew that Amanda Heavrin was a lesbian and she was concerned about Shanda's friendship with her. "Shanda had always been a mother-hen type, even to me," Amanda Edrington said. "She was always taking people under her wing and looking out for them. I thought she felt sorry for Amanda. I thought they were just friends. I never suspected what was going on until later."

There was one friend, however, with whom Shanda did confide. Michele Durham, who lived down the street from Shanda's father, went to school in Jeffersonville but she saw Shanda nearly every weekend. One night Shanda opened up to her.

"She said, 'I've got to tell you something and I hope you don't think badly of me when I do,'" Michele remembered. "I asked what she was talking about. She said, 'Please, don't think I feel this way about you. Please don't be scared of me. But I've done things with Amanda, and she says we're lesbians but I don't feel that way. I must be bisexual because I really like guys more.' She didn't really say much more about it. But I could tell it was bothering her. You've got to know Shanda. She'd do anything for anybody. She just wanted to fit in so bad. I think Amanda kind of pushed her to it."

Melinda's suspicions were also on the rise.

"Amanda told me that she and Shanda were just friends," Melinda said later. "But I would see them in the halls laughing and passing notes. I'd be at Amanda's house and Shanda would call all the time, and she'd hang up when I answered. Stuff like that started happening, so I was upset."

At first Melinda tried being diplomatic. She knew that Shanda liked boys and she wasn't sure how far Amanda had gone with her. She hoped that Shanda would back off from Amanda once she knew that her friend was a lesbian. One day she dropped the following note through a slot in Shanda's locker:

Shanda,
    Don't be scared of me please! I just want to be your friend. I just don't like when you speak to Amanda when I'm not there! I mean, why can't we all three be friends?! You act as if you got something going with her! Amanda and I are going together and she loves me and I love her and she only wants to be friends with you. You need to accept that! I don't want you sneaking behind my back! Why don't you speak to Amanda when she's with me? You need to find you a boyfriend because Amanda is mine and you can even ask her! Please talk to both of us or you can forget about Amanda! You, me and Amanda need to have a talk together and get this squared away, then we could all be friends! Can you meet us at lunch?
                                    Your friend,
                                    Mel

But when the note didn't deter Shanda from seeing Amanda, Melinda stepped up her efforts to break up their friendship. She cornered Shanda in the hallway one day and threatened to hurt her if she didn't stay away from Amanda. Intimidated by the older girl, Shanda promised that she would do as she was told.

Melinda thought her threats had worked until she opened Amanda's locker one day and found a note in the shape of a heart. Written on the note were the words "Shanda Loves Amanda." Infuriated, Melinda surprised Shanda in the hallway, grabbing her by the hair and pushing her against a wall. She shoved the note into her face.

"Did you write this?" Melinda demanded.

Shanda stuttered and insisted that it wasn't her handwriting.

"You're a lying bitch!" Melinda crumbled the note and threw it in Shanda's face. "You better cool it, girl. Amanda is mine," she said as she stormed away.

Melinda had had enough of this bullshit. She told Amanda that they were through and that she could have Shanda if she wanted her. But after a few days Melinda calmed down and apologized to Amanda. In turn, Amanda promised to stay away from Shanda. But it was an empty promise.

After her meeting with Melinda, Amanda wrote Shanda the following note:

Shanda,
   When I went to Melinda's house she asked me to go back with her. What's killing me is that I want to go with both of you. I'm confused because I love you both. Shanda I love you.

                                        Love ya,
                                        Amanda Poo

Later that day, just to be sure there was no confusion about her affections, Amanda wrote Shanda another note:

Shanda,
   God you look good in those pants. Your butt especially.

                                        Amanda

Amanda asked Shanda to accompany her to a dance at Hazelwood, knowing that Melinda did not like dances and had made plans to spend the evening with her friend Kary

Pope. Seventeen-year-old Kary was also a lesbian, and although she and Melinda had petted and kissed each other, they had never been serious lovers. They'd met through a group of gay and lesbian teenagers that hung out together in New Albany and Louisville. Kary looked, dressed, and carried herself like a young man. She had a lanky build, a plain face, and short brown hair that she combed to one side. She also had her own car and knew someone who would buy her and Melinda wine coolers.

On the night of the dance, Melinda was drinking heavily. She pleaded with Kary to take her by the school so she could see if Amanda was with Shanda. Kary tried to talk her out of it. She knew that if Melinda found the two girls together there would be trouble. But Melinda insisted, and they ended up in the parking lot, waiting for the dance to end. When Melinda saw Amanda and Shanda walk out together she became livid. She jumped out of the car and confronted them as a crowd circled around.

"I just went off on Amanda," Melinda said later. "I started yelling at her in front of the whole school, and the principal was there. I just started yelling and crying. Amanda wanted us to take it to her house but I told her we'd settle it there and now. I smacked her across the face."

After the Hazelwood principal had broken up the fight, Amanda left with Melinda and Kary.

"Amanda told me that she and Shanda were just friends and that it was no big deal and that Shanda needed someone to talk to," Melinda recalled. "I told her that was fine but that she shouldn't talk to her unless I was there and that's how I wanted it to be."

A few days later Melinda was turning a corridor corner at Hazelwood when she spied Amanda up ahead. She was about to yell out a greeting, but before she did she caught sight of Shanda. Melinda hung back, watching as Amanda and Shanda began talking and laughing. There would be no confrontation this time. Tears came to her eyes, and she turned away.

"There for a while Amanda and I kind of stopped seeing each other," Melinda said. "I was just hurt. I cried a lot and was depressed."

Melinda felt abandoned. She told her sisters, Michelle

and Melissa, that Amanda had betrayed her. Hoping to ease her loss, one of her sisters told Melinda that a lesbian friend, eighteen-year-old Carrie East, had expressed an interest in dating her. Melinda began going out with Carrie, hoping that Amanda would find out, become jealous, and come running back to her arms.

Meanwhile, Amanda tried to convince Shanda that the difficult times were behind them now that Melinda was out of their lives. In the early part of October, Amanda wrote Shanda the following three letters:

Shanda,

I'm sorry for all the stuff that has been happening. I never meant for you to get in any trouble. I'm sorry and if you don't want to see me anymore I'll understand, OK. I'm all yours, not Melinda's. She fucked up my life and I finally understand because for so long my dad has been trying to tell me that Melinda was a bad person but I didn't believe him. But I realize myself that she's not the kind of person I should be hanging around. Please find somewhere in your heart to forgive me because I probably won't be able to look at you without crying. I feel so bad for what I've done. I should have listened to you when you said it was wrong, but I'm stupid and didn't. Don't worry about Melinda anymore because I can't hang around with her. I can only hang around with you. My dad thinks you are the greatest thing that happened to me, so please forgive the way I acted around you.

Love,
Amanda

Shanda,

Hi Honey. Well listen, Melinda don't want nothing to do with me so I don't want nothing to do with her. I guess I'm all yours. You can do what you want with me. Is there anything you expect out of me? What I expect out of you is to be nice and don't lie or flirt with anyone besides me.

Love ya,
Amanda Poo

Shanda,

God, I'm really starting to hate Melinda. I never thought I would but it's happening. I don't care anymore and if she even talks to me I will tell her to F--- off because I'm so pissed off at her. Shanda. Listen, OK. I'm all yours, OK.

The letters sound convincing, but Amanda was actually playing it both ways. She wouldn't admit it to Shanda, but Amanda was extremely jealous of Carrie East's relationship with Melinda. She learned Carrie's phone number and began a series of harassing phone calls, telling Carrie to stay away from Melinda. Carrie, who at eighteen was bigger and stronger than Amanda, was hardly scared. And anyway, Carrie, who was not a particularly attractive young woman, considered Melinda quite a catch for her, so she was not about to give her up.

But Melinda had eyes only for Amanda. When Melinda saw that Amanda was jealous, she told her that her affair with Carrie was just a fling and that it was Amanda whom she truly loved. Melinda pleaded with Amanda to break off her relationship with Shanda, and Amanda agreed to do so.

But once again it was a lie. Instead, Amanda sent Shanda these two notes:

Shanda,

Hey honey. Yes, I do love you but I just feel like Melinda has me in a trance and I don't know how to get out of it and I'm scared. If I try to get out something bad will happen and I'm scared to death.

Love,
Amanda

Shanda, I don't think I would ever tell Melinda that we're going out. She would probably kill you. Yes, I love you a lot, Shanda my honey.

Love ya,
Amanda

While Amanda was trying to sort out her feelings about Melinda, she was confronted with another problem. Shanda had begun to make new friends, and several of them were boys. Suddenly Shanda wasn't returning her phone calls or responding to her notes. Instead of meeting Amanda between classes, Shanda was devoting her time to two male suitors, Ray and Mike. Feeling scorned, Amanda used veiled threats and sweet talk to woo Shanda back. In mid-October, she sent the following notes:

Shanda,
 Melinda said she saw you flirting with some boys. And you better stop calling Ray when you like me. How do I know you don't like him if you aren't calling me? I'm scared of losing you.

Love ya,
Amanda

Shanda,
 Hey, what's wrong with you? You were acting all stuck up when you were walking with Shawna. You just looked at me and kept walking. What's your problem? Can you look me in the eye and tell me them rumors about you and Ray are not true? I know it's true so just tell me.

Shanda,
 I thought you never liked Mike. Yesterday you said you didn't like him anymore. So that means you did like him at one time. Tell me the truth. I can have people who can find out.

Shanda,
 I talked to someone that saw you standing real close to a blond headed boy. So who was that boy? Don't lie.

Since Shanda was occupied with her new friends, Amanda began spending more time with Melinda and other friends. When Amanda was caught cutting school one day, Amanda's father called Jacque at her job. Jerry Heavrin was

unsure who'd skipped school with Amanda, and he warned
Jacque that Shanda might have been with her. Jacque
immediately called the school but was told that Shanda had
been in class all day. That night Shanda admitted to her
mother that Amanda and some other girls had tried persuading her to cut school with them.

"I told Shanda that I was proud of her for not skipping
school with them," Jacque said. "I also told her that I didn't
want her hanging around with Amanda anymore."

Shanda promised her mother that she would break off the
friendship, but she actually had no intention of doing so.
Even though she was beginning to develop new friendships,
Amanda still had a strong hold over her.

Shanda's father and stepmother, Steve and Sharon Sharer, didn't know that Jacque had forbidden Shanda to see
Amanda. So they thought nothing of it when Shanda asked
if Amanda could accompany them to Harvest Homecoming, New Albany's annual fall festival that October. Before
they left the house that night, Sharon overheard Shanda
talking to someone on the phone.

"She was asking the person on the other end what kind
of cologne they were going to wear," Sharon recalled. "I
thought it must be a boy, so I asked who she was talking
to. She said it was Amanda. Then Shanda asked me if she
could wear some of Steve's cologne. She said it was the
new fad."

Steve and Sharon had met Amanda once before. The girl
had been dressed nicely and had been on her best behavior,
in the hope of impressing Shanda's father and stepmother.
So when they arrived at Amanda's house on the night of
Harvest Homecoming to pick her up, Steve and Sharon were
startled by her appearance.

"When she came over to our house that first time she
looked like any normal little girl, but that night she came out
looking like a little boy," Steve Sharer said later. "She had
on a ball cap and a baggy sweatshirt and jeans. She even
walked like a boy does, kind of swaggering. I looked at
Sharon and said 'What is this?' "

Steve and Sharon were also put off by Amanda's smug

attitude. She seemed to be trying to impress Shanda with her toughness. On their way home from the festival, Shanda asked if Amanda could spend the night, but Steve and Sharon said no.

"I was really concerned about the way Amanda acted," Steve said. "She carried on like she was a boy."

The next day, one of Melinda's friends told her that she'd seen Amanda with Shanda at Harvest Homecoming. Melinda couldn't believe it. Amanda had told her that she was staying home that night. Unwilling to accept the girl's word without confirmation, Melinda recruited a friend, Kristie Brodfuehrer, to check out the story. Kristie didn't really know Shanda, but she called her at home, saying she was a friend of Amanda's. During the brief conversation she managed to get Shanda to admit that she'd gone to the festival with Amanda.

Melinda couldn't believe that Amanda had lied to her. She felt betrayed and angry. Despite all her threats, Amanda and Shanda continued to flaunt their friendship for the whole world to see.

"Shanda's going to pay for this," Melinda told Kristie. "She's ruining my life."

The fifteen-year-old Kristie, a small, delicately built blonde, listened to her friend rant about how she wanted to hurt Shanda. Finally she turned to her and said, "It's not Shanda's fault. She wouldn't be with Amanda if Amanda wasn't encouraging her. If you do anything, you need to teach Amanda a lesson, not Shanda."

That evening, Kristie and Melinda devised a plan to do just that. Kristie called Amanda and asked if she wanted to sneak out later that night. Amanda agreed that it sounded like fun, not knowing that Melinda would be joining them. Kristie told her she would talk some boys into driving and would come by later that night to pick her up.

Melinda and Kristie had worked out all the details of their scheme. Kristie would persuade one of her boyfriends to pick up her and Melinda and drive to Amanda's house, where Melinda would hide in the backseat while Kristie went to the door to get Amanda. When Amanda came out to the car, Melinda would grab her. Then they would drive to some secluded place, where Melinda would beat up Amanda.

Melinda and Kristie hadn't figured on the boy bringing two male friends with him, however, and one of the boys knew about a party where Kristie could find some cocaine. Melinda was upset about the change in plans, but Kristie persuaded her that the night was still young and there'd be plenty of time to abduct Amanda—after they got high.

They drove to an older boy's apartment. Melinda was not interested in doing any drugs, as she wanted to keep her head clear for her confrontation with Amanda. Kristie didn't have any money, so she paid for her cocaine by having sex with one of the boys. It wasn't the first time she'd worked such an exchange. The innocent-looking young girl was strung out on the drug and would, a few weeks later, be checked into a detox center by her mother. As the hours dragged on, Melinda became impatient and started begging Kristie to leave, who by this time was also angry. The high just didn't feel right, and she suspected that the cocaine was bogus, a mixture of baking soda and speed.

Finally they all left the party and drove to Amanda's house. Kristie went around to Amanda's window and knocked but there was no rousing the fourteen-year-old, who was now in a deep sleep.

The whole plan had been screwed up because Kristie couldn't keep her nose clean. Melinda vowed to herself that the next time she'd choose her accomplices more carefully. And the next time the victim wouldn't be Amanda. It would be Shanda.

3

Shanda's physical relationship with Amanda was still a secret from Shanda's parents, but they had begun to suspect that something was not right with their daughter.

"Shanda used to spend hours in the bathroom fixing her hair," said Shanda's stepmother, Sharon Sharer. "I'd have to tell her to quit spraying all the hair spray because everything in the bathroom would be lacquered up. All of a sudden she didn't care about her hair anymore. She didn't care about her clothes, either. She started dressing like Amanda, wearing flannel shirts and baggy old pants."

Jacque was also concerned about the changes in appearance, but Shanda's older sister, Paije, assured her mother that it was just a phase. "Mom, leave her alone," Paije said. "All the kids dress that way."

But Shanda's taste in clothing wasn't the only thing that had changed. She became withdrawn. Her bubbly personality was replaced by a sluggish detachment. After making the basketball team, she began to complain about going to practice and eventually quit the team. Jacque encouraged her to go out for the swim team, but Shanda would have nothing to do with it.

"Shanda, you love sports," Jacque said one night. "Why don't you want to go out for anything?"

"I'm just not into it anymore," Shanda said, then immediately changed the subject.

Jacque said later, "It was like I saw her dwindling. She went from this robust child that could never do enough, to this child that didn't even want to talk. That would close the door to her room and not come out all night. She changed completely within a matter of a month. I tried to get her to go outside and meet the kids in the neighborhood, but she wouldn't. It was like she was hiding from everything, like she was ashamed of everything. I can look back now and see that, but at the time I knew something was wrong but I didn't know what."

Shanda seldom seemed to have much homework, explaining, in response to her mother's questioning, that her teachers rarely gave take-home assignments. As the school year progressed, Jacque began to wonder why her daughter hadn't yet received a progress report.

One day in late October, while Shanda was at school, Jacque's worries got the best of her. She went into Shanda's room and found a note written by Amanda, instructing Shanda how to forge her mother's name on a detention slip. Jacque immediately called the school. She was told that Shanda had been placed in detention numerous times since her fight with Amanda, and each time she had turned in a note with Jacque's signature.

"I drove down to the school and met with a school counselor," Jacque said. "He showed me one detention slip after another where Shanda had been tardy to classes or had skipped classes with Amanda. Shanda had signed my name on every one of the slips. She'd even signed my name to her progress report. It was all *F*s."

The counselor decided to get to the bottom of things and called Shanda to his office. When she saw her mother, Shanda collapsed into a chair and began crying.

"What is wrong?" Jacque asked, kneeling down in front of her daughter and touching her knee. "What is going on with you?"

Shanda wiped the tears from her face. "I'm so ashamed,"

she said. "I've been so bad. I've let you down. I lied to you."

"Did you sign these notes?" Jacque asked.

"Yes," Shanda answered, whimpering. "I wrote your name on all of them. I know I shouldn't have done it. Please forgive me."

"Shanda, I look at these notes, and every time you've gotten in trouble it had something to do with Amanda. Why are you continuing to hang around with her when I've asked you not to?"

"I'm afraid," Shanda said softly.

"Afraid of what?"

"Some girls want to beat me up and Amanda won't let them," Shanda said.

"What girls?" Jacque demanded.

"Melinda and her friends," Shanda said.

It was the first time that Jacque had heard Melinda's name. The counselor intervened at this point and explained that Melinda Loveless and Amanda Heavrin had been in a series of problems over the past two years.

"He told Shanda that they were not the type of girls she should associate with," Jacque said. "He said they had been in trouble before and would continue to get into trouble, and if Shanda kept hanging around with them she would find herself on a road to trouble and she wouldn't be able to find her way back. He told her that she needed to get away from these people and that if they gave her any more problems she should come to him."

Shanda promised her mother that she would stay away from Amanda and Melinda and would buckle down with her schoolwork.

"Shanda had always been in the popular group at St. Paul," Jackie said later. "She had always been a leader. But these kids were older and rougher, and she got herself in a position where she was no longer a leader, she was a follower. I knew she was in a predicament that was difficult, but I wanted her to be strong enough to walk away from it. I think she honestly tried to do that, but I think the other girls were so overwhelming that she just didn't know how to get away from it."

The day after the meeting, Jacque hired a tutor to help Shanda with her schoolwork. Shanda had always been an above-average student, but she had fallen so far behind in her studies that the tutor had to spend three nights a week with her.

Although Shanda had promised her mother that she would have nothing more to do with Amanda, that didn't prevent Amanda from calling Shanda at home. Amanda would disguise her voice, or she would have other girls call on a three-way connection.

"I'd catch her trying to disguise her voice to me," Jacque said. "I'd tell her not to call back, but she didn't know what it meant to listen to an adult when they told her something. I was aggravated with her."

Fed up, Jacque drove to Amanda's house and confronted her father, whom she'd talked to on the phone before but had never met personally.

"I told him that Shanda had been in a lot of trouble and that everything she had done had something to do with his daughter," Jacque recalled. "I told him that I did not want Amanda to hang around with Shanda. He looked at me and said, 'You know, it's funny, but every girl that my daughter has ever been friends with, the parents ended up telling me that they didn't want their daughter to have anything to do with mine.' He said, 'I just don't understand it.' I looked at him and I said, 'Well, Mr. Heavrin, it's probably not my place to say this, but have you ever noticed how your daughter never dresses like a girl and always looks like a boy?' He looked at me and said, 'Yeah, you know, I've asked my daughter if she was a lesbian and she told me no, so I don't know what else to do.' I told him that maybe she needed to be around her mother more. I told him that she needed to dress like a little girl and act like a little girl. He said he'd tell Amanda to stay away from Shanda."

The phone calls from Amanda stopped. With the help of her tutor, Shanda was getting good grades again. Jacque thought that everything was under control. Then while going through the mail one Saturday, she found a letter from Shanda to Amanda, which had been returned because there was no stamp on it. Jacque opened the envelope and found one of Shanda's school pictures. On the back her daughter had written a note: "Amanda, I miss you and I will always love you no matter what happens. I miss the touch of your soft body."

"It was very obvious from what Shanda had written that there had been physical contact between her and Amanda," Jacque said.

Jacque showed the note to her oldest daughter. "I don't think Shanda's a lesbian," Paije said. "I think she's just real confused."

"Don't fool yourself, Paije. I think we have a big problem here. I think something has happened between Shanda and Amanda."

Shanda was spending the weekend with her father, but this was not something that could wait. Jacque called her ex-husband and told him about the writing on the back of the photograph. Shanda, overhearing Steve's side of the conversation, slipped out of the room and pulled Sharon aside. In a whisper, she asked her stepmother, "If you mail a letter and don't put a stamp on it, will it come back?"

"Yes," Sharon said. "Why?"

"I think Mom found a letter I sent to Amanda," Shanda said. "I sent Amanda a picture of me and I wrote a note on the back. It was written like it was from a boyfriend to a girlfriend. It was just a joke."

Sharon initially believed Shanda's story. "Shanda was not one to lie," she said later. "But when Jacque told me what Shanda had actually written, I knew that it wasn't just a joke."

"We all need to sit down together and get to the bottom of this," Jacque told Steve and Sharon, who agreed to bring Shanda back to Jacque's townhouse that evening. Jacque then called Amanda's father and told him about the note.

"I asked him to bring Amanda over to my house that evening, and he assured me that he would," Jacque said. "Well, he and Amanda never showed up. When I tried to call him a few days later, I found out that he'd had his phone changed to an unlisted number."

That night, Jacque gave much careful thought to what she would say to her daughter and the others.

"I could tell that Steve was devastated by my call, but I had told him over the phone that this was not a situation where we wanted to scream and get upset," Jacque said. "It was apparent that Shanda was going through a difficult time emotionally and she needed our help. We needed to treat her with kid gloves. Suddenly I knew why the last month or two had been pure hell. This is what had been troubling this child."

Jacque had always prided herself on her emotional strength, but now she was fraught with worry. "I had never in my life dreamed I would be in a situation where I would have to deal with something like this," she said. "How do I do this so I don't hurt her and let her know that I'm here for her, and no matter what she has done, it's going to be okay?"

Shanda was crying when she came in with Steve and Sharon. Jacque took her daughter by the hand and sat down next to her on the living-room carpet.

"Shanda, you need to tell us what's going on with you and Amanda," Jacque said. "Shanda, we will always love you. Whatever you have done, it is not unforgivable. It's nothing you should be ashamed of. You are only twelve years old. You are just a little girl. Shanda, you've got to tell us the truth. Has Amanda ever touched any part of your body in any way that she shouldn't have touched you?"

"No, Mom," Shanda said through her tears. "We're just friends."

"This note leads me to believe that you and Amanda have more than just a friendship."

"No, Mom, it's just that Amanda needed a friend and I wanted to be a good friend."

Jacque handed the photograph to Shanda and told her to read the note to her father.

"That was the hardest thing I ever made her do because it was so degrading for her to read it," Jacque said later. "You could tell that it just devastated her."

When Shanda had finished reading, Jacque said, "Shanda, you told us that she never touched you, but this leads me to believe that she did. Now's the time to tell the truth."

"I don't know why I wrote it, Mom," Shanda insisted. "None of it's true."

Jacque tried again and again to draw out the truth, but Shanda would not open up.

"I held her in my arms and told her that I loved her and that whatever had happened it was nothing to be ashamed of," Jacque said. "I told her that she was just a little girl, and even though she may think she was all grown up she wasn't. I told her that the mere fact that she was sitting there in tears and couldn't talk showed me that she was still a little girl and she didn't know how to deal with this."

For over an hour, Jacque, Steve, and Sharon questioned Shanda about her relationship with Amanda. And for over an hour, Shanda insisted that she and Amanda were just good friends. Finally Jacque took Shanda into the kitchen so they could talk privately. Shanda was still crying and her head was down. Jacque got down on her knees in front of her.

"Shanda, it doesn't matter what you've done," Jacque said. "I'm not ashamed of you and I love you and you can tell me whatever you need to tell me. Shanda, don't you know I love you?"

Shanda looked in her mother's eyes and replied, "No."

"Shanda, how can you say that?"

"I've been so bad," Shanda said. "I've done so many things I shouldn't have done. I just don't believe you love me anymore."

Jacque reached up and lifted her daughter's chin. "Shanda, you are my baby. I will love you forever, no matter what happens. You have to know that I will always love you."

Mother and daughter held each other for a few minutes, then walked back into the living room. Steve and Sharon hugged Shanda and told her that they loved her too. After Shanda had gone to bed, the adults decided the first thing they had to do was transfer Shanda out of Hazelwood and into Our Lady of Perpetual Help. Steve said he would increase his child support to help cover the tuition.

The next day Jacque met with the principal of the

Catholic school and, without going into all the details, explained some of the problems Shanda was having at Hazelwood. The principal said that Shanda could start school there the following week.

"When Shanda realized that we were serious about switching schools she got mad," Jacque said. "She couldn't believe we were really going to do it."

When Melinda heard about Shanda being transferred, she felt as if all her wishes had come true. Suddenly all her worries were over and she had Amanda to herself again. A note Melinda wrote to Amanda on November 18, a week after Shanda had left Hazelwood, reveals her happiness.

Across the top of the page, Melinda had written "Eat at Mel's." In the right-hand border were two other notations: "Melinda Loves ____ . You fill in the blanks" and "I Love Myself." The rest of the note, however, indicates that Melinda still harbored a lingering resentment:

> Amanda,
>   Why did you write her fucking name on your folder! It hurt so much when I seen it! I didn't think you would put her ugly name on your folder and you wrote it!! You must have liked her enough to write her name! Why? Well, I'm gone!
>
>   Melinda
>   P.S. Just tell me you liked her once cause I know!

But there was no mention of Shanda in a letter written the following day. Melinda's thoughts were on Amanda and Amanda alone:

> Amanda,
>   Thanks for my sweet and very neat letter. I liked how you joked and said cute things. I'm doing my best in trying to write this but the teacher is eyeing me down and trying to catch me in the act but I'm too damn slick. And I hate dick. Na! (I really do though.) You look so damn cute in the morning honey. In class I always day dream about you. I can't help thinking

about you all the time. Yes, I would love to go to your game and see you play in your little shorts. And see you sweat. Hmmm! Makes me hot just thinking about it. And I'm always a good girl. You better keep being a good girl. And I'll be good with Carrie East and I'll do her good too! Na! You did like how I let you go last night? Well, I'll do it more often then. Na! I don't have any lunch money honey! My mom didn't bother to give me any cause I forgot to ask her. (I guess that's why she didn't give me any.) Ha! Ha! Ha! Aren't I so damn cute! Well I'll write more later after you write me.

> I love you, Melinda
> Amanda -n- Melinda
> Do you wanna fuck? yes. no.

In the border of that letter, Melinda had written: "Melinda loves Amanda always and forever." And written upside down on the bottom of the page were the words "Horny people with an attitude read upside down. That's why I read it first."

With her rival out of her life, Melinda was in ecstasy. Her unbridled joy shows through in the following two love letters, all written in late November:

Poo,

I was in the hall and I went past this class and there was the most beautiful girl in there and she was holding her hair back in a sexy way and doing some work. Do you know her? I think her name is Amanda. Well anyway, I don't feel too good today but I'm real hyper and in a playful way like chasing someone and jumping on them. Did you know we get off Thursday for Thanksgiving? I love turkey and all that good food! Do you want to come over to my house and eat? (Me) Na! I'm gone.

> Love always,
> Melinda

Amanda,

I changed the heading on my note a little cause I got

sick of the same damn thing. I enjoyed eating lunch with you and I'm real sorry about jumping down your throat and being a sour puss but I get that way once in a while. I love you no matter what I do or say. And I don't mean to take it out on you. We just need to agree and give each other's opinions more often and then take turns. Well, I still have cramps and I'm still in a bitchy mood. So don't mess with me! Na! I'm back. I'm in art class now and we're listening to country and "I'm Shameless" came on the radio! I love that damn song! Will you get the tape for me? Please!! Please!! Please!! I'll get down on my knees and beg and then I'll eat your puss! Na! I'm in a real excited mood! I'm acting real stupid and making everyone laugh! Well almost everyone. I'm going to leave you with one more thing to say: I love you!!

> Love,
> Melinda
> XOXOXOX

But Melinda's high spirits would soon come crashing down. At the same time that she was expressing her love in these letters, Amanda was carrying on a secret correspondence with Shanda, who was having a hard time adjusting to her new school. Through a series of phone calls, Shanda and Amanda had arranged to get together. Shanda was going to spend one night with her cousin, Amanda Edrington. Without Jacque's knowledge, Shanda and her cousin would go to a Hazelwood dance, where Amanda would be waiting.

But Melinda caught wind of the plan and was waiting for Shanda in the school parking lot.

"Melinda jumped out at us," Shanda's cousin remembered. "She had Amanda with her and she told Amanda to tell Shanda that she didn't like her anymore. Amanda told Shanda to get lost and Shanda started crying."

Even though Melinda had won this face-off, she was growing tired of the constant worries. "It was the same thing all over again," Melinda said later. "I just got fed up with it."

Melinda vented her frustration in this letter dated November 26:

Amanda,

Yes! I think we should at least talk this out. If you have noticed all these uncalled for fights have been because of Shanda! Yes, I'm hurt and pissed at you! I can't believe you! You better straighten your act up missy! I'm sick of hearing and seeing Shanda!! I think we should let me cool off cause I'm still let down with you. You have not shown me no improvement yet. Shanda is not gone! You haven't got rid of her. It's your problem not mine! Until her name and writing is off of your shit I'm not going to hang with you and your problem. I'm real mad at you! I feel like I need to cry! I want Shanda dead!!

Love,
Melinda

In early December, Amanda's father found this letter and dozens of others in Amanda's room. Disturbed by the sexual content of many of the notes, Jerry Heavrin was determined to put an end to Amanda's friendship with Melinda. He took the letters to Virgil Seay, the county's juvenile-probation officer. At Heavrin's request, Seay contacted Melinda and told her that if she didn't stay away from Amanda she could face charges of harassment in juvenile court.

Melinda was livid. She felt that Shanda was responsible for all her troubles. Over the next few weeks she would tell one friend after another that she wanted to kill Shanda.

One night Melinda asked her longtime friend Crystal Wathen how to go about disposing of a dead body. Crystal coldly answered that the best way would be to put the body in a barrel full of leaves and set it on fire.

Melinda didn't know it yet, but the confrontation in the Hazelwood parking lot had been a turning point in Shanda's friendship with Amanda. Amanda had contacted Shanda afterward and apologized for telling her to get lost. But

Shanda had about had it with Amanda and her fickle ways. It turned out that Shanda was beginning to like her new school. She was making new friends, nice girls like those she knew at St. Paul, and boys who were eager to court the pretty new girl. Shanda joined the basketball team and started going with a boy at the school.

"She was trying to get away from Amanda," said Shanda's cousin, Amanda Edrington. "She stopped writing Amanda and wouldn't talk to her when she used three-way calling to get to Shanda. Amanda started calling me and asking what was wrong with Shanda. I told her that Shanda was meeting new friends now."

Jacque could see the changes in her daughter. Shanda was now spending every school-day morning jockeying with Jacque for position in front of the bathroom mirror so she could fix her hair. Shanda spent hours on the phone with her new friends at Our Lady of Perpetual Help, including a boy who called constantly.

"After she got away from those girls at Hazelwood, Shanda became herself again," Jacque said. "She wanted to do things. She wanted to go shopping. She wanted to lay on the couch with me and watch television. She'd laugh and joke. She was Shanda again." By the time Christmas break rolled around, Jacque was feeling secure in the normalcy that had returned to their lives.

Then on Christmas Day, the phone rang and Jacque answered. It was Amanda.

"She asked if she could wish Shanda a merry Christmas," Jacque said. "I told her that she could not. She said, 'I know you think I'm a lesbian but I'm not.' I said, 'Amanda, I don't give a damn what you are. It's none of my business. I could care less. But I will tell you one thing. I don't want you around my daughter. Don't you ever call back again.'"

A few days later, Shanda told Jacque that Amanda had been having other girls call on a three-way connection so that Amanda could talk to Shanda. "She told me that if certain girls called I should hang up because it was Amanda trying to get to her," Jacque said.

In a letter that Shanda wrote to her friend Lisa Livergood on January 2, she complained about Amanda trying to draw her back into their relationship. "I can't take all this pressure," Shanda wrote. "I wish she would stop calling me and following me."

Jacque hugged her daughter one night in early January and said, "Shanda, I know you were mad at me because I made you change schools, but don't you feel like you've got a second chance?"

Shanda returned the hug and said, "Yeah, I didn't think I could ever find my way back. I had been so bad. I had done so many bad things. I didn't know what to do."

Shanda had never wavered from her claim that Amanda had not touched her, and Jacque didn't pressure Shanda to tell her more now. That would come in time, she thought. Now was the time for healing old wounds and for getting their lives back together again.

Little did she know that time was running out and that Melinda Loveless was already plotting her revenge.

4

Rural Kentuckians tend to think of Louisville, the state's largest city, as a wide-open town. And it's true that it probably has more bars per capita than most Midwestern cities its size. But even though it cultivates a laid-back, good-time image, at its heart Louisville is a blue-collar, churchgoing, family-oriented, softball-playing town with tree-shaded streets and middle-of-the-road views. Nearly all of its politicians are Democrats, yet the most popular show on the most popular radio station belongs to arch-Republican Rush Limbaugh. Louisville is not so much wide open as it is relaxed, and its relaxed ways seem to keep it a couple of years behind other cities its size when it comes to most fashions and trends.

Despite the Middle America conservatism of the area, the teens that Melinda had fallen in with had carved out their own niche of places to go and things to do.

The alternative music scene in Louisville was flourishing, and many of the local bands would play at off-the-beaten-track teen clubs, where these young iconoclasts would congregate. Another place they felt at home was amid the eccentric shops, coffeehouses, and music stores in Louisville's Highlands and Crescent Hill neighborhoods, two of the few places in town where punk hairstyles and clothes did not draw stares. Every so often, when the *Rocky Horror Picture Show* would make one of its frequent appearances at the avant-garde Vogue theater in Louisville, the teens would follow in that cult film's tradition and come to the theater dressed in bizarre costumes.

The previous fall, Melinda had been initiated into this motley mix of young rebels by Kary Pope, a friend who'd boldly come out of the closet and openly flaunted her homosexuality, taking pleasure in shocking people with her punk clothes, dyke hairstyle, and butch behavior.

Among those introduced to Melinda by Kary were two seventeen-year-old twin brothers with weirdly poetic names, Larry and Terry Leatherbury. The two slightly built, darkly handsome brothers had recently moved to Louisville from Madison, Indiana, a small town about fifty miles upriver from Louisville.

Compared to Louisville, Madison was Old World. Madison had been portrayed in a military propaganda film during World War II as a typical small town, to remind soldiers of the way of life they were defending. Madison had changed little in the subsequent fifty years and still prided itself on its homespun values.

Teen life in Madison revolved around high-school basketball and football games, bowling alleys, and hanging out in shopping-center parking lots. None of these pastimes appealed to Larry or Terry. Both were extremely bright, but they spent less time on schoolwork than they did playing Dungeons and Dragons—a board game based on medieval legends—and reading books about the occult and pagan rituals. Larry especially was fascinated with the dark side of occult beliefs. He dabbled in black magic and carried himself with the smugness of an all-knowing shaman. He often dressed in black and wore exotic accessories such as black fishnet gloves. Often ridiculed by other students at Madison Consolidated High School, Larry got even with one of his taunters. He pulled a knife on the boy in a classroom and slit the youth's throat. The boy recovered, but Larry was suspended from school (he later dropped out) and was brought up on juvenile charges.

Both Leatherburys now lived in an apartment they shared with another young man in a run-down area of Old Louisville. Larry made no secret of his bisexuality, and Terry had confided in Kary Pope that he too was bisexual. Both brothers were a central part of the clan with which Melinda and Kary now ran.

It was through Larry and Terry that Kary and Melinda first heard of Laurie Tackett.

Laurie had been a close friend of the Leatherburys in Madison, and she shared their fascination with the occult. Although Laurie was a loner with few friends, she'd had sex with a number of boys, including Larry. But she'd recently found herself more attracted to girls. A lesbian relationship with a girl in Madison had convinced her that she was gay, and she was heartbroken when the girl left town.

While Madison was boring to the Leatherburys, it was a bottomless pit for Laurie. She lived with her parents in a small, inexpensive home in the rural countryside, a long drive from the heart of town and seemingly a million miles away from where she wanted to be.

Classmates made fun of her strange haircuts—she once shaved her head—and since her lesbian lover left town, Laurie was lonelier than ever. Madison was not a place where people were open about homosexuality. The previous fall, Laurie had moved to New York City to live with her cousin, thinking she'd fit in with the underground crowd there. But that adventure ended in disappointment when her cousin broke up with her boyfriend and Laurie no longer had a place to live.

When she arrived back in Madison she contacted the Leatherburys, who told her of the radical group they were running with in Louisville and New Albany. They introduced her to one of their friends, Crystal Lyles, and Crystal agreed to let Laurie stay with her in New Albany. But Laurie's father was fed up with his daughter's rambling ways and refused to drive her the fifty miles to Crystal's home. Crystal came up with a solution. She told Laurie to call her friend Kary Pope and ask her for a ride.

Kary and Laurie had heard each other's names through the Leatherburys but had never met. Melinda was at Kary's house the day Laurie called and introduced herself, then asked Kary to chauffeur her from Madison to New Albany. The round trip would take two hours and Kary was a bit reluctant, but Laurie sounded nice on the phone and Kary felt sorry for her predicament. With Melinda tagging along for the ride, the two girls drove toward Madison but only got as far as Hanover—a small town ten miles south of Madison—before they lost their bearings and called Laurie for better directions. Laurie told them she knew the spot they were calling from. She told them to wait there, saying that her father would take her that far.

A half hour later Melinda and Kary saw a car pull up to the convenience store and watched as a dull-faced girl with a stocky build and short, blond spiked hairdo stepped out with a bag full of clothes. Laurie, dressed in dark, loose-fitting clothes, smiled at Melinda and Kary and walked toward them with a cocksure strut. Melinda was a bit intimidated by the girl's tough appearance, but Kary felt herself attracted to her. Laurie also liked Kary and admitted to her early on that she was a lesbian.

When the girls arrived back in New Albany they discovered that Crystal Lyles, who still lived with her parents, hadn't gotten clearance from them for Laurie to move in. With nowhere to go, Laurie asked Kary if she could stay with her. Kary, who lived with her grandmother, welcomed the opportunity to spend some time with her new gay friend.

Although they didn't have sex, Kary and Laurie became very close. Over the course of the next few days, Laurie would tell Kary all the intimate details of her troubled home life.

Laurie's father, George Tackett, had spent two years in prison for robbing a gas station when he was a young man. He was a squat, stout, plain-faced man who tended to keep to himself. The household, which also included Laurie's younger brother, Bubby, was dominated by Laurie's mother, Peggy Tackett, who was a devout member of a Fundamentalist church called the Lighthouse on the Hill, whose members often spoke in tongues and had visions. The church, which Laurie's father did not attend, forbade females to wear makeup or jewelry. For years Peggy had made Laurie wear long dresses to school and did not allow her to take physical education because the church didn't let girls wear sweatpants or shorts. The only type of music Laurie was allowed to listen to was gospel hymns, and her mother had sold the family's television set because she'd made a vow to God that she wouldn't watch TV anymore.

Other students would make fun of Laurie's clothing, and one day she began to rebel against her mother. It started with small transgressions, like sneaking pants into her schoolbag and changing into them when she got to school. She was feeling the power of freedom now, and her changes soon became more dramatic. The clothing she wore away from home became more provocative. She'd wear mini-skirts, net stockings, and open blouses. Guys came on to her and she went along, having sex with a number of them. She also began to have homosexual urges.

It was about this time that Laurie's younger brother, Bubby, looked in her diary and discovered that she resented her family, that she no longer believed in God, and that she wished she were a boy instead of a girl. When Bubby showed the diary to Peggy Tackett, she had a heated argument with her daughter and asked why she couldn't be normal. A short time later Laurie made her last visit to her mother's church. The occasion was a mother-and-daughter banquet. Without her daughter's knowledge, Peggy had spoken to the preacher about what she'd found in Laurie's diary. And when the preacher began his sermon, it was aimed directly at Laurie.

"He preached that all homosexuals would go to Hell," Laurie recalled. "I didn't go back anymore because I was tired of all the preaching. I was tired of being condemned. I was tired of being judged."

Seeking an escape from what she considered her dismal reality, Laurie took up an interest in the occult and spent long evenings with the Leatherburys, having séances, reading books about black magic, and trying to cast spells on people they disliked. She began wearing only black clothes, dyed her hair wild colors, and once even shaved it all off. After a group of black girls confronted her in Louisville and accused her of being a skinhead, Laurie began carrying a knife for protection. Sometimes she would use that knife or a razor blade to cut herself as "a method of relieving stress." She'd learned the trick from others in the radical group she'd begun hanging around with at school. It had also become fashionable among this group to carve initials into their own skin as a show of independence. She and Larry Leatherbury had once cut themselves and used their blood to draw a picture. They dubbed their creation "blood art." Another time, after Laurie had cut her wrist with a razor, her mother called the preacher and had him come over to the house. Laurie barricaded herself in her room and wouldn't let him in.

"I got the impression they wanted to exorcise something out of me or pray for me so the devil would leave me alone," Laurie remembered. "It just made me mad. I put the most vile music I had on the stereo and turned it up full blast so I wouldn't have to listen to them."

Laurie got into punk, hardcore, and other forms of alternative music. The darker, the more neurotic the themes, the more volatile the music, the better. Her favorite artists—Sinead O'Connor, The Cure, the Violent Femmes, and Nine Inch Nails—had one thing in common: They sang about frustration, anger, and resentment and railed against the evils of authority with a mind-numbing vengeance. There were songs about suicide, self-mutilation, and violence. There was no Beatles' "Good Day, Sunshine," no Bobby McFerrin's "Don't Worry, Be Happy" on Laurie's play list. The music she listened to was brooding, bitter, and bleak. Within the walls of her bedroom, Laurie would crank the volume high and take it all in.

When she was sixteen, Laurie cut her arm so badly with a knife that she was taken to the hospital. The doctors thought it might have been a suicide attempt and committed her to a mental hospital for several weeks. Shortly afterward Laurie dropped out of school and worked a series of minimum-wage jobs. She began dating a boy named Aron Hall, but he broke up with Laurie when he learned that she'd had sex with a girl named Danielle. Aron's rejection stung Laurie, and one day she retaliated by trying to run him over in her car. He jumped out of the way just in time. Fed up with guys, Laurie threw herself into her relationship with Danielle, but when Danielle suddenly moved to another state, Laurie again fell into a depression. She ran away from home in the summer of 1991 but, after staying a few days with her friends Larry and Terry Leatherbury, she returned home. She left home again a few weeks later to go to New York.

Kary was fascinated with her new friend, but their relationship was interrupted when Kary, who'd been abusing drugs, checked into a hospital to sober up.

While Kary was hospitalized, Laurie and Crystal Lyles finally got together and began sharing an apartment. As soon as Kary got out of the hospital she fell back in with Laurie, Crystal, the Leatherburys, and the rest of her old crowd and once again began doing drugs. She and Laurie dropped acid together a couple of times.

It was not difficult for the girls to get drugs. Since the late 1960s drugs had been readily available to teenagers in Louisville and even its smaller neighboring cities in Indiana. The secret to finding marijuana, acid, or cocaine was a simple matter of knowing the right people. Alcohol could be obtained in the same way. It might take an evening's work, but eventually a fake ID would do the trick, an unscrupulous liquor-store clerk would look the other way, or an older friend would make the purchase.

Money was not always necessary in these transactions: Melinda's friend Kristie Brodfuehrer, for example, exchanged sex for cocaine. Nearly every group of teens included someone who either worked or received a generous allowance from their parents, and there was no surer way to secure one's cool status than to turn on one's friends, whether by paying for a wine cooler or buying a hit of acid.

Although she liked to get high occasionally, Laurie wasn't hooked on drugs and could do without them if they were scarce. She did need money for other things, however, and after a few months during which she was unable to hold down a job in New Albany, Laurie swallowed her pride and returned to her parents' home in Madison.

After his daughter had persuaded him that she couldn't hold down a job without her own transportation, George

Tackett bought his daughter a seven-year-old, four-door sedan. Laurie finally landed a job at the Madison K-Mart, but she didn't like the work and hated spending time in a dull town like Madison. Whenever she could, therefore, she took advantage of her new mobility and drove to New Albany or Louisville to see Kary, the Leatherburys, and their strange circle of friends.

By this time, however, those friends were beginning to tire of Laurie. Even in this group where eccentricity was glorified and weird behavior prized, Laurie had become too bizarre. She often spoke about a dream she had about charred, mutilated infants hanging from trees. She said there were times when multicolored hands would come up through the floor of her bedroom and try to pull her down into Hell.

Laurie told Kary she'd enjoy killing someone because it would be fun to get the publicity. She went on at great length about how she'd love to stick a knife in someone's stomach just to see what it felt like to push it in. She also said she'd like to watch someone being set on fire. She even offered to kill Kary's grandmother, who was giving her friend troubles at the time.

Laurie was also taking her habit of self-mutilation to extremes. At a party attended by Kary and the Leatherburys, Laurie drank her own blood after cutting herself, then tried to talk others into letting her drink their blood.

Larry Leatherbury had often held the others spellbound with his so-called ability to channel—to speak in the voices of people caught in the spirit world. But Laurie was starting to upstage Larry, saying she had learned to channel with the dead.

"She'd sit there and go into a trance and her voice would change and her mood would change," Kary recalled. "Everything about her would change. She said she could bring back people. She would bring back her great-grandmother. She'd put curses on people. She'd bring vampires back. She'd say she was Deanna the Vampiress and that she would love to kill somebody."

Larry took his occult practices seriously, so he was peeved

at Laurie. He felt she was degrading these channeling ceremonies by faking her communication with spirits. At the same time Kary was also withdrawing from her friendship with Laurie, who, she felt, was trying to control her mind. Kary had struck up a relationship with another lesbian by now, and she told Laurie that she didn't want to hang around with her anymore.

Suddenly Laurie was on the outs with the circle of friends she'd tried so hard to impress. Desperate to find her way back in, she began calling Melinda.

Melinda had always been wary of Laurie. She knew about her penchant for cutting herself and her channeling. Kary and both Leatherburys had told her that Laurie once killed a cat as a sacrifice to Satan. But Melinda had also had an argument with Kary recently, so she responded to Laurie's offer of friendship. Laurie was unlike anyone Melinda had ever met. She just didn't seem to give a damn—not about herself, not about other people, not about anything. (Actually Laurie cared deeply what others thought about her; she just refused to show it.)

Now an outcast among a group of outcasts, Laurie was determined to become better friends with Melinda, to whom she was sexually attracted although too intimidated by the girl's beauty to make any advances. (All of Laurie's other sexual conquests had been as plain-looking as herself.) She was sure that Melinda didn't like her in that way, but she held out hope. Maybe if they became close enough, Melinda's feelings for her would change. But even if they didn't, Laurie had to be sure she didn't screw up this friendship. She'd tried hard to make friends outside of Madison, and if she lost Melinda she'd lose her connections in New Albany.

Melinda also had her reasons for cultivating Laurie's friendship: She knew that this was someone with a capacity for violence, someone who could help her get back at Shanda.

Laurie knew all about Melinda's problems with Amanda and Shanda, which was all Melinda wanted to talk about. Even after Shanda had transferred to Our Lady of Perpetual Help, Melinda was obsessed with the thought that Shanda and Amanda were still sneaking around behind her back. She often told Laurie that she wanted to beat up Shanda, and sometimes she said she wanted her rival dead.

On January 8, 1992, Laurie called Melinda and invited her to a hardcore concert in Louisville that Friday night. Hardcore was the rough-edged stepchild of punk and heavy metal music, and there were plenty of young local bands playing this new sound. Melinda called some of her friends to see if they wanted to come along, but they'd heard about Laurie's reputation and none of them were eager to spend the evening with her. Melinda called Laurie back the following night and said she'd go, but on one condition: She wanted the evening to include a trip to Shanda's house.

She told Laurie that she needed her help in a plan she'd concocted to lure Shanda out of her house. Laurie played along, saying she'd do whatever Melinda wanted. Melinda said she wanted to kill Shanda and Laurie coldly agreed that it could be done. Then Laurie told Melinda that she'd already asked two girls from Madison to come with them that night. Melinda asked if they would go along with the plan to get Shanda, and Laurie assured her that it wasn't a problem.

Actually it was a problem. Laurie was sure that one of the girls, Toni Lawrence, wouldn't go if she knew about the plot against Shanda. Too much like the preppy kids at school who had ridiculed her, Toni was too skittish for Laurie's liking. The other girl, Hope Rippey, was a different story. Laurie held considerable sway over Hope, and she knew that Hope, who'd been in a number of fights herself, was game for anything and wouldn't shy away from a little terrorism.

Now that the Leatherburys lived in Louisville, fifteen-year-old Hope was Laurie's closest friend in Madison. They'd met in grade school and formed an immediate kinship. While other youngsters were ridiculing Laurie's strange ways, Hope was always there to lend a sympathetic ear, particularly when Laurie was going through her problems with her mother.

Hope also had her share of family problems. After years of heated arguments, Hope's parents had divorced when she was seven. The couple's oldest son, John, stayed with his father, Carl Rippey, who worked as an engineer at the Clifty Falls Power Plant in Madison. The three other children—Dan, Tina, and Hope, the youngest—moved to Michigan with their mother, Gloria.

Three years after the divorce Carl and Gloria decided to get back together for the good of the children. They never remarried, but they made a pact that they would no longer argue in front of the children. However there were still times when the home—a two-story frame house near the railroad tracks in west Madison—was rocked by violence. The two Rippey boys, John and Dan, had developed a rivalry that would often result in fistfights in front of Hope and the rest of the family.

"John was bigger and would beat Dan up," Carl Rippey recalled. "I allowed them to fight it out because I knew John would not hurt him badly. When Dan said 'uncle' the fight would stop."

The rough atmosphere of the Rippey home rubbed off on Hope, and she developed her own feistiness. When she was in junior high she organized a student walkout over a school policy she disagreed with. While the stunt irritated her teachers, it made her popular with the more rebellious students.

Hope, a medium-sized brunette with an earthy attractiveness, played basketball, ran track, and was in the school band in junior high, but she gave up all three pursuits after entering Madison Consolidated High School. As for the sports, it was probably a practical decision. She wasn't an outstanding athlete, and she realized she would have had difficulty competing at a higher level.

The decision to give up her formal music training, however, was unfortunate because she had real talent. She could play several instruments and had such a good ear that she could play a song on the piano after hearing it only a few times. But by her freshman year Hope had formed definite opinions about what was cool and what wasn't. And in her eyes, the school band wasn't. Every once in a while, Hope would talk about forming a rock band, but her initiatives never evolved into anything more than jamming in the garage with a few friends.

Hope had also realized that she would never be accepted by the preppy high-school crowd. There was a coarseness about her that kept her outside that circle. Hope had been smoking cigarettes for several years, and when angry she could curse like a construction worker. She liked to hang out at the poolroom in the local bowling alley and she had become a pretty good pool player.

Hope was not a beauty, but she had a pleasant enough face and a nice figure, as well as a forwardness that boys found attractive. Hope's older sister, Tina, had gotten pregnant in high school and kept the child. Hope too began having sex at a young age. By the time she was a sophomore she had made love with a number of boys. She never had a lengthy relationship with any of them and liked playing the field.

Though an average student, Hope had no firm plans to attend college. She expected that she would eventually find a guy to settle down with, have some kids, and raise a family in Madison. But she didn't give much thought to any of this, since her main concern was having fun.

It was Hope's thirst for adventure that had drawn her to Laurie Tackett. While other students at Madison High shunned Laurie and her strange behavior, Hope thought of her as the ultimate rebel, as someone to emulate—in all ways except sexuality. Laurie had confided in Hope that she was gay and, according to Kary Pope, had tried to interest her in a lesbian relationship. Hope had rejected these advances, but this had not damaged the girls' friendship.

Hope's parents, Carl and Gloria, tolerated their daughter's friendship with Laurie, even though they were put off by Laurie's punk hairstyles and weird clothes. The Rippeys would rather have seen their daughter spend more time with other friends, particularly Toni Lawrence.

Hope had known Toni since kindergarten, and though they weren't best friends they were still good friends. Toni had been acting a little too preppy lately for Hope's satisfaction, but she shared Hope's interest in shooting pool and meeting guys so they still found time to be together.

Toni was the youngest of Clifton and Glenda Lawrence's three daughters. She lived with her parents and her oldest sister and her family in a brick ranch home a few blocks from the Rippey residence. Although they weren't wealthy by any means, they enjoyed a modestly comfortable existence. Clifton Lawrence had been a boilermaker until an on-job injury ended his career and he was forced to make ends meet on his pension.

Toni, slim with light brown hair and glasses, was an average student and was well liked by her peers, though she wasn't the type to stand out in any crowd. Although generally timid and reflective—she wrote many poems—she enjoyed the company of friends, participated in school activities, and did all the things other girls her age did: went to the movies, shopped for clothes, and talked on the phone for hours on end.

A year and a half earlier, Toni had gone through the most traumatic time of her life. A boy had raped her while she was at a friend's house. Toni didn't tell her parents about it until her mother discovered a letter she'd written to a friend in which she mentioned her attacker's name. Clifton Lawrence tried to press charges against the boy but ended up seeing him only mildly reprimanded by police as a juvenile. When the story got around school, some classmates took the boy's side and ostracized Toni for turning him in. Already shy, she withdrew further and her studies suffered. She found a steady boyfriend and began to come out of the shell she'd built for herself. Unfortunately, her relationship with the boy ended when she learned he'd been with another girl, and Toni was eager now to find another boy she could be serious with.

Toni spent a great deal of time with Hope and Laurie during this troubled time. Toni had not liked Laurie much before and had thought her too strange. But at this vulnerable stage Toni became intrigued with Laurie's weird philosophy and behavior. Once she asked Laurie to spend the night with her. It was a disastrous evening. While sitting in Toni's room, Laurie tried to show Toni how she relieved stress by cutting herself. Trouble was, Laurie cut herself so deeply she had to be taken to the hospital. After that episode Toni's parents frowned on the friendship, and Toni pretty much agreed with them. She'd still see Laurie from time to time when she was with Hope, but she kept at a distance.

When Hope called Toni and asked her to go to the hardcore concert with her and Laurie, Toni was a bit reluctant. She told Hope that Laurie's strange ways scared her. But Hope was persistent. Laurie had let Hope in on Melinda's plans for Shanda, but Hope purposely didn't mention this to Toni. Instead, she pointed out that there would probably be a lot of cute boys at the concert. In Toni's mind that outweighed any reservations she had about Laurie. She told Hope that she'd ask her mother if she could go.

Glenda Lawrence said no. She didn't want Toni going down to Louisville at night, particularly with someone as irresponsible as Laurie. Toni decided not to push it. Instead, she asked her mother if she could spend that Friday night with her friend Mikel Pommerehn. Mikel was a nice girl, one of the preppy crowd that Toni usually ran with, and Glenda Lawrence gave her approval. But Toni had no intention of staying with Mikel. She had come up with a scheme to fool her parents.

"Can you cover for me tonight?" Toni asked Mikel the next day at school.

"What do you mean?" Mikel asked.

"I told my mom I was spending the night with you, but I'm going to a concert with Hope and Laurie."

"Ugh, Laurie Tackett," Mikel said. "I don't see why you hang around that girl."

"Come on, Mikel, be a friend," Toni pleaded. "All you have to do is tell my mom I'm in the bathroom if she calls. It's no big deal."

Mikel reluctantly agreed, and Toni was set. Hope had also lied to her parents, telling them that she was going to spend the night with a friend in a nearby town. That afternoon, Laurie picked up Toni and Hope in the school parking lot.

Laurie seemed in great spirits, ready for an evening of fun. But she was seething inside. The day before, she'd gone to the home of her ex-boyfriend, Aron Hall, and asked him to get back together with her. Aron was fed up with Laurie, who'd cheated on him with Danielle. Aron had never understood Laurie's obsession with witchcraft, and now he was hearing rumors around Madison that she was trying to join a Satanic cult. He told Laurie he didn't want anything to do with her.

"She said she was going to leave Madison because there was nothing to hold her there anymore," Aron said later. "She was crying and said she was going to kill herself or kill someone else."

The girls' first stop was the Madison WalMart, where Laurie and Hope stole some batteries for Laurie's CD player. Next they grabbed some hamburgers at a fast-food restaurant, bought gas and cigarettes at a convenience store, then headed toward New Albany. They were driving past the Indiana Army Ammunition Plant northeast of Jeffersonville when Laurie nudged Hope.

"Have you told her about it yet?" Laurie asked.

"About what?" Toni asked.

When Hope didn't volunteer the news, Laurie spoke up. "We're going to kill a little girl."

"No you're not," Toni said, not eager to be the butt of one of Laurie's jokes.

"Yes we are."

Sure that they were pulling her leg, Toni changed the subject and nothing more was said about it.

But it was still very much on Laurie's mind. She had already selected the place to take Shanda, a place that Laurie and her friends called the Witches' Castle. It was actually just the ruined remains of a grand old stone mansion that overlooked the Ohio River in Utica, a small town upstream from Jeffersonville. Laurie had taken Hope there before, and since it was on the way to Melinda's, they stopped by to show it to Toni. During daylight hours the ruins were not that scary, but the house still gave the timid Toni the creeps, particularly when Laurie began calling the cellar a dungeon and told of the séances she and the Leatherburys had conducted there. After about half an hour spent wandering around the site, the girls got back in the car and drove to Melinda's house.

Melinda greeted the trio at her door, then invited them upstairs to her bedroom. No one else was home. Melinda had met Hope once before when she was with Laurie at the River Falls Mall in Clarksville. She had liked her immediately, though she was a bit surprised that Laurie had a friend who was—well, not weird. She was even more taken aback by Toni, who talked and acted like the preppy kids whom she knew Laurie so despised.

In turn, Melinda was nothing like Toni had expected for a friend of Laurie's. Toni couldn't believe how many neat clothes Melinda had in her closet.

"I love those shoes," Toni said, eyeing all the different styles on display.

"Go ahead and try a pair on," Melinda said, eager to please. "If they fit, you can wear them tonight."

Hope joined in the fun, trying on a pair of Melinda's jeans.

In the middle of this girlish scene—one like so many Toni had experienced in other friends' bedrooms—a dark specter was suddenly raised. As Toni was trying on the shoes, Melinda pulled a rusty old kitchen knife from one of her purses and said, "This is what I'm going to use to scare Shanda."

Having captured everyone's attention, Melinda began a diatribe against her rival.

"Melinda said that she was going with a girl named Amanda and that Shanda was flirting with her and had been trying to steal her away," Toni said later. "She said they'd gotten into a lot of fistfights and that she wanted to kill her."

Toni's first impression of Melinda as a nice, normal girl vanished immediately. As Melinda continued to rant about killing Shanda, Toni began to worry about what she'd gotten herself into. Surely she couldn't be serious about wanting to kill the little girl. Surely she just wanted to scare her. Then she heard Melinda say how cute Shanda was and that she wouldn't mind having sex with her if only she didn't hate her so much. "I'd like to run the knife down her stomach and tease her with it," Melinda said.

The other girls listened as Melinda mapped out her plan to get Shanda alone. It was the same scheme that had gone awry that night with Kristie Brodfuehrer. They would go to Shanda's house and somehow entice her to the car where Melinda would be hiding, waiting to spring. Melinda knew that Shanda usually spent the weekends with her father, so she called there several times, hoping to confirm that Shanda was home. The line was busy, but Melinda was undeterred.

"I'll bet she's there," Melinda said. "Let's go get her."

5

Steve Sharer was a man of medium height with a solid build, wide shoulders, cord-strong wrists, and hands callused by his work as a heating and air-conditioning technician. Thirty-eight years old, he was growing bald and so had a habit of keeping his crown covered with a baseball cap. Not that he was a bit shy. He had a gregarious disposition and easy smile, and he spoke in the Southern drawl of the area.

Steve worked long hours and enjoyed nothing more than relaxing with his wife, Sharon, his stepchildren, Larry Dale and Sandy, and his daughter, Shanda, on the weekends. During the warm months that meant regular family trips to a lakeside cabin in Kentucky. In the winter, Steve would often tinker around in his garage on Saturdays and Sundays or tackle minor household chores—taking time out to watch car racing and college basketball.

But this weekend, he'd talked himself and several relatives into a major project. Steve's father and stepfather were coming over early Saturday morning to help him rip up carpet and knock down a wall to expand the living room in his house.

When Steve arrived at Jacque's townhouse to pick up

Shanda on Friday afternoon, the first words out of his daughter's mouth were, "Can I help on the living room?"

"Sure you can, honey," he said. An extra hand, even a young, overeager one, was always welcome.

That evening, as Shanda was helping Steve unload lumber from his truck, she got a call from her friend Michele Durham, who lived a few blocks away. Michele had big news: A boy who lived nearby was having a birthday party and Shanda was invited.

"Can I go?" Shanda asked.

Steve and Sharon had planned on ordering a pizza and spending the night with Shanda in front of the television. But they knew Michele to be a nice girl, and after all that Shanda had been through lately she deserved to have some fun. Within a minute of Steve's approval, Shanda had conveyed the news to Michele, hung up the phone, and set up shop in front of the bathroom mirror. "What am I going to do with my hair?" she moaned to Sharon.

It was just starting to get dark when Laurie pulled her car down Capital Hills Drive and edged over to the side of the road a few doors down from the Sharers' house.

Melinda turned to Toni and Hope and ordered them to go to the door.

"Why don't you go up?" Toni asked nervously.

"Because she won't come out if she sees Melinda," Laurie said tersely.

"Well why don't you go up?" Toni asked Laurie.

"Because I'm driving," Laurie said impatiently. "Are you going to chicken out or what?"

Hope intervened. "Come on, Toni, let's go."

"Don't forget now," Melinda said, reminding them of the plan they'd been going over on the way there. "Tell her you're friends of Amanda's and that Amanda wants Shanda to go with you and meet her somewhere."

Toni followed Hope reluctantly to the Sharers' front door.

Steve was relaxing on the living-room couch, Sharon was in the kitchen, and Shanda was still busy in the bathroom when they heard the knock. Before Steve or Sharon could make a move, Shanda had breezed past them and opened the front door.

"Is Shanda here?" Hope asked.

"I'm Shanda."

"Hi, my name is Hope. I'm a friend of Amanda's."

Shanda told Hope to lower her voice, then stepped out on the front porch so that her father wouldn't hear Amanda's name mentioned. Hope was about to introduce Toni when Toni spoke up. "Hi, I'm Stacy," she said. The fake name momentarily startled Hope, but she continued with the story Melinda had concocted and told Shanda that Amanda was waiting for her at a neat place down by the river called the Witches' Castle.

"Amanda really needs to talk with you," Hope said. "It's real important."

"I can't leave now," Shanda said. "Besides, I'm going to a party tonight."

"But you really need to talk to Amanda," Hope insisted. "She needs to tell you something."

Shanda's curiosity was piqued. "I know what," she said. "Why don't you bring Amanda back by my house later tonight, around midnight? I'll try to sneak out for a little while."

Sensing that this was the best they were going to do, Hope and Toni said goodbye, then spun around and raced back to the car.

"Who was that?" Steve asked as Shanda came back inside.

"Just some friends from school," she lied matter-of-factly, then quickly turned the corner into the bathroom, hoping to avoid any more questions.

"Wait a minute," Steve said. "Come back in here."

Shanda peeped around the corner. She studied her father's stern face and stepped meekly back into the living room.

"Why did they ask you if Shanda was here?" he demanded. "Don't you know them?"

Shanda became defensive. "Yes, I know them. I don't know why they asked that."

"I heard them say Amanda's name," Steve said, rising to his feet and placing his hands on his hips. "Are they friends of Amanda?"

"They didn't say anything about Amanda," insisted Shanda. "They just wanted to know if I could go with them to the mall and I told them I couldn't."

"I know what I heard," Steve said, his voice rising.

Sharon stepped between the two. "Now just cool it. Let's not get into a big argument about this."

At that moment the doorbell rang. It was Michele and another girl from the neighborhood. They'd come over to help Shanda get ready.

The tension faded and Steve sat back on the couch as Shanda and the other girls slipped into her bedroom. Shanda persuaded her stepsister, Sandy, to help fix her hair, an operation that took nearly half an hour. Finally Shanda was ready. She shyly approached her father.

"Can I stay out till eleven?" Shanda asked.

"Let's make it ten-thirty," said Steve, who hadn't quite gotten over the earlier argument.

As they walked to the party, Shanda mentioned to Michele the visit of the two unfamiliar girls.

"I remember her saying something about these two girls and something about Amanda, but I wasn't really paying attention," Michele said later. "Then we started talking about something else and she didn't mention it again."

A little while after Shanda had left, Sharon's two children went out for the evening, Sandy on a date and Larry Dale to a friend's party. Home alone, Steve and Sharon had a pizza delivered and snuggled together in front of the television.

Melinda was fuming when Hope and Toni arrived back at the car without Shanda, but she eased up when she learned that Shanda had told them to come back later. The plan would just have to be delayed for a while.

They drove on to Preston Highway in Louisville. The hardcore music concert was being held in a place called the Audubon Skatepark, located next door to a neighborhood bar in a run-down shopping center. It was filled with large ramps on which teenagers tested their skateboarding skills.

This night, however, the ramps had been pushed to the sides to make room for a dance floor and bandstand. The room was crowded with hundreds of teens jostling for space, pushing against each other as they rocked to the relentless rhythms of a punk band called Sunspring.

Seeing a girl that she knew, Melinda sneaked up and pinched her butt. The girl threw her arms around Melinda and they danced together. Laurie also felt at home here, and she liked the fierce, slashing chords played by the lead guitarist. She adopted a tough attitude and began searching the crowd for a familiar face.

Hope and Toni had taken off their shirts and walked inside with only their jackets over their bras, hoping that this sexy attire would attract guys. After a few moments of flashing their assets with little success, however, they became bored. The room was stiflingly hot, the music louder and harsher than they liked. They asked Laurie for her car keys, then pushed their way through the sweaty crowd to the exit. The sun was down now, and it was bitterly cold. The girls idled the engine to keep the heater running. Two teenage boys tapped on the window and asked if they could sit in the car for a minute to get warm. Toni and Hope thought the boys were good-looking and eagerly opened the door. After all, wasn't that why they had come along in the first place?

Hope and Toni talked to the boys, Jimmy and Brandon, for hours—about school, about skateboarding, about music, about everything but what was really on Toni's mind. Brandon could tell that something was bothering her and asked what was wrong.

Hope gave her a look that said Keep your mouth shut. But Toni's mind was spinning, and she had to talk to someone.

"You know those two girls we told you we came with?" Toni began. The boys nodded. The next words came out haltingly: "Well, they're going to kill a little girl tonight."

The boys stared back in disbelief, then they laughed. "Yeah, sure," Brandon said.

"No, I'm not kidding," Toni said seriously. "That's all they've been talking about. They even have a knife. Don't they, Hope?"

Hope decided, What the hell, she may as well show off a bit. She reached into Melinda's purse and pulled out the knife.

Brandon and Jimmy were unmoved. They knew plenty of kids that carried weapons, even guns. But Brandon could sense that Toni was truly frightened.

"Listen," he said, "if you're scared, why don't you just come with us? We'll find someone to give you a ride home."

Toni said okay eagerly, but Hope gave her a stern look. "We can't do that," she said. "We can't just take off. Laurie will be pissed."

Toni didn't want to leave without Hope and she didn't want to make Laurie angry. She thought to herself that maybe she was making too much of this. Maybe Melinda just wanted to beat up Shanda. Maybe nothing at all would come of this. She told the boys she'd stay with Hope. The knife was soon forgotten and they began to talk about other things.

Jimmy and Brandon were still in the car at about eleven-thirty when Melinda and Laurie came out of the concert. Seeing that the new arrivals were eager for them to leave, the boys said their goodbyes. The girls went to a nearby Long John Silver restaurant, and while they were waiting for their food, Melinda began talking about Shanda again. She told Toni that, much as she hated Shanda, she had to admit she was sexy. "I'd like to eat her out," Melinda said.

Melinda was all worked up. The concert was over now. There would be no more distractions. It was time to do what she'd set out to do. It was time to get Shanda.

When Shanda got home from the birthday party at eleven, she had her friend Michele by her side. Shanda was supposed to have been home half an hour earlier, and her father was not pleased.

"Can Michele spend the night?" Shanda asked.

"No," Steve said. "We're going to have a house full of people here early tomorrow morning to work on the living room. You'd better call Michele's mother and have her pick her up."

Then, feeling he was being too harsh on the girls, Steve

added, "While you're waiting, why don't you two finish off the pizza?"

The girls were still eating when Steve decided to go to bed.

"Shanda, when Michele leaves you can watch TV for a half hour, then you'd better turn in," he said.

"Okay, Dad," Shanda said. "Good night. I love you."

"I love you too," Steve told his daughter before he went into his bedroom and closed the door.

A few minutes later Michele's mother arrived and the two girls said their goodbyes.

"I think she'd forgotten all about those girls coming back," Michele said later. "She hadn't mentioned them again all night. If she remembered that they were coming back I doubt that she would have asked me to spend the night."

Michele had been gone less than half an hour when Laurie's car rolled down Shanda's street and slowed to a stop a few houses away. The headlights were off, but no one was getting out. Toni had just told the others that she wasn't going to the door with Hope this time.

"But she's expecting to see you," Melinda insisted.

"I'm not going," Toni said with all the firmness she could muster.

"I'll go with you, Hope," Laurie said, giving Toni a contemptuous look.

The two girls began walking up the sidewalk when they saw a pickup truck pull up. Sixteen-year-old Dale Gettings had just gotten off from his job at a pizza shop and was stopping by to pick up Shanda's stepbrother, Larry Dale. They were going to a big party out in the country.

Dale saw the two girls approaching.

"Hi," one of them said. "Do you know if Shanda is home?"

"I don't know," he said. "I'm just going to pick up her brother."

Assuming the girls were Shanda's friends, Dale motioned them to follow him. "Come on, we'll see if she's still up."

Dale went to the side-door porch and knocked, Laurie and Hope standing a few feet behind him in the driveway.

Shanda opened the door. The family dog, a rottweiler, stood quietly by her side. Dale petted the dog and asked about Larry Dale. Shanda told him that her stepbrother had already gotten a ride to the party with someone else.

As Dale pulled away in his truck, he saw Shanda step out onto the porch to talk to the two girls.

Out in the car, Toni sat on the front passenger side, with Melinda crouched in the backseat. Laurie came running back to the car by herself.

"Hurry up, we've got to hide you," Laurie said. "She'll be out in a minute."

Holding the kitchen knife in her hand, Melinda scooted down on the rear floorboard, while Laurie arranged an old red blanket and some dirty clothes on top of her. A few minutes later, Hope and Shanda came running to the car.

"Where's Amanda?" Shanda asked.

"We've going to meet her," Laurie said. "Come on, get in."

Toni stepped out of the car and let Shanda get in the middle of the front seat. Hope went around to drive, and Laurie got in the back with the hidden Melinda.

"Did you know that Amanda and Melinda have broken up?" Hope asked innocently as they pulled away.

"Yeah, I know," Shanda said. "Amanda and I went together for about four months."

Melinda had heard enough. Springing up suddenly, she pulled Shanda's hair back and put the dull side of the knife to her throat. Shanda shrieked.

"Surprise!" Melinda shouted. "I bet you didn't expect me here, you bitch."

Shanda recognized the voice and cried, "Please, Melinda, don't hurt me."

"Shut the fuck up," Melinda ordered. "Now answer me, and you better tell the truth: Did you and Amanda go to the haunted house at Harvest Homecoming?"

"Yes."

"Did you and Amanda have sex?" Melinda demanded.

Shanda hesitated, then felt the pressure of the knife increasing. "Yes," she said. "Please, don't hurt me."

Melinda was so angry she began to stutter. "You . . . you

bitch." She kept the knife to Shanda's throat as Hope drove them down to the river, then headed east toward Utica and finally arrived at the Witches' Castle. Shanda was sobbing as Melinda and Laurie each grabbed one of her arms, pulled her out of the car, and marched her up the hill to the foreboding ruins. Toni and Hope stumbled behind, using lighters to see in the darkness.

Entering the main room of the old stone house, Laurie and Melinda sat Shanda down on a stone bench and tied her wrists and ankles with two pieces of rope.

"Doesn't she have pretty hair?" Melinda taunted. "I wonder how pretty she'd look if we cut it off."

"No," Shanda stammered. "Please, don't. Please, let me go. I'll stay away from Amanda, I promise."

Hope, who'd been given the knife while Melinda tied Shanda's wrists, moved closer to Shanda and waved the knife in front of her. "I like that watch," Hope said, pointing to the Mickey Mouse watch Shanda had gotten for Christmas. She handed the knife back to Melinda and took the watch from Shanda's wrist. She pressed a button and a Disney tune began to play. "Ooo, I love this," Hope said.

Melinda pulled several rings from Shanda's fingers, giving a couple to Toni and putting the others on herself.

Laurie was bored with these childish pranks and decided it was time for a real scare. She stood in front of Shanda and pointed to the pitch-black cellar.

"That's a dungeon," she said creepily. "There's human bones down there." She stared ominously at Shanda. "Yours could be next."

Shanda's eyes were wide with fright and she drew quick, deep breaths. "Don't hurt me," she moaned.

"It's too damn cold and dark in here," Laurie declared, then abruptly bolted down the hill to her car. She returned with a black T-shirt.

"I love this shirt," Laurie said, holding it up for the others to see. It had a smiling yellow face on it, but the face had a bullet hole painted on its forehead and blood was running from it.

But this was a special occasion, so Laurie showed no hesitancy in dousing the shirt with the remaining contents of a whiskey bottle she'd found in her trunk, then setting it on fire. But once the fire started, Laurie was struck with the fear that someone in a passing car might spot the flames and stop to investigate.

"Let's get out of here," she said. "I know where we can take her. There's a place near my house where nobody will see us."

Melinda and Laurie untied Shanda, then grabbed her roughly by the arms and marched her back to the car. When they discovered that they were low on gas, they made Shanda lie down on the backseat and covered her with a blanket before they pulled into a gas station. As Laurie walked inside to ask the attendant for directions, Toni told the others that she needed to call a boy she knew in Louisville.

Toni would say later that she'd felt a compelling urge to talk to someone—not to tell them what was happening, but just to hear a familiar voice. She didn't intend to tell Mike about Shanda's abduction, and she didn't. She and Mike talked for several minutes. It was just chitchat. She told him about her trip to the hardcore concert and said she hoped to see him the next time she went to Louisville. Despite all that had happened, Toni's interest was only in her own well-being. She had called Mike so that she would feel more at ease and it had worked. After exchanging final pleasantries with the boy, Toni hung up and returned to the car in which Shanda remained captive.

Toni had passed up the perfect opportunity to call the police and put an end to this wretched affair, since the others were too far away to hear what she was saying. Instead, she rejoined the others and the car pulled away.

But in a few minutes they were lost again and had to pull into another gas station. This time Hope and Toni spotted a couple of boys in another car and got out to talk to them.

"I told them I wanted to go with them but I said it in a joking way," Toni said later. "They said they didn't want to go all the way to Madison, but they followed us for a little while before they turned around."

Once again an opportunity to bring the vile affair to an end was passed up.

As they continued on the fifty-mile drive to Madison, Shanda pleaded constantly with Melinda to take her home. When that failed, she tried threats.

"I'm going to get in trouble for being out so late," she whimpered. "My stepbrother is going to be mad and come looking for me."

"Ooo, I'm so scared," Laurie said with a laugh.

Melinda was enjoying this too. She forced Shanda to slip off her bra, then handed it over the front seat to Hope. Joining in the fun, Hope squirmed out of her own bra and put Shanda's on—all the while still steering the car. Melinda and Laurie laughed at this while Toni stared out the window, saying nothing.

Caught up in the thrill of the moment, Laurie turned up the boombox that was sitting on her lap and started singing along to a strange song that Toni would later say sounded like an opera. After a while, Laurie started mimicking Shanda and acted like she was crying. Then she started laughing.

It was a weird, maniacal laugh. Hope and Toni had heard it before. Laurie called it her Devil Laugh.

6

They drove through Madison, then headed north to the rural countryside where Laurie lived. Passing farms and forests, they turned down Laurie's road, sped by her house, and swung up a dirt road. The car bumped along the rugged path a quarter of a mile and stopped at the edge of some woods.

The girls stepped out into the cold night air, Melinda and Laurie pulling Shanda from the car.

"I gave Shanda a hug," Toni said later. "She begged Melinda not to hurt her. I told Melinda to take her home but Melinda told me to shut up. She said we couldn't take her back because she knew all of our names. That's when Melinda told her to take her clothes off. Melinda said she wanted them as a souvenir. I got back in the car. It was cold out there."

Hope joined Toni in the car and the two of them watched through the windows as Shanda stripped down to her panties and T-shirt, while Melinda held the knife threateningly in front of her. Suddenly Laurie grabbed Shanda and held her arms behind her back. "Do it now," she shouted. "Hit her."

Melinda punched Shanda in the stomach, and the girl

70

crumbled to the ground. "Please stop," Shanda cried. "I have asthma. Please stop. I can't breathe."

Melinda grabbed Shanda's head and smashed her knee into her rival's face. The force of the blow drove Shanda's lips into her braces and blood flowed from her mouth.

Next Melinda and Laurie were both on top of Shanda, trying to cut her throat with the knife. They managed to stick the point of the knife into the back of Shanda's neck, but she squirmed loose before it could be driven deeper.

Hope suddenly bolted out of the car and joined in the fray. It looked to Toni as though Hope was trying to help Melinda and Laurie. Then just as quickly, Hope rejoined Toni in the car.

"Why are you helping them?" Toni asked.

"I wasn't," Hope said. "I was trying to pull Shanda away."

Shanda managed to wrestle away from the knife, but Melinda and Laurie pinned her to the ground again. Melinda wrapped her arms around Shanda's legs as Laurie pulled a rope from her pocket, slipped it around Shanda's neck, and twisted it tightly.

Inside the car, Hope and Toni cranked up the radio so they wouldn't hear Shanda's screams. "I was about as freaked out as I could get," Hope said later. "I was flipping. I wasn't crying. I was too scared to cry. Toni was holding my hand because I was shaking so bad."

Shanda's frantic movements finally ceased.

"Do you think she's dead?" Melinda asked.

"I don't know," Laurie answered.

They hoisted Shanda's limp body from the ground and tossed her into the car trunk. Then the two girls hopped in the front seat beside Hope, who was behind the steering wheel. Toni sat alone in the back. Hope revved the engine and spun the car around, heading down the gravel road at top speed.

In the darkness, the car careened off the path and ran over a log, dislodging the muffler. The car's tailpipe roared as Hope drove to the road, then swung up Laurie's driveway and parked behind the Tackett house, where Laurie's parents were in bed asleep. Leaving Shanda in the trunk, the four girls slipped quietly into the house through the back door.

Laurie was extremely cool in the aftermath of the violence. After she and Melinda went to the bathroom to wash off Shanda's blood, Laurie strolled to the kitchen to fix them all soft drinks, as if nothing out of the ordinary had occurred. But she could tell that the others were losing their composure. Back in Laurie's room, Melinda and Hope were talking nervously while Toni sat silently on the bed with the frightened look of a small animal caught in a car's headlights.

Laurie's room had always been her one hideaway, and she had decorated it with artifacts of her strange beliefs. She'd converted an old preacher's pulpit that she'd found into an occult altar, filled with books on witchcraft. One of the books had come with a small cloth pouch of smooth colored stones, each marked with a mystic symbol.

Sensing that she had to do something to calm the others, Laurie dumped the stones on her bed and began to read the signs.

"These tell your fortune, Melinda," she said softly, careful not to wake her sleeping parents. "Everything is going to be all right."

At that moment the girls heard Laurie's dog barking outside her window. They listened closer and could hear the muffled screams of Shanda in the trunk.

"I'll take care of this," Laurie said.

She went to the kitchen and grabbed a paring knife, then stuck her head back in the room and showed it to the others. "I'll be right back," she said.

A few long minutes passed before Laurie came back inside. She went back to the bathroom to wash off more of Shanda's blood, and the other girls noticed that the screaming had stopped and the dog was quiet.

When she returned to the room, Laurie announced, "We need to go country cruising. Come on, let's go before my folks wake up."

"I'm not going anywhere," Toni insisted. "I'm staying here."

Laurie was disgusted with Toni's backtalk, but there was no time to argue. "Hope?" she asked.

"I'm staying with Toni," Hope said.

Laurie turned to Melinda, giving her a look that would accept no more shows of cowardice, and said, "Let's go, Melinda."

If Melinda wanted to stay she said nothing. She followed Laurie out the door.

"Is she dead?" Melinda asked as they climbed into the car.

"I don't know."

"Well, what did you do to her when you went out?"

Laurie didn't answer. Instead, she suggested that they dump Shanda somewhere in the country.

Melinda suddenly remembered what her friend Crystal Wathen had told her about disposing of a body. "Let's burn her," she said.

Nodding her head in approval, Laurie drove the car some fifty yards from the house to a burn pile that the Tacketts used to incinerate trash. Leaving the engine running, she and Melinda got out and searched the site for something to start a fire with. Suddenly Laurie noticed a light on in the trailer on the adjoining property. She could see the shadow of a man at the window. He was looking at them.

Ace Newman and Michael Starkey, both in their late teens, had just gotten home from their jobs at a pizza shop in Madison. They were too keyed up to turn in, so they had started to repair a leaky sink in their bathroom. Newman would remember later that it was two-thirty when he and Starkey heard the sound of Laurie's noisy muffler out by the burn pile. Newman looked out the window and could see two bodies moving about.

Thinking fast, Laurie scampered up to the trailer and knocked on the door.

Laurie had talked to Newman and Starkey only a few times in the past, when she had dropped by to get soft drinks out of the Coke machine they kept on their porch. This was the story Laurie fed Newman when he opened the door.

"Hi," she said, with all the casualness she could muster. "Can I have change for the Coke machine?"

"Sure," Newman replied, fishing a few quarters out of his pocket. "Say, what are you all doing out there?"

"My muffler's broken."

"Need any help?" Newman offered.

"No, I can fix it," Laurie said, anxious to end the conversation. "Thanks anyway. See ya."

Back at the car, Laurie told Melinda that they should make tracks. "We'll just drive around and let her die slowly," she said.

With the muffler growling, the girls drove away, staying on the side roads, traveling by darkened farmhouses and through deep woods. Every so often a car would pass in the other direction and Laurie would ease up on the gas pedal so as not to draw attention to the noisy muffler.

After a while, a pair of headlights appeared behind them and for long, nervous minutes they watched the rear-view mirror as the headlights gradually drew closer. Then, just as suddenly as they had appeared, the headlights vanished as the car turned into a driveway. Laurie and Melinda continued on their way, searching the roadside for a place to dump the body.

As they approached a long bridge over a valley, Laurie eased the car to a stop.

"I know this place," she said. "There's a creek down there. Let's throw her in."

Melinda argued against it, saying that the body would float and be found by someone. Then she again raised the possibility of burning Shanda.

"Let's see if she's dead yet," Laurie said, grabbing a tire iron she kept under her seat.

The two walked back to the trunk and opened the lid. The rush of cold air caused Shanda to stir, and she slowly began to sit up. Her hair and arms were smeared with blood and the pupils of her eyes rolled back in her head as she tried to speak, managing to mutter only one word, "Mommy," before Laurie hit her with the tire iron and slammed the trunk lid down on her.

After driving awhile longer, Melinda and Laurie came up with a plan to finally kill Shanda without getting their hands soiled. They stopped again and opened the trunk, hoping that Shanda would stumble out on the road where they could run over her. But Shanda was too injured to do anything but lie there, so they closed the trunk again and drove on, cursing Shanda for clinging to life so determinedly and hoping that she would just go ahead and die.

Back at Laurie's house, Hope and Toni talked in whispers so not to wake the Tacketts. Neither could believe what had happened on the logging road. They hadn't considered that it would go this far, and both wondered what was happening now. Was that little girl already dead? What were Melinda and Laurie going to do with her? They were afraid of the answers. Afraid of their involvement. Afraid of waking Laurie's parents and telling them what was going down. Afraid of what would happen to them if they walked into the kitchen and called the police.

The quiet was suddenly broken by a soft tap on the window.

"What . . . what was that?" Toni stuttered.

"I don't know." Summoning her nerve, Hope looked out the window. "It was just Laurie's cat," she said, sighing with relief.

Then they heard heavy footsteps walking down the hallway toward the bedroom. Scooting under the bedcovers, they pretended to be asleep. The door cracked open slowly. Laurie's father stepped inside and flicked on the light.

George Tackett was startled to find two girls in Laurie's bed.

"Where's Laurie?" he asked.

Thinking quickly, Hope said, "She and Melinda went to get something to eat."

"It's way too late for that kind of stuff," Tackett grumbled before closing the door and returning to his bedroom.

Laurie and Melinda had passed through the country crossroads known as Canaan and were into another stretch of thick woods when they heard a noise barely audible over the tailpipe's roar, a thumping in the trunk. Then came Shanda's voice.

"It wasn't really a scream or a yell," Melinda said later.

"It's like something was messed up with her throat. It was like a gurgle. I know at one point she was saying my name. That's when we stopped and Tackett told me I had to get behind the steering wheel and keep my foot on the gas so the muffler would be louder than Shanda's kicking."

Laurie walked back to the trunk, grasping the black metal tire iron.

"I watched through the rear-view mirror but I couldn't see much," Melinda recalled. "I heard something thump and there was like a weeping sound. I heard this hit like you would hear when someone hits you in your stomach. I heard a yell and a thump and then I heard the trunk door slam down. Then here comes Tackett back in."

Laurie slid into the passenger seat and told Melinda to drive off. As she did, Laurie stuck the bloody tire iron under Melinda's nose. "Smell this, will you," Laurie said gleefully. "I hit her head and it was so cool. I could feel it going in."

Laurie thumped the tire iron against the dashboard. "I hit it like this. I hit it this hard. It felt so neat."

"Stop it!" Melinda screamed. "You're making me sick."

Laurie stuck it in Melinda's face again, and Melinda ripped it from her hand and threw it in the backseat.

Laurie laughed. "You've got to see her. She's soaked with blood. She's red."

Laurie's bloodlust made Melinda shiver. She wanted Shanda dead but she'd never imagined that murder would be such dirty work.

And so it went. Driving and listening for signs of life in the trunk. Every time they heard a stirring, they would stop and do what was necessary to silence Shanda. This continued for hours, until the light of daybreak sent them rushing back to Laurie's house.

Laurie's father was gone by now, having left early for work at the factory. Laurie's mother was still in bed and the house was silent as Laurie and Melinda walked into Laurie's bedroom, where Hope and Toni were half asleep.

Toni slowly opened her eyes. "Where's that little girl?" she asked.

"It was just a nightmare," Laurie said prankishly. "There was no little girl."

"Oh, good," Hope muttered groggily.

It was a nightmarish experience, all right. But it was real. Toni could see Shanda's blood splattered on Melinda and Laurie.

"They had blood on their hands and Melinda had blood on her face," Toni remembered. "They went to the bathroom to wash it off."

Upon returning, Melinda and Laurie told Hope and Toni that Shanda was still in the trunk and that she might still be breathing. At least she was the last time they'd checked.

"They said that every time Shanda screamed they hit her on the head with the tire iron," Toni said later. "They were laughing about it. Both of them."

Toni was scared. Scared of the situation. Scared of Laurie and Melinda. But Hope's fear was more focused. For the first time she began to look at their dilemma from a practical standpoint. It had gone too far to turn back now. The job had to be finished.

Leaving the others in the bedroom, Laurie went to the telephone and dialed the number of her neighbor, Brian Tague.

"Brian, this is Laurie Tackett. Do you have any gasoline? I need some gas. I need to burn some clothes on our burn pile."

Tague was irritated by the early-morning call, but he wanted to be neighborly. "I don't have any gas, Laurie," he said. "I might have some kerosene. I'll check. Why don't you call me back in a little bit."

Laurie said she would, but she was growing impatient. Maybe they could get a fire going at the burn pile with matches and lighters. Laurie stuck her head back in her room and told the others to follow her. The four girls walked through the cold morning mist to the car parked by the burn pile.

"Want to see her?" Laurie asked Hope and Toni.

Toni gazed blankly at the blood-stained trunk lid, then said, "No. I don't want to see anything." She looked at Hope, expecting her friend to agree with her. But Hope had chosen her path. She was with Laurie and Melinda now. She nodded at Laurie to open the trunk.

Laurie gave Toni a chilling stare. "If you don't want to look, then get in the car and rev the engine," she said tersely, handing Toni the keys. "She might scream again."

Following orders, Toni slipped behind the wheel and cranked the engine. Laurie slowly opened the trunk. Shanda was lying in a fetal position.

"There was not an inch of her that did not have blood," Hope said later.

Laurie pulled an old sweater out of the trunk, laid it on the burn pile, and tried to set it on fire. While she was doing this, Hope reached into the trunk and pulled out a bottle of window cleaner that was lying beside Shanda. She pointed the bottle at Shanda and sprayed the blue liquid on her wounds.

"I don't know why she did that," Laurie said later.

"She had this strange look on her face when she did it," Melinda recalled. "She was into it. Sort of like when you dissect an animal."

Shanda moved. The girls held their breath in horror as the bloody, beaten girl pushed herself up into a sitting position. She had one hand on her head and the other on the spare tire and slowly swayed back and forth.

"Her eyes weren't really open, but they sort of were," Hope recalled. "They were kind of back in her head."

"We tried to talk to her then but she wouldn't talk or couldn't," Laurie said later.

Melinda turned to Hope and asked, "Where's your heart?"

Hope touched the left side of her chest. "Here. Why?"

"Well," Melinda said, "how do you get a knife to go into somebody's body?"

Eager to end it now, Hope told Melinda, "You've got to jab it in."

This bizarre scene was suddenly interrupted by the voice of Laurie's mother. Peggy Tackett had walked out on her back porch. From her position facing the front of the car, Laurie's mother could see only the three girls standing around the trunk and Toni behind the wheel.

"What's going on?" she yelled.

Laurie slammed the trunk down on Shanda's head, imprisoning her again. "I'm trying to get a fire started," Laurie yelled at her mother.

"You aren't starting any bonfires at this time of the morning," Peggy Tackett shouted back. "Are you just getting in?"

Fearing that her mother would investigate, Laurie stormed toward the house, arguing as she went. "Just shut up and leave me alone," Laurie sneered. She and her mother stood nose to nose, wrangling for several long minutes. After a while, Peggy Tackett's anger began to fade. She looked at Melinda, Hope, and Toni. These were the kind of nice girls she'd been wanting Laurie to hang around with. They weren't weird like the Leatherburys and Kary Pope.

"Well," she said finally, "do you want me to fix you and your friends breakfast?"

"Nah," Laurie said as she turned away. "I've got to take them home. We're going to stop by McDonald's."

Laurie drove the car away with Melinda beside her and Hope and Toni in the backseat. "We've got to get some gas," she said. "We're going to have to burn her. We have to kill her. She knows all our names."

Laurie pulled the car into a Clark Oil station on State Road 62, a busy highway lined with fast-food restaurants north of downtown Madison. But at this time on a Saturday morning, there were few people on the road. Laurie told Toni to go with her into the station, where they bought a two-liter bottle of Pepsi and paid for several dollars of gasoline.

While they were inside, Melinda and Hope heard Shanda moving in the trunk. At that moment a car pulled up beside them at the pumps. Fearful that the man getting out of his car would hear Shanda, Hope ran around to the driver's seat and moved Laurie's car away from the pumps.

"What's going on?" Laurie asked upon her return.

"Listen," Hope said.

Shanda's moans were growing louder.

Laurie quickly passed the Pepsi around, and after each girl took a drink, she poured the rest out. By this time the other car had left and the girls drove back to the pumps. Laurie filled the plastic bottle with gasoline, topped off her gas tank, then drove away. They headed back north, taking some of the same side roads that Laurie and Melinda had driven the night before. Hope said she knew a place where they could burn Shanda—a little-traveled gravel lane called Lemon Road.

There were no farmhouses around, only harvested soybean fields on both sides of the country lane. The car stopped beside a wide dirt path that ran between a crop field and thick woods. Laurie swung the sedan around and backed a few feet up the path. All four girls stepped out. A tractor and a combine were parked about thirty feet up the path on the edge of the woods. But otherwise it was deserted. As Laurie started to open the trunk, Toni got back in the car.

"I didn't want to take part," Toni said later. "I didn't want to touch her. I didn't want to look at her."

Laurie held the blanket used earlier to cover Melinda at Shanda's house. "Come on, let's wrap it around her and lift her out," she said.

"Oh, gross," Melinda moaned, backing away in disgust.

Angered by Melinda's wavering, Hope snarled, "I don't know what your problem is. You started the whole thing."

Hope grabbed one end of the blanket and helped Laurie wrap it around Shanda's trembling body. Toni glanced out the window as Shanda, rolled up in the blanket, was lifted out of the trunk and dropped behind the car in the middle of the dirt path.

"I saw her arm move, then I looked away," Toni said later. "The radio was on. I just listened to it and didn't watch what was happening. I didn't want to be there."

Laurie stood over Shanda with the bottle of gasoline. "Here," she said, extending her arm toward Melinda.

Melinda backed away.

"Here," Laurie said, shoving the bottle at Hope.

"No," Hope said.

Laurie leered at her. "Just pour it, damn it. Just do it."

Hope grabbed the bottle and doused the blanket with

gasoline. Laurie stepped closer and drew a pack of matches from her jacket. She struck a match and tossed it. A flash of flames leapt up, scorching Laurie's hair before she could step away. As the fire raged, the girls scrambled back to the car, all three piling into the front seat. As Laurie wheeled the car onto Lemon Road, Toni, alone in the backseat, turned to look at Shanda's burning body. They'd driven only a few hundred yards when Melinda noticed that the flames had already begun to die down.

"My God, what if she doesn't burn all the way!" Melinda yelped. "We've got to go back. Go back."

Laurie spun the car around and jerked to a stop a few feet from the flaming blanket. This time Melinda got out alone and walked over to the smoldering body. Holding the bottle, still half full of gasoline, she stood for a moment, looking into the face of the girl she so hated. Then she tossed the open bottle on her. The fire surged again with an angry flash.

Melinda was laughing when she got back into the car. "You should have seen it," she roared. "Her tongue was going in and out of her mouth."

Toni shrunk deeper in the backseat and bit down on her knuckles so hard that she drew blood.

"I'm so glad she's gone," said Melinda with a giggle. "I'm so glad she's out of me and Amanda's lives."

As they drove away, Melinda wondered aloud if someone would see the smoke.

"Nobody goes down that road," Hope assured her.

"I'm going to come back later tonight with a shovel and bury her," Laurie said.

Toni's conspicuous silence worried Laurie and Melinda.

"Everybody has to keep their mouth shut," Laurie said, making menacing eye contact with Toni in the rear-view mirror.

Melinda spun around in her seat and told Toni, "If we all stick together, everything will be okay."

Hope spoke up for her friend. "We're not going to say anything, are we, Toni?"

Toni said nothing but nodded her head in acknowledgment.

"Let's go to McDonald's," Laurie said with a smile. "I'm hungry."

Taking care to back the car into a parking space so that no one could see the blood stains on the trunk, Laurie strutted inside the restaurant and ordered a full breakfast. While Hope and Melinda were deciding what they wanted, Toni slipped away to a pay phone.

"Where's Toni?" Laurie growled as they sat at a table.

"She said she had to call Mikel Pommerehn," Hope said. "Her mom still thinks she spent the night there. She wants to make sure her mom hasn't called."

"That better be who she's calling," Laurie said. Then she stuck a fork in her sausage patty and showed it to Melinda and Hope. "It looks like Shanda."

Looking nervously back at the table, Toni whispered into the phone, "Something really bad has happened."

"You didn't get in a wreck, did you?" Mikel asked.

"No. Worse than that. Something terrible."

"Well, what?" Mikel was getting impatient.

"Laurie and her friend Melinda, they killed a little girl."

There was a pause at the other end. "You're kidding," Mikel said finally. "You're kidding, aren't you? I don't think it's funny, Toni."

"No," Toni said sharply, then turned to see if Laurie and the others were looking at her. They were. She lowered her voice and pleaded with Mikel to believe her. "They beat her with a crowbar and took her out and burned her. Me and Hope watched it."

Mikel was too stunned to say anything.

"Listen, I can't talk anymore," Toni said. "They're getting suspicious. Call my mom and tell her I'm on my way home but don't say a thing about this. Come up to Arby's and meet me in an hour."

When she walked back to the table, Laurie eyed her distrustfully. "Who were you talking to?" Laurie asked.

"Just Mikel," Toni said coolly. "I wanted to see if my mom called. She didn't."

Satisfied, Laurie finished her food and the girls drove Toni to her house. Before she got out, Laurie and Melinda reminded her again that everyone had to stick together. Everybody had to keep quiet. Toni said she understood, then ran into her home.

"Hi, Toni," Clifton Lawrence said as his daughter came through the door. "Did you have a good time at Mikel's last night?"

"Yeah, Dad," Toni said, rushing to her room. "Can't talk. I've got to get ready for work."

Later, as Clifton Lawrence drove his daughter to Arby's, where she worked as a cashier, he noticed that she had little to say. He figured she and Mikel had just stayed up late. She's probably just tired, he thought.

7

Steve Sharer awoke to the sound of the television in the living room. The clock at his bedside said four in the morning.

Damn. Shanda must have left it on. He rolled out of bed, stumbled into the living room, and switched off the late-night movie. The house felt drafty. Then he saw why: The kitchen door was slightly ajar. Probably the work of his stepson, Larry Dale, Steve thought. He had probably come in late and forgotten to close it. He would have to talk to that boy in the morning. Steve shut and locked the door. On the way back to his bedroom he glanced in Shanda's bedroom but didn't see her. He assumed she'd gone to sleep on the bed downstairs, didn't think any more about it, and went back to sleep.

Three hours later the alarm clock started ringing. Seven o'clock. Time to get up. Steve's father and Sharon's stepfather would be arriving soon, ready to start on the remodeling job. Steve slipped out of bed and Sharon followed. As Steve started a pot of coffee, Sharon went downstairs to check on Shanda. Seconds later she came running back up to the kitchen.

"Steve! Shanda's not down there."

"What do you mean she's not down there?"

"She's not there and neither is Larry Dale," Sharon said. "I don't think Larry Dale even came home last night. His bed hasn't been slept in."

"My God, I bet she got up to let the dog out and I locked her out last night," Steve shouted as he ran out the back door. He checked the cars. He checked the garage. Then he noticed Sparky, the family dog, limping up the driveway. She was whimpering and dragging her hindquarters.

"What the hell is going on?" Steve wondered out loud.

If Steve had locked the door on Shanda while she was putting Sparky outside, surely she'd have banged on the door or come around and knocked on her parents' bedroom window. They would have heard her.

"It was freezing out and her coat and purse were still on the kitchen table," Steve recalled. "I figured that if she was locked out she'd have gone over to one of the neighbors. I went to all their houses but she wasn't there."

Sharon called Michele's house. Michele hadn't seen Shanda since the night before. Sharon started calling all of Shanda's friends. Just then Steve's father, Bill Sharer, pulled up in the driveway. It was Shanda's grandfather who first uttered the unspeakable: "Maybe somebody grabbed her when she let the dog out."

Steve and his father got in Steve's truck and drove around the neighborhood, then to some woods not far away.

"Dad said we needed to check the woods, so we got out and combed the area," Steve said. "I felt like I was in a nightmare. I was going crazy with worry."

Sixty miles away, near the small town of Canaan, a man who would play a pivotal role in this drama was just waking up.

Donn Foley was roused from sleep by the sound of his hounds rustling in their chainlink pens outside his trailer.

The bird dogs were restless because it was Saturday, the day their master took them quail hunting. The hounds knew it was Saturday because the sun had crept over the treetops and Donn's truck was still parked beside the barn. Had it been a weekday, the pickup would be gone by now and Donn would be at work, digging up and dismantling unexploded mortar shells at the firing range at Jefferson Proving Grounds, an Army artillery-testing installation a few miles west of his small farm. It was dangerous and exhausting work and Donn, a hard-muscled, forty-nine-year-old veteran of the Vietnam War, enjoyed sleeping late on Saturdays.

He lingered in the warmth of his blankets, in no hurry to start the day. Then he remembered something that made him almost as eager as the dogs: This was the day he'd be taking his youngest pointer pup on her first hunt.

Donn pulled his aching body out of bed and quickly slipped on his overalls, sweatshirt, boots, and hunting vest. He shuffled into his kitchen and put on a pot of coffee, then pulled a worn baseball cap over his balding head and stepped out into the brisk morning air. As he walked toward the barn to feed his ponies and mules, he saw the anxious dogs spinning in crazy circles in their pens, yapping in frenzied excitement. After completing his morning chores, he returned to the warmth of his kitchen and poured himself a cup of coffee. He lit a cigarette, then sat down at the kitchen table to wait for his older brother, Ralph, to arrive.

As he looked out the kitchen window, Donn saw his son Greg's truck approaching on the gravel road that ran by the front of the farm. But Greg's truck breezed by without stopping. The next vehicle down the road was Ralph Foley's truck. As it pulled up the driveway, Donn Foley stuck his head out the trailer door. "Want a cup of coffee?" he asked.

"Yeah, I guess I will," Ralph said. "No point in hurrying. It's still pretty cold."

The brothers knew that quail were slow to move from their coveys on cold mornings. The birds would huddle for warmth with their tail ends together until the temperature rose to a comfortable degree. The quail would not become targets for hunters until they spread out into fields to feed on scattered grain.

Donn and Ralph finished the pot of coffee, then, deciding they'd waited long enough, they loaded the dogs into the traveling cages in the back of Ralph's truck and headed toward the Jefferson Proving Grounds, where Donn had hunting privileges on the hundreds of acres that weren't used for testing.

The Foleys had traveled less than a mile when they turned onto Lemon Road. As they drove along slowly, Donn gazed out his window at the stubble of a harvested soybean crop. Donn knew that the owner of the field didn't allow hunting on his property, but a few weeks earlier Donn had spotted quail in the field and he and Ralph had turned the dogs loose and bagged a few.

Dense woods filled Ralph's side of the road, so he left the bird-watching to his brother. It wasn't until the woods on the left opened into another barren soybean field that Ralph looked out his window. Almost immediately he spotted something strange—a horrible sight that still burns in his memory.

"Goddamn, did you see that?" Ralph said. He lifted his foot off the gas pedal and the truck eased to a stop. "That looked like a body."

Donn studied the curious expression on his brother's face and laughed nervously. "Ah, bullshit." Then he turned and looked through the back window and saw what had startled his brother. "What the hell is that?" Donn asked.

Ralph put the truck in reverse and backed up slowly, stopping alongside a dark figure that was lying on the edge of the road in a dirt path used by tractors and combines.

"That ain't no body," Donn said. "Somebody's playing a prank. That's one of them mannequins."

The brothers got out of the truck and stepped closer. The figure was that of a young woman. It was nude except for a pair of ripped blue panties. It lay on its back, its head pointed toward the road. It was charred black from waist to head. Its pale white legs were spread open and bent at the knees. Both arms seemed frozen in motion, stiffly reaching up to the gray winter sky with fists tightly clenched around what appeared to be fragments of cloth. Specks of long, wavy, honey-blond hair could be seen beneath a matted gray filmy substance. The face had been blackened by fire and smoke. The eyes were cloudy and without color. The mouth was open, teeth clenched. The figure's breasts, scorched by the fire, didn't appear to have nipples.

"You know what this is?" Donn Foley said. "It's one of them rubber dolls that guys have sex with. Somebody burned it as a joke."

"I don't know," Ralph said. "It looks real."

"But it doesn't smell." One of Donn Foley's comrades in Vietnam had been killed by napalm and he'd never forgotten the stench. "If it was human it would smell."

Donn knelt beside the figure. He could see toenails and body hair. With a trembling finger, he scratched the foot. It was cold but it was soft and fleshy.

"Goddamn, I think it's real," he gasped. "We better call the police."

The brothers hopped in the truck and Ralph started to pull off the road to turn around when Donn ordered him to stop. "Wait a minute," he said, pointing to the dirt path where the body lay. "There's some tire tracks right there. You don't want to mess them up. Maybe you better back out of here."

Ralph saw where the icy gully beside the road had been broken by tire tracks. The tracks were fresh, and the water hadn't frozen back over. Ralph put the truck in reverse and backed away until he was far enough up the road to turn around.

Back at the trailer, Donn called the Jefferson County sheriff's office in Madison. Chief Deputy Randy Spry, an acquaintance of Donn's, answered the phone. It was 10:55 A.M.

"Randy, this is Donn Foley."

"Yeah, Donn. How are you doing?"

"Not so good. I think we've found a body."

"Are you sure?"

"No, I'm not sure." Donn hesitated a few seconds. "There is a doubt in my mind. It may be a mannequin or one of them rubber dolls, but I'm almost positive it's a body. It's been burned."

After Donn gave him directions, Spry told the Foleys to wait for him at the corner of Lemon and Jefferson Church oads. Knowing that it would take Spry twenty minutes to drive from downtown Madison, Donn fixed two cups of coffee and joined Ralph at the kitchen table. The dogs, still in their traveling boxes in the back of the truck, were raising a ruckus, hungry for the scent of quail and howling because they'd been cheated of their fun. The Foleys paid them no mind. They drank their coffee and smoked two cigarettes apiece. Once they'd killed enough time they drove back to Lemon Road to wait.

There hadn't been a murder in Jefferson County, Indiana, in three years, and Chief Deputy Randy Spry had his doubts when he left Madison to go meet the Foleys. But he knew Donn Foley as a hard-working, practical man; not the type to call police unless it was a serious matter. Spry turned east at the Jefferson Proving Grounds and drove along a narrow road that winded past farmhouses, crop fields laid bare for the winter, and woods thick with tall timber.

"I remember thinking that if someone wanted to dump a body, those woods were the place, not in a barren soybean field," Spry said later.

The Foleys were waiting where Spry had told them. They waved for him to follow, then led him a quarter of a mile down Lemon Road and stopped. Spry pulled his car up beside the brothers' truck and looked where they pointed. He too thought it looked like a burned mannequin.

"I was thinking I'd get out of the car and make sure it was a mannequin and then I'd go eat lunch," Spry recalled. But his uncertainty grew as he drew closer. It was too lifelike to be a mannequin, but it didn't look like any burn victim he'd ever seen. He turned to the Foleys and told them he could see where they were confused because he didn't know if it was a body either. Returning to his car, Spry called the dispatcher on his radio and told him to send the sheriff to the scene. He purposely didn't mention what the Foleys had found, knowing that if he did every radio buff with a police scanner would be making tracks to Lemon Road.

Shortly after sending the message, Spry saw a truck approaching on Lemon Road. It was Donn's son Greg, returning from Madison after buying some cigarettes. Greg pulled up beside the three men standing on the gravel road and rolled down his window.

"That farmer called the cops on you, didn't he?" Greg said, halfway enjoying the opportunity to preach to his old man. "See, I told you he was serious about not hunting there."

Donn Foley shook his head and told his son to step out of the truck. They showed him the charred body. Greg was unable to pull his eyes away from the figure. Spry asked him whether he'd noticed it when he drove by half an hour earlier. Greg told the officer that he hadn't seen it and that if he had he would have stopped.

"I can't believe I passed it by," Greg Foley said.

Richard "Buck" Shipley, fifty-two, had been elected sheriff of Jefferson County a year earlier, after spending twenty-five years as a trooper for the Indiana State Police. He was sturdily built, with light brown hair and an easy smile.

It was noon before Shipley arrived at the scene from his home in Madison. At first glance he was as perplexed as the others. He'd seen a lot of dead bodies, but he'd never seen one in such a curious position, flat on its back, with its legs spread wide and its arms in the air.

Shipley pulled off his glasses, squinted, then put them back on. Only then was he sure it was a human body.

Shipley didn't know where the trail of such a grisly crime would lead, but he knew that he had neither the manpower nor the resources to handle a complex investigation. He decided to call the state police and request a detective and lab technician.

After dropping off Hope, Laurie and Melinda drove back to Laurie's house so they could wash the blood off the car.

"Laurie goes in like nothing happened," Melinda recalled. "She was cheerful. She complained to her dad that her muffler had come loose, so he got under the car and fixed it."

The girls didn't realize until George Tackett was under the car that blood stains remained on the outside of the trunk. They stood around and watched him reattach the tailpipe to the muffler, making sure to block his view of the blood when he crawled out from under the car. Then, not willing to take any more chances, they quickly moved the car around to the back of the house, got out a garden hose, and washed the inside and outside of the trunk.

There were bloody hand prints all over the inside of the trunk. Laurie found a blood-stained white sock that had belonged to Shanda and tossed it on the burn pile. They deposited Shanda's other clothes there and started a small fire to burn them. Looking into the trunk again, Laurie told Melinda to come closer. Laurie was picking at something, which finally came loose from the bottom of the trunk. She held the bloody mass between her fingers and turned to Melinda.

"Look—a piece of her skull," Laurie said, laughing. She extended her hand toward Melinda. "Smell it."

Melinda slapped her hand, and the fleshy substance fell to the ground.

"I guess the dog will eat it," joked Laurie.

They walked into the house, and Laurie asked if she could spend the night with Melinda. Peggy Tackett looked at Melinda and noticed how nervous she seemed.

"It's okay with me if it's okay with Melinda," she said.

Melinda nodded to say that it was, but she was already wanting to get away from Laurie. She'd accomplished what she'd set out to do. Shanda was out of her life. Laurie had come through like gangbusters. But now Melinda wanted to put it all behind her. Laurie was beginning to give her the creeps.

Before they left, Peggy Tackett told Laurie that Hope had called and said that it was very important for Laurie to call her.

When Hope entered her home after being dropped off by Melinda and Laurie, she found herself alone for the first time in more than twenty-four hours. Her mind raced with images of Shanda's fiery death. Hope ran through her home, screaming, "This isn't happening."

Suddenly she saw a reflection in the living-room mirror and her heart jumped.

"What the hell is your problem?" asked her older brother, John, whose nap in the basement had been disturbed by the commotion.

"Nothing, nothing," Hope replied. She couldn't tell him what happened. He wouldn't understand. "I'm okay," she said, then slipped into her bedroom.

Hope and John did not get along. It was years since they'd had a long conversation. But John was worried about Hope. He'd never seen her so upset. He stuck his head in her door and saw his sister sitting on the bed, sniffling. "Hope, what's wrong?" he asked.

Hope knew she couldn't tell him the truth, but she had to say something. "John," she said, "I saw some people burn in a car crash last night."

"Is that all? So what?" he crowed unsympathetically before marching back downstairs.

"I decided I would call Laurie and have her come over," Hope recalled. "When I called I was really upset, and Laurie's mom asked what was wrong with me. Her mom's really sweet and we're sort of close. I told her I'd broken up with my boyfriend and I needed to talk to Laurie."

Hope was hysterical when Laurie got her on the phone. Laurie told her to calm down and promised that she and Melinda would be right over.

"I can't take it," Hope said when Laurie and Melinda arrived. "What if we get caught? My God, what if someone finds out?"

"Take it easy, Hope," Laurie said. "If everyone keeps their mouth shut, nobody will ever know."

Laurie had brought her pouch of mystical stones with her. She spread them out on Hope's bed.

"The signs are favorable," Laurie assured her. "Everything is going to be just fine."

Desperate minutes had stretched into hours. The search by Steve Sharer and his father had been fruitless. Shanda's friend Michele and her mother were in the Sharer kitchen, helping Sharon make phone calls to everyone who had been at the party the night before. They found other phone numbers in Shanda's purse and called them all. The answers were all the same. No one had seen or heard from Shanda. Sharon even called Amanda Heavrin, who told her that she hadn't talked to Shanda for weeks.

Steve called his longtime friend Joey Craig, a police officer from the neighboring town of Clarksville. Craig checked with all the police departments in the area but found no leads on Shanda's whereabouts. At ten o'clock, Craig picked up Steve in his car and the two began another search of the area, stopping everyone they passed to ask if they'd seen a young blond girl. It was nearly noon when they returned to the house. Still no word about Shanda.

"Steve kept saying that somebody grabbed her," Sharon recalled. "But I didn't believe it. I kept reassuring him that she'd turn up. I thought she'd gone to somebody's house when she got locked out and that she would turn up at any minute. I just refused to think that someone had taken her."

Steve had put off calling Jacque because he didn't want to upset her, but he couldn't wait any longer. There was a chance Shanda had somehow made her way to her mother's home.

Jacque and her sister, Debbie, had gone out to dinner the night before. They hadn't stayed out late because Jacque was tired. The next morning, while she was reading the paper and drinking coffee, Jacque had an urge to call Shanda.

"It was about ten o'clock and I remember wanting to call Shanda and tell her I loved her," she said later. "I thought it was odd at the time, because I usually called her at night when she stayed with Steve and Sharon. Well, I called over there and got no answer. [Steve and Sharon were both out searching for Shanda at that time.] I didn't think anymore about it and went on getting ready."

Jacque was thinking about moving out of the townhouse, and she and Debbie had planned to go house hunting that day. When Debbie arrived around noon, Jacque went into the bathroom to brush her teeth and was met by an odd sight—a vision that she would later believe was a sign from God.

"My tongue was black," Jacque recalled. "I was able to brush it off, but it kind of scared me. I called my doctor, and he said that perhaps a viral infection had settled into my tongue and he called in a prescription of antibiotics for me."

Little did Jacque know that sixty miles away, her daughter, Shanda, lay dead, burned beyond recognition.

Jacque and Debbie were walking out the door when the phone rang. It was Steve.

"Jacque," he said, "I didn't want to call earlier because I didn't want to upset you. Shanda's disappeared. We can't find her anywhere."

Fifteen minutes later, Jacque arrived at Steve's house and they called the police. A Clark County police officer come to the house and had them fill out a missing-persons report. By this time the Sharer home was filled with nervous relatives and friends. Every once in a while someone would think of another phone number to call, but mainly they just waited.

To take their minds off the worry, some of the men started in with the remodeling. But Steve was too jittery to be of much help. Every so often he would make up some excuse to leave the house and he'd walk to the garage, where no one could see him, and he would cry.

8

Indiana State Police Detective Steve Henry was going bald at forty-two, and his strong face was creased with the weathered wrinkles he'd earned working his mule teams in the fields of his farm in the evenings and on weekends. Although his face showed his years, his build was that of a college halfback.

Steve Henry had followed in his older brother Howard's footsteps and become a state trooper when he was twenty-two. The close-knit brothers now worked together at the state police post in Sellersburg, about forty miles west of Madison.

Howard Henry was the region's chief detective, and normally this would have been his case, but when the senior detective couldn't be reached that day, the assignment fell to his younger brother. Steve Henry had assisted in dozens of homicide cases, but this would be his first as the lead detective.

Steve Henry and Curtis Wells, a lab technician who also worked at the Sellersburg post, both arrived at the crime scene at about the same time. Steve Henry already knew Donn Foley. They'd met years earlier and discovered that they shared a common interest—raising mules. Henry also knew Randy Spry and Sheriff Buck Shipley. Spry had grown up not far from Henry's farm in western Jefferson County, and Henry and Shipley had become friends during their years together as state troopers.

The four police officers crowded near the body. It was a gruesome sight. As Steve Henry studied the troubled look on Buck Shipley's face, he remembered feeling the same way himself years earlier when he and an older trooper had investigated an especially grisly murder in Indianapolis. At that time the older trooper had made a remark that eased the tension. Recalling the trooper's words, Henry turned to Shipley and said matter-of-factly, "Heart attack."

Shipley laughed. To a layman it might have seemed a callous remark, but it served its purpose of relieving the stress, and Shipley knew it was no measure of Henry's true feelings. Shipley could tell that Henry was deeply disturbed by what he saw.

"Looks like she might be in her early twenties," Shipley said.

"I'd guess a little younger, maybe seventeen or eighteen," Henry said. "What kind of animal would do something like this?"

They studied the curious position of the victim's arms, which were raised into the air with clenched fists. Curtis Wells felt that the pugilistic position of the arms could mean that the young woman had been alive when she was set on fire and that she'd fought to free herself from a burning housecoat or blanket. That would explain the burned red cloth held tightly in her fists.

Thinking that the victim might have been abducted from her home in her housecoat, then murdered and burned by a rapist to cover his tracks, Shipley used his car radio to ask local police departments to check missing-persons reports for a young woman in her late teens to mid-twenties.

As Wells videotaped the body and surrounding area and followed up with color photographs, Steve Henry questioned the Foleys, then sent them on their way. Henry figured that since the body had been cold when Donn Foley touched it at 10:40 A.M. and Greg Foley had not noticed smoke when he drove by half an hour earlier, the young woman had to have been burned sometime before ten o'clock.

The fire had thawed the ground around the body, and there were footprints other than those of the Foleys and the police. Wells made plaster casts of the footprints and tire tracks in hopes they might provide a clue to the murderer's identity.

Henry noticed that gravel on the road was disturbed at a point about a hundred feet from the body, possibly indicating a scuffle. The detective called the county highway department and learned that the road had been graded three days earlier. The gravel had been kicked around since then.

Fragments of a heavy red cloth were gathered near the body. So was the melted remains of a plastic two-liter soft-drink bottle.

Radio messages came back with missing-persons reports, and none matched the description of the victim.

"No telling where she's from," Shipley said, hoping she wasn't a local woman. "Cincinnati, Louisville, Indianapolis. She could have been brought here from anywhere."

Every so often Steve Henry would walk over to the body and talk to it in a gentle tone.

"Help us find who did this to you," Henry would say, squatting beside Shanda's charred figure. "Are we missing anything that will tell us who killed you?" He'd lean closer and whisper, "Help us find this monster."

It was early afternoon when Melinda and Laurie arrived at Melinda's house. Laurie camped out on the couch and watched television while Melinda made a phone call to her friend Crystal Wathen.

Melinda and fifteen-year-old Crystal had been best friends since kindergarten. Crystal was tall, slim, and pretty, with flowing sandy-blond hair. She went to Jeffersonville High School and generally ran with a different crowd than Melinda, but they remained very close. Crystal was heterosexual and had tried to fix Melinda up with boys in the past, but she understood when Melinda told her she was in love with Amanda.

"Melinda called me and asked if I would come over," Crystal remembered. "She was crying. She was very upset. She said, 'Shanda's dead and I need to talk to you.' I told her to sit tight and I'd have my mom bring me over to her house."

Melinda had just hung up when the phone rang. It was one of her longtime friends from Hazelwood, Leslie Jacoby. Leslie knew that Melinda had planned to go to the concert with Laurie the previous night and wanted to know about the evening.

"I remember asking if they'd had any alcohol," Leslie said later. "Melinda said no, she said they'd just gone to the slam dance and drove around. She sounded like she'd just woke up. Sort of dazed. She kept crying. She was really upset. She said, 'I've done something really bad and I can't tell you what it is.' I tried to persuade her to tell me. Finally she said, 'What would you do if I told you I killed somebody?' I didn't know what to say. She said, 'I can't tell you who I killed. I want to tell you but I can't.' She said she had done something bad and that she was going to hell. She said it was all Laurie's fault and that Laurie was into all that devil-worshiping stuff."

After begging Leslie not to tell anyone what had happened, Melinda heard a knock on the door. It was Crystal. Melinda ushered her friend into the living room, where Crystal had her first meeting with Laurie, who was sitting on the sofa with the covers pulled around her. Melinda started crying, but Laurie's disposition was stonelike as the two girls began to tell Crystal about Shanda's murder. Hours earlier, Laurie had cautioned Hope and Toni to keep their mouths shut, but she didn't follow her own advice. She saw Crystal as someone to impress, so she spared none of the gruesome details. At first Crystal didn't believe her own ears, but as the tale continued she began to realize that she was hearing the truth.

"Laurie started laughing," Crystal remembered. "I asked her what she was laughing about, and she said she did not feel bad anymore about killing Shanda."

Melinda's mother and her sister Melissa were home, but

both were unaware of the horrifying conversation taking place in the living room.

Melinda decided to call Amanda but learned that she wasn't home. Amanda's father was not pleased to hear from Melinda, since he thought he'd put an end to her and his daughter. "She's not here," he said bluntly. "She went to River City Mall with Jeffrey Stettenbenz."

Melinda called the mall office and, saying it was an emergency, had Amanda paged. When Amanda picked up the mall phone, Melinda told her that something terrible had happened and she was on the way to the mall to pick her up.

Jeffrey Stettenbenz was the boy whom Amanda had pawned off on her father as her boyfriend. Actually, Jeffrey would have liked nothing better. He had a crush on Amanda, but she'd made it clear to him a long time earlier that they were just friends.

Now a sad-faced Jeffrey was left behind at the mall as Amanda climbed in the backseat of Laurie's car next to Melinda. Crystal was in the front with Laurie. As they drove off, Melinda hugged Amanda and told her that Shanda was dead. At first Amanda thought Melinda was playing a joke, but her friend's tears convinced her that something awful had happened. When they arrived at Melinda's house, Melinda led Amanda upstairs to her bedroom. She hugged and kissed Amanda and told her she was sorry that Shanda was dead.

"I just wanted to beat her up," Melinda said, desperate to explain herself. "But Laurie went crazy and killed her."

Amanda returned the hug and stared into Melinda's eyes. Melinda had told her several times before that she wished Shanda were dead, but Amanda never thought her friend was actually capable of murder.

"I guess I was in shock," Amanda said later. "I couldn't believe what I was hearing."

Fearing the worst but still thinking it might be some kind of sick joke, a dazed Amanda followed Melinda back downstairs where Laurie was waiting, eager to show Amanda and Crystal proof of the terrible deed.

It was with macabre pride that Laurie led the group out to her car and opened the trunk. "Now do you believe?" Laurie asked, pointing to the blood stains that she and Melinda had been unable to clean off. Amanda saw a blood-stained sock lying in the trunk. She felt a sick feeling in her stomach as she recognized it as the type Shanda wore.

"I don't want to see any more," Amanda said, all her final doubts erased. All she could think about was leaving and getting away from this nightmare. It was her love affair with Shanda that had incurred Melinda's wrath. If she hadn't drawn Shanda into a relationship none of this would have happened. But if she felt any regret for her role in setting the stage for Shanda's murder, she held it inside. Even at that moment, when she knew in her heart that Shanda was indeed dead, she spoke no words of sorrow—at least none that anyone could remember later.

"I want to go home," was all Amanda said. "Please, just take me home."

Before they left, Laurie pulled Melinda aside and asked, "Is she going to talk? I'm afraid she's going to talk."

"Don't worry about my friends," Melinda replied sharply. "They would never tell on me."

Amanda was skittish as she climbed into the backseat of the car—the same car she now knew that had carried Shanda to her death.

Melinda got in beside Amanda and consoled her lover while all four girls drove away.

The winter sun was going down and the afternoon shadows were growing longer as the car pulled to a stop in front of Amanda's ramshackle house. A light in the living room told the girls that Amanda's father was home. Melinda knew that he had no use for her. She would have to say her goodbyes to Amanda at the curb. Amanda was anxious to leave and started out of the car quickly, but Melinda was right behind her and she touched her shoulder, signaling her to stop.

"Poo?" Melinda said softly. "You won't tell anyone, will you? You can't tell anyone. I'm in this too deep."

"I won't," Amanda stuttered.

"You know I love you," Melinda said, running her fingers lovingly across Amanda's frightened face.

"I know," Amanda replied. "I love you too."

Melinda kissed the girl she'd killed for, once lightly on the lips, then she climbed back into the car, where Laurie and Crystal were waiting. As the car pulled away, Amanda slowly walked inside her house, then into her bedroom. Alone at last in the solitude of her room, Amanda sat on her bed and read, one by one, the many letters that Shanda had written her. Then, and only then, did the fourteen-year-old begin to cry.

It was nearly dark by the time Laurie, Melinda, and Crystal arrived at the Taco Bell in Clarksville. They parked the car and went inside to eat. When they returned to the automobile, Laurie's boombox was blaring. It was playing one of the rock songs she'd sung the night before while she was tormenting Shanda.

"I turned it off before we went in," Laurie exclaimed, her voice filled with awe. "It's Shanda's spirit. She's coming back to haunt us. Let's have a séance and try to talk to her."

Melinda and Crystal looked at her strangely before climbing into the car, Melinda in back, Crystal next to Laurie. Laurie reached into the front-door pocket and pulled out the tire iron. She began waving it, and Crystal moved as far away as possible.

"I can remember how it felt when it was going into her head," Laurie said, her eyes glazed over. "When I was hitting her it was really taking hunks out of her head."

"Stop it!" Melinda yelled. "This is sick. I can't take it anymore. I just want to forget it."

But Laurie was just getting started. She thumped the metal bar against the dashboard. "This is how I did it," she boasted to Crystal. She stuck the tire iron near Crystal's face. "Here, smell this."

Crystal and Melinda tried to ignore Laurie, but she continued ranting. "Shadows keep jumping at me," she said. "They're coming to get me."

Melinda grabbed Crystal's arm. "Do you think God will forgive me?" she asked.

"I don't believe in God," Laurie crowed. "I believe in black magic."

When they got back to Melinda's house, Laurie went to the bathroom, leaving Melinda and Crystal alone.

"Laurie's planning to spend the night," Melinda said. "Please, stay here with me tonight. She's crazy. I'm scared of her."

But Crystal had seen enough, and she didn't want to spend another minute with Laurie Tackett. She told Melinda she had to go home.

Toni couldn't escape the horror. The image of Shanda's burning body was scorched into her consciousness. She stood behind the cash register at Arby's, casting nervous glances at the customers. She was certain that at any moment Laurie and Melinda would march through the door. She was afraid that they had sensed her weakness and had decided to kill her too.

Toni's friend Mikel Pommerehn had stopped by Arby's earlier, and Toni had told her everything. Mikel told Toni that she knew a lawyer and had promised to have him call Toni later that day. Toni was trying to hang on but her fear was overwhelming. She went through the motions of her job, but she was in a daze.

"What's wrong with you today?" her supervisor asked.

Toni didn't answer. She just stared off into space.

"You better go on home," the supervisor said. "You look sick."

Toni acknowledged that she didn't feel well and tried to call her parents to pick her up. When they didn't answer the phone, she called Hope. "Just stay where you are," Hope said. "My mom will come and get you."

But Toni didn't feel any safer at Hope's house. She began crying when she heard a car go by with a noisy muffler. She thought it was Laurie coming for her. The two girls decided they needed to go somewhere where they could think clearly. They decided to go to the pool hall at the Anderson

Bowling Alley. They had a lot of friends there, and guys who could protect them if Laurie and Melinda came looking for them.

As soon as they walked into the pool hall they saw two friends from school, Shawn Pyles and Chris Alcorn. Toni and Hope fell into the boys' arms and began crying. At first they resisted the boys' questions about what was wrong, but eventually they opened up and told all. The boys listened in disbelief as Toni and Hope related the grisly details of Shanda's murder.

"You've got to go to the police," Shawn said. "You've got to tell them. It's the only way."

Toni and Hope assured the boys that they would, but instead the exhausted girls went back to Hope's house and fell asleep in front of the television. But they didn't sleep long before a nightmare descended on Toni. She awoke with a scream, shaking and covered in sweat. It had been the ring of the phone that had awakened her. Mikel Pommerehn was on the other end of the line. She told Toni that she'd talked to the lawyer, a friend of her family named Darryl Auxier, and he wanted to talk to Toni and Hope. Auxier called a few minutes later and told Hope that she and Toni would have to tell their parents what had happened. Auxier said their parents should call him if they needed advice on what to do next.

Glenda Lawrence and Toni's older sister, Tina, were spending a typical Saturday evening at home watching television in their living room when Toni walked through the front door, followed by Hope and her parents, Carl and Gloria Rippey.

Toni ran into her mother's arms and crawled up on her lap, quivering and moaning. Toni's father, Clifton Lawrence, who was in the basement, heard the anxious voices and hurried up the steps. Toni stumbled toward him and put her arms around his neck.

"I'm sorry, Dad, but I didn't stay at Mikel's last night," she said. "I went to Louisville."

Clifton Lawrence was livid. He removed Toni's arms from

his shoulders and looked deep into her reddened eyes. She turned away from his glare and cried, "Forgive me. Please, forgive me!"

Toni's father would say later that he thought his daughter was pregnant. "I guess that's the worst thing a father can think his daughter will tell him, especially a fifteen-year-old daughter."

He couldn't make sense of Toni's babbling. He sent his daughter to her room, then turned to the Rippeys for an explanation. "What's going on?" he asked.

Carl Rippey spoke up, repeating the story the girls had told him: that they had witnessed two girls murder another girl. Rippey said he was sketchy on the details, but he believed what the girls had told him was true. A young girl was dead, and Toni and Hope knew the murderers.

The words tore Clifton Lawrence's quiet, stable world apart. He asked the Rippeys to go with him to the police but they refused. Carl and Gloria told the Lawrences that they had already talked to their attorney, Darryl Auxier, and had been advised not to talk to the police. They decided to take Hope to a motel until the next day. Carl suggested that Toni's father do the same. But Clifton would have none of it. He showed the Rippeys the door, then walked stiffly into Toni's room, knowing what had to be done. His daughter was on the bed, sobbing and shivering.

"I told Toni we had to go to the police," Clifton said later. "I didn't know what happened to the little girl she said was murdered, but if there was a chance she was alive she needed every minute that we could give her."

During the drive to the police station, Clifton and Glenda Lawrence waited for Toni to tell them it was just a prank and to take her home. But Toni said nothing, she just held her hands cupped to her mouth as if in prayer and bit down on a knuckle and whimpered.

Steve Henry and Sheriff Buck Shipley brought out spotlights at sunset and the officers continued working for another hour, driven by the fear that they might have overlooked a clue. But after seven hours there was nothing more to do. They called an ambulance to pick up the body.

Wells took photos as the other officers carefully lifted the burned body. The hair on the back of the head was soaked with blood, and a small puddle of blood had formed on the ground. They found an injury to the back of the head and a small puncture wound at the base of the neck. After placing plastic bags over the hands—to protect any fingerprints that might identify the victim—the body was lifted into an ambulance and taken to the morgue at King's Daughters Hospital in Madison. The next day the body would be taken to Louisville, Kentucky, for an autopsy by Dr. George Nichols, Kentucky's chief medical examiner and an expert on burn victims.

Cold, tired, and hungry, the men drove to a Hardee's restaurant on the north side of Madison and got a meal and coffee. They wondered why the murderer, whom they assumed to be a man, had made no effort to conceal the body.

"He could have carried it another twenty yards to those woods and it may never have been found," Buck Shipley said. "It just doesn't make sense. It's as though he didn't care if it was found."

"Maybe whoever did it thought the fire would burn the body down to ashes," Henry said.

The men hunched over their coffees and talked a while longer before leaving for Shipley's office in Madison. During the drive, Steve Henry considered his next move. He had an unidentified body and no suspects. Prospects were not good.

He had no way of knowing that all the pieces of the puzzle were about to fall into place.

9

The temperature had dropped below freezing by the time Sheriff Buck Shipley, Steve Henry, Randy Spry, and Curtis Wells arrived at the Jefferson County police station and jail, a two-story, concrete-block building across an alley from the county courthouse in Madison. They'd been inside only a few minutes when they learned that they had two visitors.

Darryl Pyles, a Madison resident, walked into the police station with an arm around the shoulder of his teenage son, Shawn.

"My son has something to tell you," Darryl told Shipley grimly. "It's about a murder."

Shipley and Steve Henry quickly ushered the father and son into the sheriff's office and closed the door. After a moment of nervous hesitation, Shawn Pyles told the officers the same macabre tale he'd related to his father half an hour earlier. The same story he'd heard that afternoon at the Anderson Bowling Alley.

"Toni and Hope said that two other girls had killed and burned a little girl," Shawn Pyles told the police. "They said the girls were lesbians."

Shawn said that he and another boy, Chris Alcorn, had

advised the girls to go to the police, and he asked Shipley if he'd heard from them. Shipley shook his head and asked the boy to repeat the girls' names.

"Toni Lawrence and Hope Rippey," Shawn said.

Steve Henry leaned closer to Shawn. "Did they say where or when this murder took place?" he asked.

"This morning," Shawn answered. "In a field in the country."

Henry and Shipley were still questioning Shawn when the door to the office opened. Deputy Randy Spry leaned in the doorway and told Shipley that the Madison police were on the phone. Shipley waved off the call, but Spry was insistent.

"You better take this call, Buck," Spry said.

Shipley walked out of his office and picked up the phone. An officer at the Madison police station, which was a few blocks away, told Shipley that a teenage girl and her parents had just walked into their station. They knew something about the murder.

"What's her name?" Shipley asked.

"Toni Lawrence," was the response.

Shipley's pulse raced but he said calmly, "Send them over."

Toni's parents wrapped their arms around their daughter's narrow shoulders as they led her into the police station.

To Buck Shipley and Steve Henry, the thin, disheveled blonde looked like a frightened bird. They guided the Lawrences into Shipley's office and closed the door. With a trembling hand, Toni signed a waiver of her rights. She sniffled as Henry switched on a tape recorder.

In a soothing voice, Henry asked Toni if she had something to tell him. She muttered something under her breath, then began her story in a halting whisper.

She hadn't been talking long when Henry stopped her, wanting to make sure he had gathered it all in. "Okay," he said. "Shanda had been flirting or trying to go out with Amanda, right? What was Melinda's reaction to this?"

Toni looked Steve Henry in the eye. "Melinda hated her and she said she wanted to kill her."

"How old is Shanda?"

"Thirteen," Toni said, not aware that she was actually younger.

Henry and Shipley were shocked by the age. It sounded too young for the body they'd found.

"Do you know Shanda's last name?" Henry asked.

If Melinda had mentioned it, Toni could not remember it now. She went on with her tale, recounting how the girls had lured Shanda into their car.

"Melinda jumped up and put a knife to Shanda's throat and said if she didn't talk to her she was going to slit her throat. . . ."

Toni's voice trailed off and she began crying. She bit the back of her hand and began to rock back and forth in her chair.

"Let's take a little break," Steve Henry said. He flipped off the tape recorder and followed Buck Shipley out the door, leaving Toni and her parents in the room.

Curtis Wells and Randy Spry were huddled at the booking counter, waiting to hear what the teenage girl had told the other officers about the murder.

"Call down to Jeffersonville," Henry told Wells. "See if there's a missing-person report on a thirteen-year-old named Shanda."

The lab technician's eyes questioned Henry.

"That's right," the detective said. "Thirteen years old."

Shipley spoke to Wells and Spry in a low voice so that the Lawrences, who were in the next room, couldn't hear. "It looks like the Pyles boy might be right. All we've heard about so far are girls. Teenagers. She mentioned a Laurie Tackett. That could be George Tackett's girl. I think he has a daughter about that age."

There weren't too many people in Madison that Shipley didn't know, particularly people with a record. George Tackett had spent time in prison for robbery when he was a young man. Since then he'd worked at a factory and remained out of trouble. Shipley also vaguely knew George's wife, Peggy, who worked part time at a local bakery.

Henry flipped a cigarette from his pack and poured a

fresh cup of coffee. "Do you have any idea how we can find anything on a sixteen-year-old from New Albany named Melinda?" he asked Wells. "She might be a lesbian."

"I'll call Virgil Seay, the chief probation officer down there," Wells volunteered. "If she's been in any trouble before, Virgil will know her."

Henry looked at Shipley and asked, "Ready for more?"

Shipley nodded solemnly and followed Henry back into the room where Toni was waiting with her parents. The thin girl seemed to have regained her composure, and she picked up her story, telling the officers about the Witches' Castle, the assault on Shanda on the dirt road, and about Melinda and Laurie's long drive with Shanda in the trunk.

Toni began to stammer. "They said that every time they heard her screaming . . . they would . . . they would hit her in the head with a crowbar. They said they were going to take gasoline . . . They were going to pour it on her body and they were going to burn her. And they even said they did. They told us they did."

Toni began crying again. She seemed to shrivel and become smaller as she hunched down in the hard wooden chair. Glenda Lawrence reached over and put an arm around her daughter to console her. While Henry waited for Toni to get control of herself, Shipley got up slowly and walked out of the room. In the booking room, he told Deputy Spry to go to Laurie Tackett's house and try to find the car described by Toni: a white sedan with a brown vinyl top.

"Give us a call when you get there and let us know what you find," Shipley said.

Back in Shipley's office, Henry was coaxing Toni to continue.

"Did you get the impression that these girls had been to the Witches' Castle before?" he asked.

"Laurie had," Toni said. "She used to be a Pentecostal and she quit and she started hanging around with Larry and Terry Leatherbury and then she got back into church and then she quit again and got in all these cults and they drink . . . blood."

"They drink what?" Henry asked, not sure he'd heard correctly.

"Each other's blood," Toni said, her voice shaking.

Henry swallowed hard. Toni shifted uneasily in her chair. The room was still silent when Shipley returned from talking with Randy Spry. Henry looked at Shipley for a moment, then took a deep breath and continued his questioning.

"Who are Larry and Terry Leatherbury? Are they into this same type of thing?"

"Yeah."

"Do they go to school?"

"I don't know if they do anymore," Toni said. "I haven't seen them lately."

Henry needed a cigarette. "Let's take a little break," he said. The weary detective walked out to the garage, Shipley at his side, and took a drag on his cigarette, sighing deeply. "This is too weird," Henry said, gazingly blankly at the ceiling. "Lord, these are teenage girls."

Shipley spoke in a brotherly manner: "Come on, Steve, let's finish up with her. We've got a long night ahead of us."

When they started again, Toni said that Laurie and Melinda had dropped her and Hope off at their homes at around nine-forty-five that morning and then had gone on from there to burn Shanda.

She told the lie smoothly, but Henry was suspicious. Toni's home in Madison was at least a twenty-minute drive from where the body was found. If Toni's story was right, Melinda and Laurie couldn't have arrived at the burn site until after ten o'clock. That was about the time that Greg Foley drove down Lemon Road and only half an hour before Donn and Ralph Foley found an already cold body. Something didn't fit, Henry said to himself. The girl was hiding something.

Henry and Shipley listened in silence as a perplexed Clifton Lawrence suddenly took over the questioning of his own daughter.

"When they said they were going to burn her—was that

after they dropped you off or before?" the father asked his daughter.

"Before."

Clifton Lawrence was still puzzled. "They told you when they dropped you off that they were going to burn her?" he asked urgently.

Toni shifted uneasily in her chair. "Yes."

Clifton Lawrence seemed to be wrestling with a dreadful realization. He'd been home when Toni came into the house that morning. She had walked right by him and said nothing about a little girl's life being in danger. If Toni knew at that point that the other girls were going to burn the little girl, why hadn't she said anything to him or his wife?

Henry wanted to make sure he'd heard correctly. "They burned her after they dropped you off this morning?" he asked.

Toni nodded. "They even went and got gasoline," she said.

Clifton Lawrence stuttered in disbelief. "On the way home . . . on the way to bring you home? Did they get gasoline before they brought you home?"

"They got it on the way to my house," Toni replied sheepishly.

"This morning?" Henry asked.

Toni nodded.

"Where was Shanda then?" Henry asked.

"I guess she was in the trunk," Toni said matter-of-factly.

Clifton's anger overwhelmed him. "You don't know?" he asked sharply. "Where did they put the gas?"

"They put it in a two-liter bottle that Melinda had," Toni answered meekly.

"When did you see inside the trunk?" Henry asked.

"Huh?" Toni said. She seemed to be stalling.

Clifton leaned toward his daughter and tersely repeated Henry's question: "When did you see inside the trunk?"

Toni began rocking back and forth as tears welled up in her eyes. "When they had her on the ground. They took her out on the ground because Laurie had a butcher knife and that's when . . . Oh God . . . they were going to stab her or something. But they didn't stab her. They beat her over the head and then I looked up and blood was on the trunk. They put her back in the trunk."

"Did Shanda appear to be alive?" Henry asked.

"Yes," Toni said, beginning to cry.

Henry suspected that Toni was lying about her involvement, but he wasn't ready to charge her with being an accessory to murder. Not yet, anyway.

Before the Lawrences left the police station that night they told Henry and Shipley about the Rippeys' plan to spend the night in a motel. The officers knew there would be little chance of finding the Rippeys that night. Their spirits got a lift, however, when Deputy Spry returned to the police station from his trip to the Tackett residence with news about Melinda and Laurie.

Spry said that when he couldn't locate the white-and-brown sedan outside the Tackett home, he went to the front door. Laurie's parents, George and Peggy Tackett, seemed startled to find a policeman at their door. George, whose early scrapes with the law had left him resentful of police, was particularly uneasy, and Peggy was full of questions.

Spry played it cool. He told the Tacketts nothing of the murder but asked about Laurie's whereabouts. The Tacketts said their daughter was spending the night in New Albany with a girl named Melinda. They didn't know Melinda's last name.

Peggy said that Laurie and Melinda had left around noon for New Albany in Laurie's 1984 Chevrolet Celebrity.

After Spry had given his report to Henry and Shipley, Curtis Wells announced that Melinda's last name was no longer a mystery.

Wells had called Virgil Seay, the chief probation officer in Floyd County, where New Albany was the county seat. It seemed that several months earlier, a man named Jerry Heavrin had brought Seay a stack of letters written to Heavrin's fourteen-year-old daughter, Amanda, by a classmate named Melinda Loveless.

The father had been bothered by the sexual nature of the letters and had felt that Melinda Loveless was trying to seduce his daughter into a lesbian relationship. Seay told Wells that he had contacted Melinda Loveless and told her to stay away from Amanda Heavrin.

Wells got Melinda's address in New Albany from Seay and had already arranged for the state police in Sellersburg to send two troopers there to see if they could find Laurie Tackett's car. They would be reporting back at any minute.

Loveless! Henry thought the name rich in irony if Toni Lawrence's story of Melinda's jealous rage was true.

"Anything on the dead girl, Shanda?" Henry asked.

Wells answered solemnly. "Shanda Sharer, a twelve-year-old, was reported missing by her parents at one P.M. today. Clark County police took the report. Her parents are divorced. She lives in New Albany but was staying the night at her father's home in Jeffersonville. The address checks out with the one Toni Lawrence gave us."

Wells told them that Shanda's father had last seen her when he'd gone to bed around eleven-thirty Friday night and discovered her missing the next morning. He and others had spent the morning searching for Shanda before calling police.

"The description fits," Wells said. "Blond hair. Five feet tall. Around a hundred pounds."

"Twelve years old," Shipley said. "She must have been physically mature for her age. She looked older than that."

The phone rang. It was Steve Henry's older brother, Howard, calling from the state police post in Sellersburg. Detective Howard Henry had been following the progress of the case by phone and radio since coming on duty late that afternoon. He told his younger brother that the state troopers had found Laurie Tackett's car parked behind the Loveless residence. They were watching from a distance. The house seemed quiet, and the troopers were waiting for instructions.

"Just tell them to keep an eye on things," the younger brother said. "We'll be down as soon as we get warrants to arrest the girls and search the car."

Steve Henry told his brother that they'd identified the victim. "She's a New Albany girl, but I think both her parents are at her father's home in Jeffersonville."

113

Jeffersonville was only ten minutes from the Sellersburg post. Howard Henry volunteered for the difficult job of telling Shanda's parents that their daughter had been murdered.

"I'll go tell them," he said. "I get off at midnight. When I get through there I'll meet you at the Loveless house."

Steve Henry hung up the phone, and with the help of Donald Currie, the Jefferson County deputy prosecutor, he filled out warrants for the arrest of Melinda and Laurie on charges of murder. Henry and Currie then drove to the home of Jefferson circuit judge Ted Todd in Hanover, just outside Madison. With Todd's signature on the warrants, Henry, Shipley, and two deputies made the forty-five-minute drive through the night to New Albany.

"We were frantic all day," Steve remembers. "Sometimes Jacque would get upset and start crying and sometimes I would. There were so many people in the house I couldn't think straight. I still don't remember much of that day. It was all so crazy."

"The day just kept dragging on with no word," Jacque said. "I can't tell you how I felt. I can't tell you all the things that went through my mind. I knew that something bad must have happened. I knew that Shanda would call if she could."

At about ten o'clock that night, Steve called a boy whose phone number he had found among Shanda's things.

"Steve was just losing it at that point," Sharon said. "He was yelling at the guy, 'Have you seen my daughter?' When Steve got off the phone he started to cry and said, 'My daughter's gone,' I said, 'No she's not.' I still couldn't believe that anything bad had happened."

By eleven-thirty everyone was emotionally exhausted. Paije, who had come over to the house that evening, persuaded Jacque to go home with her and get some rest.

Steve looked into his ex-wife's reddened eyes. "Go ahead," he said. "I'll call you if we hear anything."

Jacque had been gone less than half an hour when two Indiana State Police officers knocked on Steve's door. One of them introduced himself as Detective Howard Henry. When Henry learned that Shanda's mother wasn't there, he asked Steve to call Jacque and have her come back over.

"What's the matter?" Steve asked. "Have you found Shanda?"

Henry avoided answering Steve's questions and asked him once again to call Jacque. As Sharon made the call for her husband, Henry and the other officer busied themselves in Shanda's bedroom, looking through her things.

"They went back there and looked through her stuff," Sharon said. "They were asking us things like what jewelry she had on and if we had her dental records. Shanda had just gotten braces two weeks before Christmas and they asked what the dentist's name was. They kept us so busy I guess it just didn't sink in. But my stepdad was sitting there in the living room, shaking his head. I think he knew."

Jacque and Paije had been home less than five minutes when they got the phone call from Sharon.

"The state police are here," Sharon said. "They want you to come back. They won't talk until you get here."

Thinking that Shanda had been found injured, Jacque and Paije ran outside and jumped into their car. As they sped along the highway, the speedometer raced to eighty, then ninety, and a hundred.

"Mom, slow down," Paije cautioned. "The police will pull you over."

"Nobody's pulling me over," Jacque said. "They may end up behind me, but I'm not pulling over until I get to Steve's."

When Jacque walked through the door, Howard Henry led her and Steve into the kitchen and sat down at the table with them. The veteran detective looked across the table and said softly, "Your daughter is gone."

Jacque stared back blankly. "What?"

"Someone has taken your daughter's life," Henry said.

Jacque looked into Howard Henry's eyes and knew that it was true. "No!" she screamed. She ran from the kitchen to the front door and crumbled down in front of it. "No! No! Oh God, it's not happening."

Sharon, who'd been in the living room, ran to Jacque's side and hugged her. "What's wrong? What is it?" Sharon asked.

Steve remained seated in the kitchen. He'd heard the detective's words, but his mind would not accept them. He yelled at Jacque to be quiet, then turned back to Henry. "What are you trying to say?" he asked.

"Your daughter is deceased," Howard Henry said. "She's been murdered."

10

It was nearly two o'clock on Sunday morning when Steve Henry and Buck Shipley pulled up outside the Loveless residence.

State police officers were stationed at each side of the darkened house, watching the doors and windows. Howard Henry was there, having just arrived from breaking the sad news to Shanda's parents.

Steve Henry, Sheriff Shipley, and a state trooper walked up to the door and knocked several times. At last a light came on and the door opened a crack. A woman's voice asked who it was.

"Police, can we come in please?" Henry asked.

A gaunt, dark-haired woman opened the door and moved aside to let them pass. The woman's bewildered eyes darted from Henry to Shipley to the trooper.

"Are you Mrs. Loveless?" Henry asked.

"Yes—I mean no. I was," the woman stammered. "I remarried. It's Donahue now, Margie Donahue."

"Is Melinda your daughter?"

"Yes."

"Where is she now?"

"Upstairs asleep. What's this about?"

117

A man came around a corner, wiping sleep from his eyes. It was Melinda's stepfather, Mike Donahue. "What's going on?" he asked.

"We have a warrant for the arrest of your daughter," Steve Henry said. "Is Laurie Tackett with her?"

"Yes," Margie answered. "They're upstairs asleep."

The trooper remained with the Donahues as Henry and Shipley walked slowly up the steps and pushed open a bedroom door. Two girls lay under the covers. Henry switched on the light and the girls stirred slightly. He couldn't tell whether they were in deep sleep or just pretending.

"Melinda. Laurie. Get out of bed," he said. "I'm Detective Henry of the Indiana State Police. This is Sheriff Shipley. We have warrants for your arrest."

The girls roused slowly and wordlessly. They'd been sleeping in their clothes.

"It was a lucky thing we got there when we did," Henry said later. "They were dressed as if they were ready to leave when they woke up."

Henry and Shipley led the girls downstairs, where the others had been joined by Melinda's older sister Melissa, who had been awakened by the commotion.

Henry looked into the tired eyes of Melinda and Laurie. "I have warrants to arrest you both on charges of murder," he said.

Melinda said nothing, but Laurie asked smugly, "Are we on 'Candid Camera'?"

Murder? The word registered slowly in Margie's mind. She turned to Melinda and asked, "What have you done to Amanda?"

Henry noted the remark and thought she must have meant Amanda Heavrin, whom Toni Lawrence had mentioned as Melinda's girlfriend. But why had Melinda's mother assumed that Amanda Heavrin was the victim?

As the family watched in disbelief, the two teenage girls were led out of the house in handcuffs. Melinda's mother grabbed Steve Henry as he was leaving.

"Please, watch my baby," she pleaded. "She might be suicidal."

On the drive back to Madison, Melinda rode with two of

Shipley's deputies. Laurie sat beside Henry in the front seat of his car, with Shipley in the back. Laurie said nothing, but from time to time she would turn and look menacingly at Henry. "It was the kind of stare that makes the hair on the back of your neck tingle," he said later.

It was nearly four o'clock in the morning when they arrived back at the police station and jail. A paring knife was taken from the pocket of Laurie's jacket, then the girls were fingerprinted and fitted in jail uniforms. Laurie called her parents and coolly told them that she'd been arrested for murder. Melinda slumped against a wall and appeared ready to faint.

"Are you all right?" Henry asked.

"Can I please call my mother?" she whispered hoarsely.

Henry led Melinda to a private office and dialed the number for her. He stood a short distance away as Melinda tearfully told her mother that the police had treated her well and that she was okay.

"It was a little girl from my school named Shanda," Melinda said into the phone. "I just meant to beat her up, but someone had a knife and it went too far."

Melinda was still sniffling as she and Laurie were put in separate cells. Laurie had not yet shed a tear. Not when she was handcuffed. Not when she told her parents of her arrest. Not even after the metal bars of her cell door slammed shut.

After the girls had been taken away, Henry and Shipley sat for a while to collect their thoughts. Everything had fallen into place within a matter of hours of leaving the burn site. They were pleased with the quickness with which they'd tracked down Melinda and Laurie. Both veteran lawmen were convinced that the two girls would have fled the state in Laurie's car the next morning.

But the officers' self-satisfaction was tempered by the knowledge that their work was just beginning and that many questions remained unanswered. It seemed unfathomable that teenage girls could commit such a heinous crime. Perhaps a male was involved. And what about the other two girls? Toni Lawrence had claimed that she was an innocent bystander, but parts of her story didn't ring true. And Hope Rippey's involvement remained a mystery. Was she there when Shanda Sharer was set on fire? Did she assist Loveless and Tackett in the murder?

Henry and Shipley talked until exhaustion slowly persuaded both of them to call it a night.

It was nearly dawn when Henry pulled up the gravel driveway to his farmhouse on the outskirts of Deputy, a small farming community about twenty miles northwest of Madison. He often thought it ironic that he and his brother had grown up in a place called Deputy. It was as if Fate had dictated that they become police officers. Steve Henry had never regretted his choice of profession, but there were times when he wondered whether it was worth the worry and strain. This was one of those times.

He entered his home quietly and peeked into the rooms of his three children. They were sound asleep. Safe in bed.

Loraine Henry was awakened from a light sleep by the stirring of her husband in the kitchen. Steve had called her earlier to say that he'd be late, but he'd told her little about the case other than that a girl had been murdered. She walked into the kitchen and snuggled up beside him.

"Coming to bed?" she asked.

Loraine observed the tired tension in her husband's face. She knew he wanted to talk. They sat at the kitchen table for hours as he related the events of the day. When he had nothing more to say, Steve Henry kissed his wife and stumbled off to bed. Loraine would follow him a short time later, after checking on the children. They were still sound asleep. Still safe in bed.

Early Sunday morning, Shanda Sharer's body was driven fifty miles by ambulance from the morgue at King's Daughters Hospital in Madison to the Louisville office of Dr. George R. Nichols II.

As Kentucky's chief medical examiner, Nichols had earned his reputation as an expert on the identification of fire victims under the most difficult of conditions. In 1977 he'd directed the autopsies of the 163 people killed in the Beverly Hills Supper Club fire in Owensboro, Kentucky. Then in 1988 he'd performed autopsies on twenty-three members of a church group who were killed in a fiery bus crash while returning home from an outing at King's Island, Ohio.

Although there was no longer much doubt that the burned body was that of Shanda Sharer, Nichols took the necessary steps for a positive identification. Shanda's fingers were so severely burned that the tips had to be cut off and sent to the Indiana State Police laboratory so they could be checked against her fingerprint records. Nichols also removed Shanda's jaw for later identification by her dentist. She had made her last visit to the dentist a month earlier to be fitted with braces.

In systematic order, Nichols went through the lengthy process of determining the cause of death. The upper half of her body, including her head, was covered with third- and fourth-degree burns. Her left ear had been shriveled by the flames, and her tongue protruded through clenched teeth. There were wounds on her feet and binding marks, consistent with those made by a rope, on her forearms and ankles. A small puncture wound was found at the base of her neck. There were three lacerations on Shanda's scalp that appeared to have been inflicted by a heavy blunt object. However, the skull was not fractured and there had been no internal hemorrhaging. Multiple lacerations of Shanda's anus and anal cavity indicated that she'd been sodomized by a blunt cylindrical object, which had been inserted three and a half inches into the anus and damaged the inner walls. The extent of internal bleeding convinced Nichols that the sodomy had occurred while Shanda was alive.

Shanda's larynx and trachea were coated with thick black soot, which indicated she'd been breathing—and thus still alive—when she was set on fire. The injuries to Shanda's head and anus were serious, but she could have recovered from them under proper care. In his final analysis, Nichols fixed the cause of death as smoke inhalation and severe burns.

At a hearing in his Madison court on Sunday morning, Jefferson circuit judge Ted Todd decided that Melinda and Laurie would be tried as adults. Todd appointed public defenders for the girls, then arraigned them on charges of murder. After pleas of not guilty were entered on their behalf, Todd ordered that Melinda be transferred to the jail in an adjacent county so that she could have no contact with Laurie.

By now newspaper and television reporters from Louisville, the largest city in the area, had learned of the gruesome crime and were scrambling for more information. Calls were made to Dr. George Nichols, who confirmed that Shanda had been alive when she was set on fire. Nichols also described the injuries to Shanda's head but made no mention of the sodomy.

"I saw no need to bring that out at the time," Nichols said later. "I wanted to talk to the parents before I released any information that could bring them more grief."

Reporters learned that Shanda's body would be taken to Kraft's Funeral Home in New Albany, and television cameramen crossed the Ohio River from Louisville to gather in the funeral home parking lot, hoping to get footage of the body being removed from the hearse. Mortician Jamie Rainey tricked the reporters by arranging for a decoy hearse to arrive at the front entrance at the same time that the hearse with Shanda's body came to the back door.

Inside the funeral home, Shanda's parents picked out a casket and waited to see their daughter's body. Twelve hours had passed since Howard Henry told him that his daughter had been murdered, and Steve Sharer's normally pleasant face was worn and tired. His wife, Sharon, had tried to get him to lie down earlier that morning, but he found no comfort in sleep.

After hours of crying, Jacque had somehow gathered the strength to call Jamie Rainey, a longtime friend, and ask him to make the funeral arrangements. Before leaving for the funeral home, Jacque had gone to Shanda's room and picked out clothes for her dead daughter to wear in her casket.

"I brought her favorite blue jeans and sweatshirt," Jacque said later. "That's the way she'd want to be dressed. She'd want to be comfortable."

Jacque and Steve saw the hearse pull up, but they followed Rainey's instructions to wait in his office until he had a chance to view the body. When Rainey returned to the room, he was crying.

"No human being should have to see what I just saw," he said hoarsely.

"Jamie, I want you to put these clothes on her," Jacque said, holding out the jeans and sweatshirt.

"Jacque, I can put them in the casket, but I can't put them on her body."

"Why not?" Jacque asked.

"I just can't," Rainey said. "The body is in such bad shape I can't put clothes on her. It will have to be closed casket."

Steve put his arm around Jacque and consoled her. Rainey suggested that they cover Shanda's body with a blanket of roses. Jacque and Steve nodded their approval. Shanda would like that.

As Steve turned the corner into his subdivision, he saw the big vans with satellite dishes on top and the familiar names of Louisville television stations emblazoned on the sides. By the time he'd pulled into the driveway and stepped out of his car, the reporters were on top of him. He brushed by them, ignoring their questions, pushing their microphones aside.

"Leave us alone," he said. "Please, go away."

Some of the reporters took their camera crews across the street and knocked on the doors of nearby houses, baiting neighbors with questions that might produce a film clip for the evening news. Other reporters, not yet willing to give up on getting a reaction from Shanda's family, stood at the edge of Steve's yard, waiting for the next opportunity. Inside the house, Steve's grieving relatives told him that the television crews had been there for hours.

"They just keep coming to the door," Sharon said. "I told them we had nothing to say but they just keep coming. They won't leave."

"I'll punch the next one of them that knocks on that door," Steve said. But he didn't. When the knock came a short while later, he simply told the reporters that he had nothing to say and asked them to leave. With every new knock he repeated his request. Finally, after the 6:00 P.M.

news, the television crews called it a day. They would try again tomorrow.

Despite their efforts on Sunday, television and newspaper reporters were still in the dark about the motive for the murder, and many other details remained unknown. Hoping for more information, the reporters descended Monday morning on the chambers of Jefferson County circuit judge Ted Todd in Madison.

Reporters huddled in the courthouse hallway, exchanging bits and pieces of information they'd gathered from their police sources. One reporter said he'd heard that the girls were members of a satanic cult. Some of the more seasoned reporters nodded cordially but immediately dismissed that theory. They'd heard similar stories about satanic cults before and none of them had ever panned out.

Veteran television reporter John McGrath told the other reporters that he'd learned that the murder involved a lesbian love triangle. This too seemed unbelievable, but then again, the bizarre nature of the crime begged for some explanation.

When Judge Todd finally released the police report that afternoon, it stated that Melinda Loveless was jealous of Shanda and wanted to kill her because she thought that Shanda was "trying to steal her girlfriend named Amanda." The report didn't mention Amanda Heavrin's last name, but it provided the bare outline of the story Toni Lawrence had told police and included the name of the fourth girl, Hope Rippey.

The police refused to answer questions about the lesbian angle and most of the reporters, including McGrath, refrained from using the word *lesbian* in their reports, saying only that the murder was caused by jealousy over a girlfriend. One television reporter, however, went on the air that night and said the murder was the result of a lesbian love triangle.

Armed with this new information, the reporters began again in earnest. They spread across the streets of historic downtown Madison, asking residents for their thoughts on the horrible murder that had occurred on the outskirts of town. Camera crews found the spot on Lemon Road where Shanda had been burned, and reporters waited outside the schools of the accused murderers and the victim, asking young boys and girls if they knew the victim or her alleged killers. Two television stations managed to get interviews with Melinda's mother. Margie Donahue sat on her living-room couch and told the camera that there must be some mistake, that her daughter was innocent. Laurie Tackett's little brother, Buddy, told another television station that his sister wasn't capable of murder.

All day Tuesday, the reporters staked out Kraft's Funeral Home, where friends and relatives and dozens of Shanda's classmates came to pay their respects. Jamie Rainey had banned the reporters from coming inside, but several tried to sneak in anyway, only to be turned away. Frustrated but not beaten, the television crews set up shop on the adjoining property and reporters corralled youngsters as they left the funeral home, succeeding in capturing their tears on camera.

Earlier that day, counselors at the three schools Shanda had attended in the last year met with students who were having a hard time dealing with the tragedy.

"This is so horrendous that some of the students still can't believe it happened," said Brother Bill Reigel, who had been working with students at St. Paul School. "They are in a state of denial. Some have even dreamed that she is still alive. It's going to take a long time for this to pass.

On Wednesday, Shanda's parents relented to repeated requests and allowed one of the television stations to film the interior of the church on condition that the film be shared with the other channels. The funeral mass was held at Our Lady of Perpetual Help Catholic Church in New Albany. Reporters who interviewed children entering the church began to gather bits and pieces about Shanda's past.

"I think they transferred her because Melinda was picking on her," said Kim Mancle, a classmate of Shanda's from Hazelwood. "I knew she had problems in the past at Hazelwood," added Mary Jeanne Osborne, who used to date Shanda's stepbrother, Larry Dale. "But she had changed after she transferred. She changed her makeup, her hairstyle, and she talked more like someone her age. Just last week, she told me about her boyfriend and how cute he was. She was a sweet girl."

Every pew in the church was filled. People were lined up along the sides and in the back of the church. Many of them were classmates of Shanda. They watched in silence as the casket was carried down the aisle, followed by Jacque, Steve, Sharon, Paije, and other relatives. During his eulogy, the Reverend John Fink stepped off the pulpit and walked over to the first-graders from Our Lady of Perpetual Help who sat together near the front of church, across the aisle from Shanda's family.

"What does spring bring us?" the Reverend Fink asked the first-graders. "Sunshine," said one of the youngsters. "Flowers," said another. "Butterflies," said a third.

"Butterflies," the preacher repeated loudly. "Each of you have caught a butterfly, haven't you?"

The children nodded in unison.

"Butterflies are beautiful creatures. They are a joy to catch and hold," the Reverend Fink said. "But eventually you have to let that butterfly go, don't you?"

The reverend walked over to Shanda's parents and reached out a hand to each.

"Somewhere along the line, you have to let go of that butterfly. You have to let go of that life," he said. "You must let go of Shanda."

"I can't," moaned Jacque Ott.

"You have to," the reverend said before walking back to the pulpit. "You must let Shanda go."

He ended the service by reading a poem, a copy of which Steve carried in his wallet.

"God made the world with its towering trees, majestic mountains, and restless seas—and then He paused and He said, 'It needs one more thing, something to touch and dance and sing,' so God made little girls. When he completed that task He had begun, He was pleased, for the world seen through a little girl's eyes greatly resembles Paradise."

Looking directly at Shanda's parents, the Reverend Fink said, "Your beloved Shanda now lives in Paradise."

Shanda's family waited in a room under the church until the television crews had left. Only then did the funeral procession begin its long journey across the Ohio River to the tiny town of Big Springs, Kentucky, more than fifty miles away. Shanda was buried in the graveyard of Big Springs Methodist Church, the same church in which Shanda's parents had been married fourteen years earlier. Shanda's body was laid to rest beside the grave of her grandmother. A light snow began to fall as the family said their prayers over the gravesite.

Finally it was time to leave. Relatives wrapped their arms around a shaking Jacque Ott and led her to the car. The snowfall had thickened, and it was coming down in a soft white flurry. By the time the cars approached the Ohio River, the hilly countryside was covered by a blanket of snow.

"I remember thinking how beautiful it was," Steve said later. "It seemed so peaceful. After all the horrible things that had happened to Shanda, I felt she was finally at peace."

In the days following Shanda's murder, Jacque and Steve turned down repeated requests for interviews.

They knew that reporters were bound to ask questions about Shanda's relationship with Amanda, and they didn't know how to deal with that. They were convinced that the media would sensationalize the lesbian aspect, and they couldn't risk smearing their dead daughter's reputation.

Jacque and Steve remained silent as the hosts of local radio talk shows began to speculate about how a twelve-year-old could get involved is such a sordid and tragic affair. Some listeners were ready to place part of the blame on Shanda's parents. "This wouldn't have happened if that little girl's parents had done their job," said one caller to a Louisville radio show.

Steve and Jacque kept their silence, even though they

ached to shout out to the world the truth: That Shanda had been cared for and loved. That they'd done the best they could, the very best they knew how. That, like other parents, they never believed that anything this horrible could happen to their child. That they'd learned the hard lesson that nothing in life is guaranteed.

11

Flipping an old Indian head nickel in 1971 was how Steve Sharer and his best friend, Mike Boardman, decided which would be the first to ask out the new girl in school, Jacque Watkins.

Steve and Mike were seniors at Clarksville High School and normally they wouldn't have considered dating a sophomore. But this girl was something special. She had long blond hair and a gorgeous smile, and though she was only fifteen, she looked more mature than half the girls in the senior class.

"I called tails," Steve remembered. "It came up heads."

At the time of the coin toss, neither Mike nor Steve knew how vulnerable Jacque was. Her parents had just gone through a divorce, and Jacque and her mother and older sister, Debbie, had moved from their spacious home in Jeffersonville to a small house in Clarksville. Jacque hated her new home and her new school.

"I was as angry and mixed up and lonely as a girl could be at that age," Jacque recalled later. "Mike Boardman was my white knight."

Mike was the class cutup, a natural charmer with a friendly smile and rich sense of humor. Jacque couldn't believe that a good-looking senior had asked her out, and she was even more amazed when after their first date he asked her out again. Suddenly Jacque's emotional burden didn't seem so heavy. She had someone to lean on, someone who cared for her, someone who would soon tell her that he loved her. When Mike and Jacque started going steady, Steve decided it was time that he too settled down. He began going steady with a girl in his class, and the two couples became inseparable, double-dating to movies, high-school basketball games, and parties.

Mike and Jacque had been going together about a year when he gave her an engagement ring. Then, shortly after Jacque turned sixteen, she learned that she was pregnant, and she and Mike got married. Jacque went to night school until right before their daughter, Paije, was born. The marriage lasted only another two and a half years.

"We were just too young," Jacque said later. "I was a baby raising a baby. I felt trapped, and Mike wasn't ready for the responsibility of being a father and a husband."

A single mother at nineteen, Jacque began working two jobs while relying on relatives to babysit Paije. Jacque had lost contact with Steve after her divorce from Mike and didn't know that he had left town to start up a heating and air-conditioning business in Middlesboro, Kentucky, a coal-mining town two hundred miles away.

When he came back to Jeffersonville one weekend to visit his parents, Steve stopped in at the town's most popular night spot, the Garage Club, where he ran into Jacque. The two old friends spent most of the night reminiscing, talking about Mike Boardman, about Paije, about former classmates, and about themselves. After several drinks Steve grew bold. He moved closer to the pretty girl he'd lost in a coin toss years before and kissed her. They kissed again.

The next three months brought good times but also misery. Steve would leave Middlesboro after work every Friday afternoon in time to take Jacque out that night. By Sunday afternoon he was back on the road to Middlesboro. Weekdays were spent at work. Weeknights were spent on the phone.

"The phone bills were enormous," Steve said later. "I

finally told Jacque that we're going to have to do something about this. She said, 'What do you want to do?' and I said the best thing that we could do was get married. That way we wouldn't have to worry about the doggone phone bills. So we did."

Steve had worried how Jacque would adjust to mountain life in Middlesboro but to his relief she seemed to enjoy the country as much as he did. They set up residence in a former dairy house that had been converted into a nice home. They lived simply but comfortably. Steve's business was doing well and they bought enough camping gear to spend many weekends in the nearby national park. It was on one of those camping trips, Steve and Jacque believe, that she became pregnant with Shanda. On the night that Jacque's water broke, Steve rushed her to Pineville Hospital. He was so nervous that he wrecked the truck in the hospital parking lot.

"When we got to the Pineville Hospital the nurse told me that I wasn't in labor and I should go home," Jacque said. "I told her that I'd had a baby before and I knew that I was in labor and I wasn't going anywhere." The doctor who examined Jacque said she was still a long way from giving birth. He sedated her, then left to perform another operation. Moments later, Shanda Renee Sharer was born.

"The nurse was on the intercom trying to page another doctor when I went ahead and delivered Shanda natural. Believe me, I had no intention to do so. She literally fell out on the table. I always used to tell her that she came into this world with a vengeance."

To this day, Steve and Jacque tell different stories about why they moved back to southern Indiana. Jacque claims that it had to do with a coal miners' strike about nine months after Shanda's birth. Life in Middlesboro, as in most eastern Kentucky towns, revolves around the coal industry. When the miners go out on strike the entire economy crashes. Jacque said that Steve's business suffered during the strike and they went back to Indiana because they were having trouble making ends meet.

Steve, however, contends that he was still making a good living when Jacque became hopelessly homesick.

For whatever reason, the move was made. And things were never the same between Steve and Jacque. They began to drift apart. There were squabbles over finances, and the trouble that was brewing between them came to a head with a terrible argument at a Halloween party. Jacque and the girls moved out and Steve filed for divorce.

The divorce was granted, but after a few months Steve and Jacque cooled down and began to have second thoughts about their decision. They knew that the girls were in turmoil. Paije had never really known her natural father. It was Steve she called "Dad." And Shanda, at three, was too young to understand why she could only see her daddy on weekends. Steve and Jacque decided to give it another try. They didn't remarry, but Jacque and the girls moved back in with Steve at a house he was renting in Jeffersonville. Things went well for about a year, but then the arguments started again.

"Things just didn't work out," Jacque said later. "We'd grown apart."

This time the parting was amicable. Jacque was given custody of the girls, but they usually spent every other weekend with Steve, who liked to take them to visit his father's farm in Kentucky.

At five, Shanda's independent spirit was already starting to emerge. She'd often heard Steve brag about how he'd learned to drive a tractor when he was five or six. If he could do it, so could she. Shanda argued until she got her way. She jumped up in the tractor seat with Steve crouched behind her, showing her how to work the gas pedal and brake. It wasn't long before Shanda felt ready to solo.

"Dad, I know how to do this," Shanda said. "You already showed me."

"Well, what about shifting gears?"

"I don't care about shifting gears," Shanda said. "I just want to steer it."

Without saying a word, and without Shanda seeing him, Steve stepped off the back of the tractor. Thinking her father was still crouched behind her, Shanda putted along in first gear for a while, then tightened her grip on the big steering wheel and began a wide turn, pushing and pulling the wheel with all her strength. Finally, after completing the turn, Shanda had the tractor headed back the other way. Only then did she see Steve standing in the field.

"Her eyes got real big, her mouth dropped open, and then that big smile of hers came across her face," Steve remembers. "She'd done it on her own. My dad was standing next to me, and he said, 'Steve, I remember when I did the same thing to you. She's a chip off the old block.' I couldn't keep her off that tractor after that."

To supplement her income from her job as a clerk at a barge line, Jacque began working on weekends with her sister, Debbie, as a mutual clerk at Churchill Downs, the thoroughbred racing track in Louisville and home of the Kentucky Derby. One day another mutual clerk asked her out on a date. His name was Ronnie Ott. At forty-one, Ronnie was ten years older than Jacque. He'd been married once before but had no children. Ronnie lived well. In addition to working at the racetrack, he received two pensions, one as a disabled veteran and the other for a workplace injury that had cost him his job as an electrician at the Naval Ordnance Station in Louisville.

It was a whirlwind romance. Ronnie showered Jacque and her daughters with gifts, he'd cook them elegant dinners at his beautiful home in southwest Louisville, and he made it clear early on that he had marriage on his mind.

"My mother kept saying, 'Jacque, this is what you need in your life. Your life has been so unstable,'" Jacque said later. "And early on Paije and Shanda thought he was the best thing since peanut butter. I was at a point in my life where I saw an opportunity to make a good life for us all."

Shanda was seven at the time of her mother's marriage to Ronnie Ott. After a few years at a public elementary school, Jacque enrolled Shanda in St. Paul Catholic school, where she would spend the fourth, fifth, and sixth grades. When she was ten, Shanda won a crossword-puzzle contest at a McDonald's restaurant. The prize was an all-expense paid trip for her family to Disneyland in California.

"Shanda felt like the belle of the ball after winning that contest," Jacque said later. "She got to ride on an airplane for the first time, and we had a limousine that chauffeured us everywhere. It made her a real bigshot with her friends at St. Paul."

Shanda never had a problem making friends. She was a bright, humorous child, who made above-average grades and who never had enough time for all the things she wanted to do. She joined the Girl Scouts and 4H, she made the cheerleading and gymnastics squads, and played on St. Paul's basketball, volleyball, and softball teams.

Shanda had a mischievous nature, a bit of moxie that endeared her to her playmates. Shanda was always the first one to hurl a water balloon at a birthday party, to sneak on the neighbor's trampoline, to flirt with the new boy in class.

"She loved to be the center of attention," said Shanda's friend Joyce Robertson. "I can't remember anybody I had so much fun with. She just had so much life in her laugh and the way she talked."

"Shanda kind of looked out for me," said another St. Paul classmate, Brittany Thompson. "We were trick-or-treating one Halloween and some boy threw a water balloon in my bag. Shanda marched up to the boy's house and told his mother that she owed me a whole new bag of candy."

Jacque said that Shanda was "always a bit of a showoff. She'd always want to put on a performance for you. She'd do her new cheer or the new dance she learned. She always wanted to be like her big sister, Paije, but in one respect they were worlds apart. Paije was hard-headed like me. If I got mad at Paije she'd argue with me until she was blue in the face. Shanda was the opposite. If Shanda thought she did wrong or had hurt your feelings, she would cry. Her feelings got hurt so easily. She was very emotional. She got that from Steve's mother."

There was a special bond between Shanda and Steve's mother, Betty Sharer. Shanda delighted in spending the occasional weekend with her grandmother. When Shanda was just a toddler, her grandmother designated one drawer in the kitchen as Shanda's and was always filling it with surprises for her grandchild. Betty Sharer taught Shanda how to sew clothes for her dolls and instilled in her a love for reading.

"Books fascinated Shanda," Betty Sharer remembers. "I

had a bookcase at my house and Shanda was constantly pulling books off the shelf and asking me to read to her. When she got older she wanted to read for me. I'd take her to the bookstore to buy a new children's book and she'd have a hard time finding one she hadn't read. She had two favorite books. One was a story about a little tugboat, the other was the Bible. She loved for me to read about little Jesus in Bethlehem."

Beneath Shanda's bubbly personality was a girl with a deep longing to find the answers to life's questions.

"There was a serious side to Shanda," Betty Sharer said. "She asked me a lot of questions about God and what happens to us when we die. One time when we were out for a drive, Shanda asked what she had to do to be a good Christian. She was only about nine at the time. I asked her if she believed that Jesus died for our sins and she said yes. Then I asked her if she wanted Jesus to forgive her sins, and she said yes. I told her that if she kept Jesus in her mind she would be a good Christian."

By the sixth grade Shanda was a budding beauty. She had long blond hair, pretty blue-gray eyes, and a trim, athletic figure. Boys from St. Paul, some of them seventh- and eighth-graders, would call her at home and she'd spend hours on the phone talking to them and then calling her girlfriends to giggle about what the boys had said.

"She was boy-crazy and the boys were crazy about her," Jacque said later.

Steve Sharer remembers when Shanda, who was then eleven, introduced him to her new boyfriend, a boy of the same age.

"Nice to meet you, son," Steve said, shaking the lad's hand firmly. "Do you have a job?"

"No sir," the boy said, casting a nervous glance at Shanda. "Not yet, sir."

"Well, you better get one," Steve advised him. "Girlfriends can be expensive."

Shanda rolled her eyes. "Ohh, Dad, cut it out. You're embarrassing me."

In the six years since his divorce from Jacque, Steve had dated a number of women but none that he was seriously interested in. Then a friend introduced him to Sharon James, an attractive, brunette divorcée who had two children of her own, a fifteen-year-old boy, Larry Dale, and an eighteen-year-old daughter, Sandy.

Sharon James had a little bit of a country twang, a lively sense of humor, and an infectious laugh. She and Steve hit it off right away. After they'd been dating for a couple of months, Shanda was dying to meet the new woman in her father's life. She could tell that he was getting serious. All he ever talked about was Sharon. A few nights before they met, Shanda called Sharon on the phone.

"She wanted to know everything about me," Sharon said. "She wanted to know how tall I was, what color my hair was, what my children's names were. I bet we talked for hours."

One night Steve took his mom, Sharon, and Shanda out to dinner. Steve had already told his daughter that he intended to ask Sharon to marry him. Shanda wasn't about to miss out on something this exciting. She kept kicking Steve under the table and giving him a knowing smile. Finally she could wait no longer.

"Dad, are you going to ask her or not?" Shanda asked.

"Ask me what?" Sharon said with a smile, knowing what was on Steve's mind.

"Will you marry me?" Steve asked.

"Of course I will," Sharon said.

Shanda was thrilled to share in such a memorable occasion. She took an immediate liking to her stepmother, stepsister, and stepbrother, and after the wedding she spent nearly every weekend at their house in Jeffersonville. It didn't take long for her to make a lot of friends in the neighborhood.

"Shanda took over the upper loft of the garage and made it a clubhouse for her and her friends," Steve said. "They'd get up there and play school. Shanda always wanted to be the teacher when they taught religion. She loved to read from the Bible."

When the weather warmed up, Steve and Sharon and Shanda would pack up their camping gear and head to the lake. Steve would put his small fishing boat in the water and tow a big air mattress behind the craft. Sharon and Shanda would lay on the mattress, sunning themselves, as Steve fished for bass.

"He'd troll slowly along, fishing," Sharon remembers fondly. "When he got a lure hung up on a stick, Shanda would roll off the raft into the water and get it loose."

As she grew older, Shanda became even more of a daredevil. She persuaded Steve to let her ride behind him on his motorcycle. The first time she went with Sharon to Steve's father's farm, Shanda talked Sharon into riding with her on the tractor.

"She had me on the back of the tractor and she was driving," Sharon said. "I said, 'Are we going down that ditch?' and she said no. Well, sure enough, when we got to the ditch, down we went."

At other times, Sharon said, Shanda could be the perfect young lady. "One time I took her with me to the racetrack. She was the only child in a group of adults, but she'd carry on these sophisticated conversations about which horse to bet on or this and that. All my friends were so impressed with her."

While Steve and Sharon were enjoying the bliss of their new marriage, Jacque and Ronnie were having problems. After a series of arguments with Ronnie, Paije, who was then eighteen, left home and moved in with her boyfriend. Jacque and Ronnie were also arguing. Jacque had been moving up the ladder at the barge line. Her new job as an insurance-claims representative called for her to spend frequent evenings away from home having dinner with clients.

"Ronnie was extremely jealous," Jacque said. "He'd call the restaurants I went to and have me paged. He was constantly accusing me of running around on him. The kids weren't getting along with him, and I was miserable. I asked him for a divorce."

Paije had since broken up with her boyfriend and moved in with Jacque's older sister, Debbie, in an apartment in New Albany. When another apartment in the complex opened up, Jacque and Shanda moved in. It was to be only a temporary arrangement. Jacque hoped that she could soon save enough money for a down payment on a house. But eight months later Shanda was dead and the walls of the townhouse held too many bad memories for Jacque to stay any longer.

"I stayed with Debbie for a while, and then I moved in with a girlfriend of mine," Jacque said. "I never slept in there again after Shanda died."

12

Chief investigator Steve Henry knew that his job was only just beginning after he'd arrested Melinda Loveless and Laurie Tackett. Everything he knew of the murder had been told to him by Toni Lawrence, and parts of her story didn't ring true.

Toni claimed that Melinda and Laurie took her and Hope home before they burned Shanda. But the times didn't fit. Toni said she was dropped off at nine-forty-five in the morning. If that was true, Melinda and Laurie couldn't have driven the fifteen miles to Lemon Road and set Shanda on fire until well after ten. Shanda's body was stone cold when Donn and Ralph Foley found her at ten-thirty. Shanda had to have been set on fire earlier than Toni claimed.

Playing a hunch, Henry drove to the Clark Oil station where the girls had bought the gas and examined the cash-register receipts from the Saturday morning when Shanda was killed.

There was no record of a two-liter soft drink being sold between nine-fifteen and nine-thirty, the time that Toni claimed they were at the gas station. However, the receipts did show that a two-liter Pepsi and several dollars' worth of gas had been purchased at eight-forty.

139

The next morning, Henry drove to the Clark Station again. At exactly eight-forty he bought a few dollars of gasoline and pumped it into his gas tank. He drove directly to the burn site on Lemon Road, parked his car, got out and opened the trunk, then walked slowly to the edge of the soybean field where Shanda was burned. After lingering a few minutes, he drove to the McDonald's where the girls had breakfast. He bought a cup of coffee and checked his watch. It was exactly nine-thirty.

So that was the sequence of events. Melinda and Laurie had not taken Toni and Hope home after the gas was purchased. All four girls were on Lemon Road when Shanda was burned alive. Toni had lied.

Henry was eager to question Toni again. But by now she had lost some of her desire to cooperate.

"Clifton Lawrence called me about a week after the murder and said that Toni wasn't going to talk to us anymore," Henry said. "The media had tracked them down and were banging on the door day and night, asking for interviews. Mr. Lawrence was pretty upset about it all and they just clammed up."

Hope Rippey was also silent. Darryl Auxier, the attorney for the Rippey family, had promised to bring Hope in for questioning. But now he was stalling, claiming that Hope wasn't ready to give a statement.

Henry decided that he could afford to wait awhile on Toni and Hope. There were plenty of leads to follow. Television and newspaper reports on the murder had spurred a flood of phone calls to police.

Since the murder had happened in his backyard, Sheriff Richard "Buck" Shipley offered to serve as Henry's partner in the investigation. The two set up their headquarters at the Jefferson County police station in Madison. It was a good pairing. Henry and Shipley had spent nearly twenty years together as state troopers and had great respect for one another's abilities.

Given the gruesome nature of the murder, both lawmen originally suspected that the killer or killers might have been high. But Toni had denied that any of the girls had drunk or used drugs that night. And a search of Laurie's car turned up no evidence of alcohol or drugs.

Henry would later hear stories of Laurie's occasional drinking and her minor experimentation with drugs. He also learned that Toni and Hope had both been infrequent users of alcohol and marijuana and that Melinda had gone through bouts when she abused alcohol. But nothing in his investigation led him to believe that any of the girls was under the influence of drugs or alcohol that night.

Henry and Shipley believed they had recovered all of the girls' weapons, even though the knife found in Laurie's pocket and a larger knife discovered alongside the road a few miles from the body and later identified as Melinda's were clean of blood stains. Forensic expert Curtis Wells had also been unable to find Shanda's fingerprints in the car or trunk, and there were no blood stains or fingerprints on the car's tire iron. However, blood samples found in the trunk were of the same type as Shanda's and fibers found in the car and trunk matched those of the burned blanket fragments clutched in Shanda's hands. There was no doubt that Shanda had been in Laurie's trunk.

With Melinda and Laurie behind bars and Toni and Hope unwilling to talk anymore, Henry and Shipley concentrated on nailing down the motive—Melinda's jealousy—and proving premeditation. They also needed to unravel Toni's quirky tale about Laurie's bizarre fascination with the occult. Could Shanda's murder have been some kind of satanic ritual?

The first name on their interview list was Amanda Heavrin. Amanda's father had already contacted a lawyer, and the interrogation took place in the law office of Steve Lohmeyer. Amanda was noticeably nervous and reluctant to talk. She chewed on her fingernails as Henry tried to draw her out. Eventually Amanda began to talk about her relationship with Melinda and Shanda. Although she said that Melinda was extremely jealous of Shanda, she repeatedly denied that there was a lesbian relationship between any of the girls.

Amanda told the police officers that on the night of the

murder Melinda had called her at about nine o'clock from a pay phone at the hardcore concert. She claimed that it was just chitchat and that Melinda made no mention of her plans for Shanda.

Amanda broke into tears as she told the officers how she learned of Shanda's murder. She described the scene at Melinda's house on Saturday, putting all the blame for the murder on Laurie. She said that Laurie admitted to beating Shanda with the tire iron and setting her on fire. Henry and Shipley were stunned that Melinda had so readily told her friends about what had happened, and they were suspicious of Amanda's claim that Laurie had been boasting of what she'd done.

"It was pretty clear that Amanda was trying to protect Melinda," Henry said later. "I think she felt that now that Shanda was gone she had to stick by Melinda. She had no one else."

The next stop for Henry and Shipley was the office of Virgil Seay, who was in charge of juvenile probation in Floyd County. It was Seay who had given Curtis Wells the information that led police to Melinda's house the night of the arrest. Seay turned over the stack of letters that had been given to him a month earlier by Amanda's father.

Henry read each one carefully. There was no longer any doubt that Amanda and Melinda had enjoyed a lesbian relationship and that Melinda hated Shanda for interfering. He read the last line of the last letter from Melinda over again: "I want Shanda dead." The detective knew that he was holding a powerful piece of evidence.

That same day, Henry and Shipley learned that a young man by the name of Larry Leatherbury had called the police station, asking to speak to the chief investigator on the Shanda Sharer case. The dispatcher told Henry that Leatherbury was very insistent and said he had some vital information. He'd left his phone number and address.

Henry hadn't been able to get the curious names of Larry and Terry Leatherbury out of his mind since Toni had told him that the twin brothers had practiced witchcraft with Laurie and had drunk each other's blood.

Henry and Shipley drove to the worn-down section of

Louisville where the Leatherburys were living in a friend's apartment and honked the horn.

"I didn't want to go to the door because there was no telling who else was in there," Henry said. "I wanted to talk to him in the car, where he was on my home turf."

In answer to the horn, Larry Leatherbury came out of the apartment and walked slowly toward the car with a swaggering gait. It was a bitterly cold day, but Larry was wearing only black shorts and a black T-shirt. On his feet were black combat boots and around his neck a black flowing cape that flapped behind him in the brisk January wind.

"Is that who we're here to interview?" Henry asked Shipley.

Shipley, who had met Leatherbury before, grimaced and said, "I'm afraid so."

At Shipley's beckoning, Leatherbury climbed into the backseat of Henry's car. The two officers turned around to face him, but before they could say a word, Leatherbury volunteered a detailed account of his whereabouts at the time of Shanda's murder.

"He gave us an alibi even before we asked him the first question," Henry said.

The cocky Leatherbury said he'd been in Lexington, Kentucky, on the night that Shanda was taken from her father's home. He had gone there with his brother, Terry, and two girls, Kary Pope and Carrie East. The foursome had attended an alternative music concert, where Larry met a male college student from Morehead State University. Making no secret of his sexuality, Larry told Henry and Shipley that he'd spent Friday night, Saturday, and most of Sunday with the young man before returning to Louisville on Sunday night. He gave the officers the young man's name and phone number and encouraged them to verify his story.

"Everything he told us checked out," Henry said. "His alibi was airtight."

Once he'd established his whereabouts that weekend, Larry eagerly told Henry and Shipley everything he knew about Laurie Tackett and Melinda Loveless. The lawmen listened with dismay as Larry described in eerie detail

143

Laurie's fascination with the occult. He told of the séances in which Laurie would claim that spirits had entered her body. During these channeling episodes, Laurie would take on alter egos and communicate with the dead. Larry described how he and Laurie cut their own arms and used their blood to draw pictures. Sometimes, he said, Laurie would drink her own blood.

"Laurie is obsessed with death and the prospect of performing a human sacrifice," Larry said. "She talked often about burning someone."

Larry also volunteered information about Laurie's home life and her rebellion against the strict Fundamentalist doctrines embraced by her mother. He told Henry and Shipley that he'd had sex with Laurie but that she now considered herself a lesbian. He even turned over photographs of Laurie with Melinda and told the officers how to get in touch with Kary Pope.

"Larry was extremely helpful," Henry said. "He seemed to get a kick out of talking to us."

Meanwhile, Steve Henry's older brother, Howard, was helping out in the investigation by following up another lead. An anonymous phone caller said that two girls, Crystal Wathen and Thea Board, had been talking about the murder at Jeffersonville High School. Howard Henry went to the school and talked to both girls. While Thea was cooperative, telling Henry that Wathen claimed to have spent the afternoon following the murder with Melinda, Crystal was not. She denied even talking to Melinda since the murder.

"Whoever told you that was a liar," Crystal said.

"Crystal," Henry said sternly, "you are aware that if you fail to tell me the truth, it can be considered an obstruction of justice."

"I told you, I don't know anything about it," Crystal insisted.

Seeing that he wasn't getting anywhere, Howard Henry went back to the police station. A short time later he interviewed Dale Gettings, the last person other than the four girls to see Shanda alive.

Gettings told Henry about the two girls he'd seen at the Sharer household Friday night when he stopped by looking for Shanda's stepbrother. Looking at mug shots, he was able to identify Laurie as one of the girls.

Steve Henry and Sheriff Shipley's list of people to interview, meanwhile, kept growing. Laurie's neighbor, Brian Tague, called the police station, wanting to talk. He said that Laurie had called him early that past Saturday morning, asking if he had any gasoline that she could use in her car. Tague told her he didn't and thought it strange that Laurie had then asked for kerosene. He didn't realize the significance of it until he read about Laurie's arrest.

Leslie Jacoby, a classmate of Melinda, came forward and said she'd talked to Melinda on the phone the afternoon following the murder. She said Melinda was crying and eventually told her that Shanda had been killed and that she'd been involved. "Melinda and Shanda hated each other," Leslie said. "Melinda was real possessive of Amanda. She didn't want anybody to be close friends with Amanda. She thought Shanda was trying to steal her away. She'd say, 'I'm going to beat that bitch up.'"

The case for Melinda's premeditation got an even bigger boost when Jeffrey Stettenbenz came by the police station. The portly, frizzy-haired fifteen-year-old, who had been with Amanda Heavrin at the mall when Melinda picked her up after the murder, claimed he'd also been at Amanda's house on the Friday night that Shanda was abducted and that he'd listened on a second phone when Melinda called Amanda. He told police that he'd overheard Melinda tell Amanda that she was going to kill Shanda.

Another that volunteered information was Valerie Hedge, a friend of Melinda and Laurie's. Henry and Shipley drove to Valerie's home in New Albany to talk to the sixteen-year-old. With her mother sitting next to her, Valerie explained that she'd met Melinda at Hazelwood Junior High and the two of them hung around with the same crowd that included Laurie, Kary Pope, and Larry and Terry Leatherbury.

"Did any of these people ever mention anything about killing anyone?" Henry asked.

Valerie nodded her head, then related an incident that had occurred a few months earlier. She'd been out in Kary's car with Laurie and the Leatherburys. They were driving through the hills of Floyd's Knobs, a scenic area north of New Albany, when the conversation took a macabre turn. Kary and the Leatherburys began talking about what crimes they would like to get away with, and someone wondered what it would be like to kill someone.

"That's when Laurie said she'd always wanted to kill somebody," Valerie said. "She said she wanted to burn somebody."

Valerie told Henry and Shipley that Kary Pope probably knew more about Melinda and Laurie's friendship than anyone else. Larry Leatherbury had said the same thing. The next day, Henry and Shipley arranged for Kary to meet him at the police station in Sellersburg. Kary came with her mother, and she was noticeably nervous. She seemed self-conscious of her boyish appearance and masculine manner. Although Kary normally liked to flaunt her lesbianism, Henry sensed that it was causing her some uneasiness.

"I tried to make her more comfortable by letting her know right up front that I had no interest at all in her sexuality," Henry said. "I wasn't going to judge her. I just needed her to be straightforward with me." It didn't take long for Kary to warm up to the softspoken Henry. Henry had two teenagers of his own, and he knew that the best results came with patience and a kind but firm manner.

"Just tell us everything you know about Shanda Sharer's murder," Henry said. "Don't embellish anything. Don't make it more than it is, but don't leave anything out. We want exactly the truth."

At first Kary shied away from questions about Melinda's jealousy of Amanda and Shanda's friendship, but eventually she opened up.

"Melinda and Amanda had been together, like girlfriend-girlfriend type of thing, and Amanda had started hanging around with Shanda and spending the night with Shanda," Kary said. "Melinda kept threatening Amanda to stay away from Shanda. Melinda and Amanda would get into fights and would break up and Melinda would come to me and say let's go kill her and stuff like that. You know how kids say stuff like that. I mean, I say it sometimes but I really don't mean it. I never took to heart what she was saying. Amanda was seeing Shanda, but to my knowledge they were just like really, really good friends, but Melinda would always get jealous and would want to go beat up Shanda because she thought Shanda was going to take away Amanda."

"How often did Melinda discuss killing Shanda?" Henry asked.

"About every day."

"Did she ever say how she was going to do it?"

"No. But Melinda always wanted me to take her to Shanda's house so she could beat her up," Kary said. "She'd say, 'I'm going to kill her.' She wanted someone to take her there and help her beat the hell out of Shanda. She'd tell me that if I didn't take her to Shanda's house she'd just go on a rampage at school and get suspended. I told her to just talk to her. I told her she didn't need to be getting into trouble."

Kary said that when she and Melinda first met Laurie they both liked her.

"We didn't know she'd be, you know, psychotic or anything like that," she said. "After a while me and Laurie got in a fight. Then me and Melinda got into a disagreement and she started hanging around with Laurie. She knew that Laurie had been telling everybody that she would enjoy killing somebody. Laurie had said it was her destiny to kill somebody and hear them screaming. She just talked like that. You see, Laurie doesn't keep friends for a very long time. When she makes a friend she'll lie to them, she'll steal for them, she'll do anything to keep that friend. When I stopped hanging around with her she told people that she was going to put a death spell on me. She was into witchcraft and stuff like that. I got scared of her and tried to keep away from her, but she kept bothering me. She'd call me up and disguise her voice and threaten me. Melinda had told me that if she had a chance she would kill Shanda. Laurie was the type of person that would probably help her just to keep her as a friend."

Henry, still bothered by Larry Leatherbury's smug attitude, asked Kary if she thought he had anything to do with the murder.

"I really don't know," Kary said. "The Leatherburys stopped hanging around with Laurie about a month ago because they thought that she was just a big fake. She'd always be doing channeling and stuff like that to get attention. She'd bring people back from the dead. She would go out of her body and have somebody come into her body. That's why she scared me, because I thought it was real. I had never experienced stuff like that, and when she first started doing it I believed her. Then I found out she was just full of it. Terry tries, but Larry is the only one that really channels. Larry said Laurie was faking it and Larry knows more about channeling than Laurie ever has."

Kary was on a roll now, and Henry kept her talking with a few pointed questions. "Tell me about the times Laurie talked about killing somebody," he said.

"She told Larry and Terry and me how it would be fun to kill somebody," Kary said. "She'd want to go trip on acid and kill someone and not remember it in the morning. We were at a party once and she started cutting herself and saying that she loves hurting herself and how she would like to do it to someone else. She said she'd like to stick a knife through someone's stomach just to see how it feels."

"How often does she do acid?"

"Only once when I was with her. I just thought she was pretty weird. Anybody that sits there and cuts herself and gets joy out of it is pretty strange. One time I got mad at my grandmother and Laurie said, 'Let's go kill her.' That would really scare me. She thought it was fun. She thought it would be a blast to do something like that before she died. She'd always go around saying that she was going to kill herself. She said she wanted to go out a different way than everybody else. One night she was channeling and she said her name was Deanna the Vampire and she would love to kill somebody. She told me she was a goddess and that she wanted me to become dead with her so I could be a vampire too. It scared me, but what was I supposed to do? You really can't report this to the police or nothing like that. I mean, if I told my mom something like that she probably wouldn't believe me."

Henry looked into Kary's eyes and assured her, "I know Laurie Tackett and I believe you."

"She scared me," Kary admitted. "I know that some

148

Shanda and her mother, Jacque, on Shanda's second birthday. *(Photo by Paije Boardman)*

Shanda relaxing with her father, Steve, after her gymnastics meet. *(Photo by Sharon Sharer)*

Shanda at nine. This is her mother's favorite photograph. *(Photo by Jacque Vaught)*

Shanda, three months after she turned twelve, four months before she was murdered. *(Photo by Betty Sharer)*

Amanda Heavrin, fourteen, wanted to be more than friends with Shanda.

Melinda Loveless, shown in her eighth-grade photograph, was Amanda Heavrin's lesbian lover. She grew insanely jealous of Shanda's friendship with Amanda.

Melinda Loveless's home was the first stop by the killers on the night of Shanda's murder. *(Photo by Michael Quinlan)*

The home of Shanda's father, Steve Sharer. Shanda was lured out of the house and abducted by four teenage girls. *(Photo by Michael Quinlan)*

The Witches' Castle, the old stone building where Shanda was told that she might not survive the night. *(Photo by* Courier-Journal *photographer Paul Schuhmann)*

Aerial view of the field where hunters discovered Shanda's body. *(Photo by Sgt. Curtis Wells)*

The X marks the spot where Shanda's burned body was found. The tire tracks of Laurie Tackett's car are visible in the gravel road. *(Photo by Sgt. Curtis Wells)*

Melinda Loveless.
(Photo by Sgt. Curtis Wells)

Laurie Tackett.
(Photo by Sgt. Curtis Wells)

Toni Lawrence.
(Photo by Sgt. Curtis Wells)

Hope Rippey.
(Photo by Sgt. Curtis Wells)

Detective Steve Henry. *(Photo by Bud Kraft)*

Sheriff Buck Shipley. *(Photo by Joe Trotter)*

Judge Ted Todd. *(Photo by Joe Trotter)*

Prosecutor Guy Townsend. *(Photo by Joe Trotter)*

Laurie Tackett's attorney, Wil Goering. *(Photo by Michael Quinlan)*

Laurie Tackett takes one last puff from her cigarette before entering the Madison courthouse. On the left is Deputy Randy Spry. *(Photo by Courier-Journal photographer Durrell Hall Jr.)*

Hope Rippey being led from the jail to the courthouse by Sheriff Buck Shipley. *(Photo by Joe Trotter)*

Toni Lawrence cries after receiving her sentence from Judge Todd. *(Photo by Courier-Journal photographer Paul Schuhmann)*

←

Melinda Loveless being led from the courthouse by her attorneys, Bob Hammerle (on left, wearing glasses) and Russ Johnson, after hearing her sentence of sixty years in prison. *(Photo by Courier-Journal photographer Larry Spitzer)*

Shanda's parents, cornered by reporters in the Madison courthouse. *(Photo by* Courier-Journal *photographer James Wallace)*

Shanda's grave in Big Springs, Kentucky. The headstone markings—hands cupping a butterfly— were inspired by Reverend John Fink's moving eulogy. *(Photo by Jacque Vaught)*

people say that people can't control your mind, but she influenced me a lot and I believe she had a hold of my mind."

Kary was starting to sniffle back tears. Henry told her to take a moment to compose herself, then asked her to tell him more about the connection between Melinda and Laurie. Kary said that when she told Laurie she didn't want to see her anymore, Laurie told her that she was moving to Utah.

"I said, 'Well go.' I said it didn't make any difference to me. I had my own life. The next thing I knew, she and Melinda were hanging out together. You see, Melinda is the type of person who will use you. If you have a car, she's going to take advantage of you."

Sheriff Shipley had been listening quietly to Kary's bizarre tale when he remembered some remarks made by Valerie Hedge and Larry Leatherbury that Laurie had talked about burning a body. "Did she ever say that to you?" he asked.

"Yeah. She said she wanted to kill somebody by burning them."

"Did she give a reason for that?"

"She thought it would be fun. She would always burn stuff. She would always cut stuff. One night Laurie asked Tracy [who was Kary's new girlfriend] to cut herself so Laurie could suck the blood out of her. Tracy told her she was crazy. No one was paying attention to her that night, so she said that somebody had taken possession of her body and that we were all in danger because the person in her was going to kill us. She just flipped out and everybody felt sorry for her, but she was just trying to get attention."

"What do you think makes her act like this?" Henry asked. "Is it something in her home?"

"Her parents hate her. They keep wanting to kick her out of her house. They think she's a devil worshiper, and I think there's really somebody in her head. Somebody has convinced her that there is stuff like witchcraft and she's been practicing it and she believes in it and she thinks she can get away with a lot of things. She don't care if she dies. She don't care if somebody kills her."

Henry had heard enough to realize that Kary probably had a better feel for the dynamics behind Shanda's murder than anyone else he'd interviewed. "Just assume for a moment that Laurie Tackett killed Shanda Sharer," he said. "In your opinion, would she have done it as Laurie Tackett, or would she have done it as somebody else? Would she have channeled?"

"Probably."

"Who do you think she would have been?"

"Deanna the Vampire."

"Would her voice change when she did this?"

Kary lowered her voice to a soft growl. "She'd sound like this. She would tilt her head to the side and go out of it. She always told me that if she was out for more than five minutes I should hold her arm and say the name 'Lucinda' and it would bring her back out of that dimension."

"What do you think happened on the night of the murder?" Henry asked.

"I think Melinda got mad at Shanda because Shanda had been flirting with Amanda. I think Melinda told Laurie she wanted to kill her and Laurie told Melinda, 'Let's do it.' Melinda probably didn't take her seriously because Melinda is not that kind of coldhearted person. I think that Laurie did most of it because Laurie would do anything for a friend to keep a friend. I think Melinda wanted to beat the hell out of her, but that was it. I think Laurie did the rest because she was always wanting to cut somebody. She was always wanting to burn somebody. When she got really mad she'd hold it in and then she'd feel crazy. She'd scream or something and would just go into another world."

"Have you heard who set Shanda on fire?" Henry asked.

"Laurie and Hope."

"Who told you that?"

"Melinda called me one night from jail and told me that it was all Laurie and Hope. She said that Laurie and Hope took the body out of the back of the car and Laurie started cutting on her and stuff. Melinda said that she and the other girl were back behind the car burning evidence and Melinda didn't know what was going on until she saw Laurie drop a match. Laurie told her that it was better that way. She told

Melinda that Shanda needed to die. Melinda told me that all she did was beat her up and that Laurie did the rest and that Hope had helped her. She said Laurie told all three girls that if they told on her she would channel and kill all of them."

"What about the fourth girl, Toni?"

"Melinda said she was there too. They were all four there when it happened."

Henry was ready to wrap up the interview, but he still couldn't get Larry Leatherbury off his mind. "Do you think he was involved in any way with the murder? He seemed eager to give us his alibi."

"He told me that he had called the police," Kary said, cracking a smile for the first time. "You've got to know Larry. He just thought it would be neat to be interviewed about a murder."

Henry shrugged. "He seemed to be having a good time."

Another girl who had hung with the same crowd was Carrie East. Carrie, who'd been Melinda's lover for a short while, confirmed that Melinda was jealous of Shanda, but mostly she wanted to talk about Laurie, who she believed pushed Melinda into the murder.

Laurie "was just crazy," Carrie said. "When we went driving with her she'd swerve all around the road. I mean, you can just look at her and see that she's evil. She was always screaming and stuff. There's hardly any time she's calm, and when she is she just sits there and stares."

In late January, Crystal Wathen admitted that she'd lied to the police when they first questioned her. Upon the advice of her lawyer, she wrote a lengthy letter to the police, recounting the afternoon she'd spent with Melinda and Laurie after the murder. The letter was obviously written to help Melinda's case. In it, Crystal gave a detailed account of how Laurie stuck the tire iron under Crystal's nose and demonstrated how she'd beaten Shanda.

Not long after receiving Crystal's letter, the police got another break in the case. Tony Downs, a New Albany police officer, told Henry that his niece, Kelly Downs, had received a letter written by Melinda's friend Kristie Brodfuehrer. In it, Kristie described her and Melinda's attempt to abduct Amanda Heavrin. Kristie was initially reluctant to talk to police. But she eventually told Henry everything that happened that night, including that she'd had sex with a boy to pay for cocaine.

This proved that Melinda had not only talked about killing Shanda, she'd actually tried the exact same abduction plan on Amanda. Although the plan wasn't carried out, it showed that the abduction of Shanda wasn't a spur-of-the-moment thing. Melinda had devised the plan months earlier.

Kristie's story was not as shocking as some of the things Henry and Shipley had heard from Kary Pope and Larry Leatherbury, but it seemed more unsettling coming from the petite, innocent-looking Kristie.

"Kary and Larry had a certain look about them. What they told me about their lifestyles, as bizarre as it was, didn't seem as startling as hearing Kristie talk about that night," Henry said later. "I looked at Kristie and I could see my own daughter or the neighborhood kid. For some reason it really bothered me."

Henry spent an entire day retracing the girls' steps. He found the remains of a small fire in the Witches' Castle but no hard evidence to prove that the girls had taken Shanda there. The next stop was the dirt road near Laurie Tackett's house. He got out of his car and kicked the frozen weeds, looking for a sign of the fight that Toni claimed had occurred at the end of the road. He was about to leave when he noticed a pair of girl's shoes side by side on the road. After placing them in a plastic evidence bag, he called Shanda's mother. They were the shoes Shanda had gotten for Christmas.

Since he was in the area, Henry called on Ace Newman and Michael Starkey, who lived in the trailer next door to the Tacketts' home. Newman told Henry that he'd gone to school with Laurie but he didn't really know her.

"I didn't know her to have any friends," Newman said. "Never talked to her before that night."

"What night's that?" Henry asked.

Newman told the lawman about Laurie's visit the night before the murder.

"She was real nervous. Her eyes were puffy and red. She said she'd knocked the muffler off her dad's car and was real upset. I got her a Big Red. Her voice was shaking. She acted like she was going to cry."

After talking with Newman, Henry walked next door to the Tackett residence. Larry Leatherbury and Kary Pope had told him about Laurie's altar and her collection of books on the occult, and he was eager to examine them. But the room was nearly empty. Peggy Tackett had already thrown out most of Laurie's things. As Henry talked to Laurie's mother, he could see that she was having a hard time keeping her composure. She told him that she and her husband had had no idea what was happening that night. She said they would have saved Shanda if they had only known that she was in Laurie's trunk. She said she'd yelled at Laurie for being out late but that Laurie was beyond her control. It appeared to Henry that Peggy had already disowned her daughter.

After leaving the Tackett home, Henry checked in with the police station and learned that Shanda's mother had found some important evidence.

Jacque had waited a few weeks after Shanda's funeral before beginning the unsavory task of cleaning the toys, games, and familiar clothes out of her daughter's closet.

She packed up the clothes she intended to give to one of Shanda's cousins, then sat down and cried when she found the page of a coloring book that Shanda had colored a few days before her murder. She was about to put off cleaning out the rest of the closet when she discovered a shoebox hidden under a larger box and tied shut with a string. Written on the top in Shanda's handwriting were the words "For my eyes only. Please do not open."

Jacque opened the box with trepidation. Inside were dozens of letters. Two were from Melinda, the rest from Amanda.

The content of the Amanda letters convinced Jacque that her daughter had been manipulated and seduced by Amanda.

"I can't imagine the amount of mental anguish she was going through without having anyone to talk to about it,"

Jacque said later. "I know she was carrying around a ton of guilt. I do believe there was physical contact between Shanda and Amanda. I will never believe that she was a lesbian. I believe that all this absolutely devastated her emotionally, but it also created a bond between her and Amanda and that's why she could never pull herself away. She was not only ashamed of what she'd done but was afraid that everyone would find out. I was close to my mom, but when I was twelve I couldn't have told her that I'd let another girl touch me. I can't imagine what she was going through."

After receiving the letters from Jacque, Steve Henry went to talk to Amanda again.

"I left Amanda and her father in the room together for a few minutes so she could tell him what was in the letters," Henry said. "She could no longer deny that she was a lesbian. When I came back in, it seemed as if there was an understanding between the two of them. Amanda owned up at that point and admitted that she'd been Melinda's lover. But she wasn't very helpful to us. It was like she was bored during the whole interview. She kept looking at the clock and telling her father that she was going to be late for basketball practice."

Although Amanda had tried to hide her sexuality from her father, Detective Henry could not get over how casual some of the other girls were about their lesbianism. This was not an area of the country where homosexuality was generally accepted. While gay and lesbian organizations in Louisville would occasionally show up on the nightly news for one reason or the other, it was not a community comfortable with open displays of homosexuality. There were several gay nightclubs in downtown Louisville, but they didn't advertise in the daily newspapers and their addresses were known, for the most part, only to their patrons. There were one or two streets in that city's more open-minded neighborhoods where a gay couple might be seen walking hand in hand, but even there it was an uncommon sight.

There were no gay organizations in New Albany, where Melinda, Amanda, Kary, and the rest of their small group lived. Spotting an outwardly gay couple strolling the streets of New Albany was about as likely as seeing them on an "Andy Griffith" rerun.

Although Melinda and Amanda would sometimes show their affection for one another at school, their lesbianism was not widely accepted by the other students, and the two girls would often hear derisive remarks. Both girls were far too self-conscious about their sexuality to flaunt it on the streets of their hometown.

"Some of the girls in their circle had told their families about being gay. Others, like Amanda, hadn't," Henry said. "She probably wouldn't have told her father for some time if we hadn't forced the issue."

In the book *Gay and Lesbian Youth*, Dr. Gilbert Herdt cites studies indicating that probably 10 percent (nearly 3 million) of the nation's 29 million adolescents are gay. But Dr. Margaret Schneider, a Toronto psychologist who contributed to the same book, contends that gay adolescents are less visible than their adult counterparts because they are unlikely to belong to gay organizations and too young to go to gay bars.

While it's difficult to determine whether there is a higher percentage of gay adolescents today than there was in the past, Schneider said there is a growing trend for gay adolescents to feel more liberated.

"Adolescents are coming out now at a time when some pop culture figures (k.d. lang, Boy George, etcetera) are openly identifying themselves as gay or lesbian and when rock songs occasionally refer to same sex eroticism," she wrote. "Sometimes this is the youth's first indication that she is not alone."

If not for Shanda's murder, however, it's unlikely that the community of New Albany would ever have realized the existence of this group of gay girls.

13

On the Saturday that Shanda Sharer's body was found, Guy Townsend, the chief prosecutor for Indiana's Fifth Judicial Circuit, was in the next county trying the cases of two women charged with helping three inmates escape from the Switzerland County jail.

Townsend had planned to wrap the trial up on Friday, but it had dragged on an extra day. At ten that evening, while the jury was still out and the exhausted Townsend was chugging coffee, trying to keep his wits about him, the phone rang. It was his chief deputy, Donald Currie, calling from Madison.

"We've got a murder and it's a bad one," Currie said. "It's a young girl and we're getting ready to arrest two suspects. You won't believe this, Guy. We think two teenage girls did it."

Townsend was still on the phone when a bailiff tapped him on the shoulder and told him that the jury had finally reached a verdict. It was time to go back into court.

"I'd been thinking about nothing but that trial of those two women for weeks and suddenly it didn't seem very important," Townsend said. "All I could think about was getting back to Madison to find out more about the murder."

LITTLE LOST ANGEL

After hearing the jury's verdicts—both women were found guilty—Townsend jumped in his car and headed back to Madison. "All the way back I'm thinking, Do I want to do this? Do I want to deal with something as horrible as this? Do I want to prosecute children for killing a child?"

The forty-nine-year-old Townsend had reason for doubt. He'd been in office for only a year and had never tried a murder case. His experience as a prosecutor was limited to four felony trials: an assault, a burglary, a child molestation, and the trial just completed. Prior to becoming prosecutor he'd tried only one case before a jury: He'd defended a drunk driver and lost.

"Suddenly I was faced with a monstrous responsibility," said Townsend. "I knew there was the possibility that I could be dealing with death-penalty trials. My first reflex was one of flight. Was there any way I could get out of this?"

Although the murder had taken place in Jefferson County, the abduction of Shanda had occurred in Jeffersonville, which was in Clark County and outside Townsend's jurisdiction. That gave Townsend an out. He could have asked the Clark County prosecutor, Steve Stewart, a well-respected attorney with death-penalty trial experience, to take over the murder case.

"Steve Stewart probably would have accepted the case and taken me off the hook," Townsend said. "But the more I thought about it, the more I knew that it was my responsibility. It was the job I had been elected to do."

Such introspection was a trait of Townsend, a tall, trim man with an easy manner and a clever wit. It wasn't that he was plagued by self-doubts. Quite the contrary, he was a man of many accomplishments and a healthy dose of self-pride. It was just that he sometimes wondered how someone who'd received a Ph.D. in British history from Tulane University after writing a doctoral thesis titled "British Reaction to the Belgian and Polish Revolutions of 1830: A Study of Diplomatic, Parliamentary and Press Responses" had ended up a prosecutor in a small Indiana county.

Born in Memphis and raised in Arkansas, Townsend's first love was academics. After getting his degree from

Tulane, he taught history for five years at colleges in South Dakota, Florida, and Georgia, while serving stints in the National Guard, the Air Force Reserve, and the Army Reserve.

Somewhere along the line he lost interest in teaching and drifted through a series of jobs. He was historian for the U.S. Army Corp of Engineers, an insurance investigator, an office manager, a warehouse manager, a bookstore manager, a magazine editor, and a newspaper bureau chief. While publishing the *Mystery FANcier,* a quarterly publication circulated to mystery buffs worldwide, Townsend, who'd recently gone through a divorce, struck up a friendship with one of the magazine's subscribers, Joseph Hensley, who was at that time the Jefferson County circuit judge in Madison.

Hensley helped Townsend get a job editing a weekly newspaper near Madison. While there, Townsend met his second wife, and after a series of other jobs in Arkansas and Pennsylvania the couple moved back to Madison. Townsend wrote a mystery novel that didn't sell well, and when the small publishing company that he'd started in Madison ran into financial trouble, Hensley helped out Townsend by hiring him as a probation officer in his court.

That's when Townsend, then thirty-nine, decided to go to night school to become a lawyer. He got his law degree and went into private practice in 1988.

After only one year as a practicing attorney, handling mostly civil cases, Townsend had the audacity to run against three-term incumbent Fifth Judicial Circuit prosecutor Merritt Alcorn in the Democratic primary in 1989.

Few political insiders thought Townsend had a chance. Not only was Alcorn a deeply entrenched incumbent, but his chief deputy prosecutor, Wilmer Goering, was chairman of the local Democratic party, a position that guaranteed Alcorn certain advantages.

The campaign between Townsend and Alcorn quickly degenerated into a mudslinging contest after Townsend accused his opponents of trying to intimidate him into withdrawing from the race. There was a great deal of silliness over a Townsend campaign billboard that Goering said was in violation of a state law, and Alcorn accused

Townsend of doing a shoddy job as Hensley's probation officer. Townsend responded by assailing Alcorn's record as a prosecutor. When all was said and done, Townsend pulled off a major upset by beating Alcorn in the primary, then winning the general election in November.

Suddenly Townsend, who knew more about British history than he did about Indiana case law, who'd written a crime novel but had virtually no criminal trial experience, was the chief law-enforcement officer of two counties.

It was nearly midnight when Townsend arrived at his office in Madison. He was met by Don Currie, his tall, lanky, blond-haired chief deputy. In short order, Currie brought Townsend up to date on the investigation. An exhausted Townsend told Currie to take care of the night's business—the warrant for the arrest of Melinda Loveless and Laurie Tackett—then he went home to bed, knowing that tomorrow would be a big day.

Jefferson Circuit judge Ted Todd held a hearing on Sunday afternoon to arraign Melinda and Laurie on charges of murder. Townsend arrived early and found a dark-haired woman waiting in the courtroom. It was Melinda's mother, Marjorie Donahue.

"At that point she didn't know who I was, but since I was in a suit and a tie she must have figured that I knew something of the case," Townsend remembers. "She asked me what was going to happen to Melinda. She wanted to know what was the worst that could happen. I told her that if Melinda was found guilty, then the death penalty was a possibility. By the look on her face I could tell that she hadn't yet considered that possibility."

It was moments later that Townsend got his first look at Melinda.

"The first time I saw Melinda Loveless I thought she was one of the most beautiful girls I'd ever seen," Townsend said. "I remember thinking that I might have trouble convincing a jury to convict this girl. She was that attractive."

After hearing evidence that neither girl had enough money to hire her own counsel, Judge Todd appointed public defenders for both of them. Both attorneys, Michael Walro for Melinda and Robert Barlow for Laurie, were capable Madison lawyers, but neither had ever been involved in a case of this magnitude.

To ensure that the girls would not be able to communicate with one another, Todd ordered that Melinda be transferred immediately to the jail in adjoining Clark County.

Wayne Engle, a reporter with the *Madison Courier,* was the first to catch wind of the murder, and by late afternoon Townsend and Sheriff Shipley were fielding calls from newspaper and television reporters in Louisville. On Monday morning, Madison felt the first effects of the coming intrusion. The sight of television crews parked outside the courthouse and reporters hunkering outside his door aggravated the normally mild-mannered Judge Todd.

"I had never been exposed to anything like the media crush of the first few days, and I was uneasy with it," Todd said later. "My first reaction was to barricade myself in my office. After a while I realized that most of the reporters were experienced with this type of thing and that the questions they were asking were procedural things that I could answer."

Within a few days of meeting with Laurie, her attorney, Robert Barlow, told the court that he might seek an insanity plea. He asked that she be evaluated to determine whether she was mentally capable of standing trial.

It took the staff of psychologists at the Indiana State Women's Prison less than a month to complete their report, a copy of which was sent to Townsend.

In the sixteen-page evaluation, staff psychologist Dr. Paul Shriver refers to Laurie by her first name, Mary (Laurie's full name was Mary Laurine Tackett, but she had always gone by "Laurie"):

Mary is a bright, articulate adolescent whose intellect is clear and unimpaired. Her spelling is near perfect and she has very high social intelligence and communication skills. [Shriver later found Laurie to have an IQ of 110.] She is probably without any intellectual, perceptual, or cognitive impairment due to any genuine psychosis. She is very anxious about her circumstances and her future and feeling helpless and doomed. She is seeking "rescue" with a strong sense of desperation and is inventing and enumerating every symptom she can think of or ever heard of.

She spoke most typically in a low, expressionless monotone without making eye contact. She appeared sad and anxious most of the time and animated and enthusiastic only when discussing her beliefs in her psychic powers and various aspects of her new age philosophy, which appears to be an amalgamation of spiritualism and hippyism left over from the 1960s with a heavy emphasis on ESP.

Laurie told the psychologists that she drank alcohol and experimented with marijuana, but her main outlet for releasing stress was to cut herself with a knife. Her case history showed that on one occasion, when she was at the home of Toni Lawrence, Laurie cut her hand so severely she had to be treated at a hospital. Shortly after that she was admitted to a Jefferson mental institution for several weeks of counseling. The counseling ended because her parents couldn't afford the treatment.

The report submitted by Dr. Paul Smith, another psychologist, states that Laurie was also in counseling for about four weeks beginning in June 1991, after she had run away from home. "The psychiatrist she was seeing placed her on Prozac. She took the Prozac until the prescription ran out at the end of the summer. She felt it was beneficial to her. Mary stated that she has been depressed her entire life. She stated that her memory of events before the age of ten or eleven was practically nonexistent."

In Dr. Shriver's report he stated that "Mary claims her mother has been physically abusive to her, including kicking, beating and choking her, for which she was arrested one time when Mary was thirteen. (Laurie said the abuse from her mother stopped after school officials noticed her bruises and contacted the county welfare department.) Abuse took place daily after school between ages nine and thirteen. Mary seemed to feel freer to rebel openly after her mother's arrest and flaunted her violations of their religious prohibitions by her clothing, makeup, social activities and sexual acting out."

Laurie also told Drs. Smith and Shriver about an incident when she tried to interfere with her father who was beating her brother with a baseball bat. "Mary says her father took the bat and struck her several times on the head and shoulders," Shriver wrote.

Even though Laurie told Dr. Smith that she had no memories of early childhood, she told Dr. Shriver that she'd begun having hallucinations at age two.

Shriver wrote:

The reported hallucinations include millions of dots, dark specks, lights, Mickey Mouse, a tall elf, a man who looked like a cricket, someone who looked like cousin It from "The Addams Family," hands coming out of the floor of her room, and UFOs. She also claims to hear voices moaning, whispering and telling her to come with them. She says she hears them off and on daily. She says they sound like little demons. At times they have ordered her to hurt her parents or friends by telling her to "destroy them." She believes she has been psychic all her life. She claims she can see auras around people and has the ability to "astral travel"—to be aware of what is happening in other places. She claims that she can channel with vampires and other dead people. Her mother has dismissed these beliefs as witchcraft or Satanism.

The bulk of Shriver's report is dedicated to Laurie's claims that she was raped at an early age (this despite earlier claims that she had no memories before the age of ten) and the bizarre reaction she had to those alleged rapes:

Mary reports having been raped by a cousin at age four and a neighbor at age six (both of which she has mentioned to other examiners). She added, to this examiner, a report of another rape by a neighbor when she was nine and another at age sixteen. She claims to have lost awareness each time this happened, with only partial recall afterward and having acquired a new personality at the age of the trauma.

Laurie told Dr. Shriver that each of her alternate personalities had names:

They were Sissy at age three, Sara at age four (but the reported rape was at age six), Darlene at age nine, Geno (a male) at age fifteen (about the time she decided she was gay) and Deanna (who was twenty-three) at age sixteen. She has rather vague and incomplete descriptions for each person, but they tend to be one-dimensional. Darlene is mischievous and impulsive. Geno is tough and protective and can be aggressive and delinquent. Deanna likes to play at being a vampire but does not really believe she is. Mary reported that Darlene, Geno and Deanna were all alternately present during the offense (murder of Shanda), but "Laurie" herself was not. Although she admits she likes to tell wild stories, she claims that her multiple identities are real and complains bitterly that no one believes her. She says she deeply fears death and wants to live forever. She is fascinated by vampire myths because of this aspect of the legend.

When the skeptical Shriver asked Laurie to produce one of her alter egos, she did so eagerly. He described it in his report:

She herself chose "Deanna" the twenty-three-year-old. Mary first dropped her eyelids as if meditating, she raised her face with a different expression and degree of mischievousness which fit a prior description of the "alter ego," but expressions and manner already observed in Mary continued to be seen. She reported that she was maintaining the personality's presence with effort and acted exhausted afterward. None of this behavior is typically reported in studies of multiple personalities.

In summation, Shriver wrote that Laurie "is desperate at the moment to avoid conviction and a prison sentence and appears quite willing to fabricate and exaggerate symptoms in order to support a defense of insanity and avoid prosecution as criminally responsible.

Shriver reported that Laurie's claims of having multiple personalities

> appear to be calculated to produce an impression of severe psychosis and achieve a commitment to a mental institution. Mary seems to believe that if her normal personality of Mary was unconscious at the time of the offense she cannot be held responsible for the behavior of her other personalities. For example, if Deanna was present at the time of the offense, the court could not punish her without punishing Sissy and Sara who were not even present at the time. She sincerely believes she cannot be held responsible for the actions of her alter egos over which she claims to have no control.

In conclusion, the report indicated that while Laurie was deeply disturbed, she was not insane and was capable of standing trial.

It didn't take Townsend long to realize that he had a strong case against both Melinda and Laurie. Steve Henry's interviews with Melinda's friends and the letters exchanged between Melinda and Amanda pointed strongly to Melinda's motive of jealousy. And the interviews with Larry Leatherbury and Kary Pope gave every indication that Laurie had a capacity for violence.

Still, Townsend knew that a lot of things could go wrong at a trial.

"This was a case where there seemed to be every indication that Melinda and Laurie would be pointing fingers at each other. A jury has to be convinced beyond a reasonable doubt. Whenever there is more than one defendant in a case there's always the possibility that one of them can persuade the jury that the other one did it. There's always the possibility that one of them could walk. Melinda could bat her eyes at the male jurors for two weeks and convince one that she couldn't possibly be responsible for this, and we'd end up with a hung jury or an acquittal."

It was Townsend's hope from the beginning to get a plea agreement and avoid a trial.

"The family would not have been subjected to eighteen months of this dragging out, this community would not have gotten eighteen months of bad publicity, and the county would have saved hundreds of thousands of dollars," Townsend said. "It was worth something to get it done."

Townsend offered both girls a chance to plead guilty to one count of murder, the sentence for which ranges from thirty to sixty years in prison. But neither of the girls' attorneys seemed eager to deal.

"They knew that my case hinged on the cooperation of either Toni Lawrence or Hope Rippey," Townsend said. "At that point I had neither."

The unwillingness of the two girls to talk to the police led Townsend to believe that they were more involved than Toni had claimed in her original statement.

"I made the same offer to Toni and Hope," Townsend said. "I told them that if Toni's story was true, if they didn't actually participate in any way, then I would treat them as juveniles and not waive them into adult court."

That was until Melinda's attorney, Mike Walro, told Townsend that Melinda claimed it was Hope Rippey who had poured the gasoline on Shanda before she was set on fire.

"Thankfully, Hope didn't accept my original offer," Townsend said. "If we'd have agreed to charge her as a juvenile and then found out later that she had actually poured the gas, it would have been a gross miscarriage of justice. And it would have been my fault."

After a month of getting nowhere with both Toni and Hope, Townsend decided to turn the screws. He would bring charges against both of them and slap them in jail. A little time behind bars might persuade them to change their minds.

Neither Toni nor Hope had gone back to school after Shanda's murder. They were afraid of harassment from the other students, and their parents feared that they might be bothered by the reporters who'd staked out the school to interview classmates.

Toni and Hope didn't see each other at all during that month, although they did talk once on the phone. In hushed tones, Hope admitted to Toni that she had poured the gas the first time. The confession came as a shock to Toni. She'd been truthful to police when she said she'd not watched the first burning. She'd assumed that Melinda poured the gas both times. Hope swore Toni to secrecy, even though it would prove to be fruitless. Melinda had no loyalty to Hope and had already told her lawyers that Hope had poured the gas the first time.

Toni became more frightened with each passing day. She had always been scared of the Leatherburys, and she feared that they or some of Laurie's other friends might seek revenge on her for talking to the police.

"Toni didn't go anyplace" that whole month, her father said later. "She stayed right with her mother. Her mother had to go to the bathroom with her. Her mother had to go get her pajamas out of her room and bring them to her so she could change. She was that scared. She slept on the floor in our room. Sometimes when she woke up with a nightmare she'd get into bed with us. She'd lay in bed and kick and jerk for a long time and I'd reach over and shake her and she'd wake up screaming."

Hope was also losing sleep, although her fears centered around her own guilt.

"She couldn't get to sleep at night and Gloria would have to sleep with her," Carl Rippey recalled. "Sometimes she'd wake up screaming, 'Make it stop. Make it go away.' She asked if she could be hypnotized or could take some kind of drug that would make the memories go away."

* * *

Television crews and newspaper reporters swarmed around the Madison courthouse on the morning of March 15. Word had leaked that Toni and Hope were going to be charged in the murder and that additional charges were being brought against Melinda and Laurie.

A few weeks earlier, a Louisville television station had broadcast pictures of Toni and Hope taken from their yearbook, but other than that they had remained out of the public eye.

The attorneys for Hope and Toni had warned them that Townsend could charge them with murder and have them arrested, but when the word finally came both girls had trouble dealing with it. The last night that Hope and Toni spent at home was a traumatic one for both of them, with many tears shed by parents and daughters. The next morning the Rippeys and Lawrences took their daughters to the offices of their respective attorneys. Townsend had agreed to let each girl give herself up.

As police escorted them into court, Toni and Hope covered their faces with their arms, trying to shield themselves from the cameras. The initial hearings were closed to the media and the public because at that point Toni and Hope were still considered juveniles. But they wouldn't be for long. Judge Ted Todd waived both into adult court, and that same day Toni and Hope were charged with murder, arson, battery with a deadly weapon, aggravated battery, criminal confinement, and intimidation. Both girls were in tears as they were escorted from the courthouse across the alley to the Jefferson County jail.

Later that afternoon, Melinda and Laurie were brought into Judge Todd's court for separate hearings, in which they were charged with seven additional crimes, including child molesting and criminal deviate conduct.

The press had been hearing rumors that Shanda was sexually molested prior to her murder, but this was the first proof. The information filed with the child molestation charge indicated that Shanda had been sodomized by a metal object.

As he'd done with Laurie, who was in the Indiana

Women's Prison in Indianapolis, and Melinda, who was in the Clark County jail, Judge Todd had ordered that Toni and Hope be kept in different jails so they wouldn't be able to communicate. Hope stayed in Madison, while Toni was sent to the Scott County jail about thirty miles east of Madison.

Away from her family for the first time since the murder, Toni was an emotional wreck. She'd been placed in her own cell, a tiny room with no windows and only a small opening at the base of the cell door, where food could be shoved through. She'd lay for hours on the floor, watching the jailers' footsteps through the door opening.

"When we'd visit her, she couldn't stop crying," Glenda Lawrence said. "She said they treated her awful up there. The jailers would say cruel things to her and she wasn't allowed to mingle with the other prisoners."

The harsh realities of her confinement and the serious charges against her weakened Toni's resolve not to testify against the others. On April 22, five weeks after she'd been slapped in jail, Toni accepted the state's offer of a plea agreement.

The attorneys for the other girls would later decry the plea agreement as the "deal of the century." In exchange for Townsend dropping all other charges, Toni pleaded guilty to the charge of criminal confinement—for keeping Shanda captive against her will—and agreed to testify against the other girls.

In Indiana, the charge of criminal confinement carries a standard sentence of ten years in prison, but the judge is allowed to subtract up to four years for mitigating circumstances or add up to ten years for aggravating circumstances. So Toni now faced between six and twenty years in prison.

"We always thought that Toni would be the one to cave in," Townsend said. "It was pretty much in the cards that she would talk. It was the only way she could salvage anything. Thank God we had her. Without an eyewitness we didn't know who did what."

14

Toni the traitor. How dare she turn state's evidence against Melinda, Laurie, and Hope.

Larry and Terry Leatherbury and Kary Pope were fuming. They'd teach that little weasel a lesson she'd never forget. They couldn't get to Toni herself, however, because she was tucked away safely in the Scott County jail. But there were other ways to take revenge.

Hyped up and full of venom, Kary and the Leatherburys went to a discount store in Clarksville and armed themselves with long knives and hatchets. Then they left for Madison in search of Toni's parents, Clifton and Glenda Lawrence, with menace on their minds.

But somewhere along the fifty-mile drive to Madison, Kary had second thoughts and convinced the brothers that they should turn back. And a short time after that, Kary called Detective Steve Henry and confessed it all.

"Kary was hysterical," Henry said. "She told me what had happened. They were going to do some horrible things to Toni's parents. Somewhere along the way they chickened out and the whole thing fell through. Kary told me she felt terrible about it."

Kary was a walking contradiction. A tough guy one minute, a confused waif the next. The seventeen-year-old lesbian had an up-and-down relationship with her own family and was drawn to the solid, easygoing Henry. The detective provided an anchor for her during the months following Shanda's murder. He had treated her with respect from the start, telling her that her sexual persuasion made no difference to him and that he needed her help to understand the dynamics of Melinda and Laurie's friendship. She would call him often and he'd offer words of advice. He told her that if she hadn't been on the outs with Laurie and Melinda at the time she might have been along the night of Shanda's abduction.

"I told her that she had a second chance," Henry said. "I told her she had the opportunity to learn from this and turn her life around and stop hanging with that crowd. I think she honestly tried at times, but then she'd do something stupid, like that stunt about hurting Toni's mom and dad. She'd act tough for the others, but I think she was probably the most fragile of the lot."

Kary had kept up a correspondence with both Melinda and Laurie after their arrest, writing letters and visiting them in jail. She told them she was lost without them and would be waiting for them when they got out—however many years that would be.

In July 1992, six months after Shanda's murder, Melinda wrote Kary this letter:

Dear Kary (poopsie),
  I received all your precious letters and I've got all these mixed up feelings about them. It's like you sometimes take Amanda's place. She hasn't written me a letter since she's been back from Florida [where she'd gone for a vacation] and it's like she don't care. I miss her so much but they say if you love something let it go and if it comes back then it was meant to be. So, that's what I plan on doing. Kary, I will always be here for you and I'll stay in touch. I promise that I'll never leave you or forget about you. You are my best friend, sister, and could be more but we are both so fucked up and

insecure we can't only have one partner. We have each other and always will and I'll see to it. Do you understand what I'm saying, poopsie? We are one of a kind. We are so much alike that we don't even realize it. Well, about that girl Angie. Drop her. You deserve the best like me. Kary, go on with your life and just date around and have fun. Well, I hope this letter finds you all right and remember we have a date when I get out!!! I love you.

All my love,
your doll,
Mel

P.S. You are so cute.

Kary and Laurie began writing to each other almost immediately after the latter's arrest. A poem Laurie sent to Kary on January 21, 1992, just ten days after Shanda's death, had obviously been inspired by the fiery scene on Lemon Road:

THE FOREST

The forest burns.
The children scream.
Shadows await, to take souls unseen.
Stones that mark death await for their calling.
Innocence allies with evil hence falling.
Their father stands watching, laughing in
victory.
His servants surround him, struggling to be
free,
From the chains that bound them to his ebony
throne.
From the ground calleth voices,
Which once had been known,
They scuffle about until one breaks free
Stumbling half flying with its hideous smile,
Then reaching the knees of an innocent baby
crying in fear
As the forest burns on,
Listen and hear.

* * *

On June 1 Laurie tried to explain herself and begged Kary to be understanding:

Dear Kary.

I guess I'll answer the question you asked me on the phone. About Melinda. No, I never loved her, only as a friend. After you came back from Jefferson Hospital and had Tracy [Kary's new lover] I just sort of clung onto the first person that came around, and the emotions and feelings I had for you never left but in my mind I substituted Melinda in your place. Never did I substitute anyone for you in my heart. And you still have a place in my heart that nobody else could ever touch. The way we split up was really fucked up. Can I ask you one question? Why didn't you tell me I scared you? Why didn't we talk it out? I could have stopped channeling for you. It was just a part of my life before I met you. I mean it was natural to me, Larry and Terry. That one night we had a séance, I can't remember half of it because of all the channeling I was doing. That lets me know it's real. Sometimes I even wondered whether it was real or not, but when you go into something and can't remember it afterwards, something there tells you it's not fake. Maybe in a way it was an attention getter—but never fake. Please believe that.

Kary, I'm so scared. I bet you never thought you'd see me falling on my knees because I always tried to be strong. I always cut myself because of my problems. I never felt like I had anybody I could go to, so I held everything in. You know I was never violent. Two nights ago I was sleeping and reliving that night with Shanda and there were people all around us and they weren't alive but they were crying and watching. It was a crazy dream.

But in a letter sent just one week later, Laurie abruptly changed her tune:

Kary,

Listen I can't take your visits anymore. They hurt too

bad. I'm sorry. I deserve this, everything I'm getting, I deserve. I want to die, so the death sentence doesn't really matter. I can't fight anymore. I'm tired. I'm pulling you from my visiting list. Everything has changed because of me. Please forgive what I have done.

> I love you,
> Laurie

When Kary visited the prison unannounced a short time later, she learned the reason for Laurie's standoffishness. Laurie had found a female lover, who was jealous of Kary's attentions. Laurie wrote Kary afterward:

Kary,

This is hard for me because I still love you but not in a way that I want to be with you. At one time I loved you so much and if you would've let me I would have shown you. For the last two weeks I've been doing a lot of soul searching and I realize that I do love Kim. She has stuck beside me from the beginning and she has never judged me. The first night I was here I was crying and upset. I didn't know her and she didn't know me but she told me that if I needed someone to talk to that she was there for me. She lived up to her word. Sure, she's overprotective, but now I understand why. Kary, I love her and if anything ever happens to us, I could never have anyone else. What we have is real. And I hope you can understand. She knows things about me that nobody else knows. Things that if given time, you would have known. But we never had that time. Now my love has been passed on to someone else and it has had a chance to grow. Please understand. I'm sorry.

> Love,
> Laurie

To make sure that Kary got the message, Laurie's lover, Kim, sent her the following letter on July 31:

Kary,

We got your letter yesterday and Mary asked me to respond. Mary—known to you as Laurie—explained to you that she wished no communication with you.

I've read your statement against her and I really don't see how you even have the nerve to write. To me, you're a very mixed up kid that Mary doesn't need or want in her life. At any rate, all of your letters will be returned, and all of your visits will be refused.

Mary is and will be doing fine, because she has realness in her life now—me—therefore you should spend your time on something that won't be a waste of your time. Understand, or would you like me to draw you a picture? You've got my address if you're not bright enough to understand this letter. I'm always willing to help a kid out!

Bye, Kim.

Mary's wife

But Kary was not ready to give up. After she showed up at the prison unannounced again, Kim got mad and broke up with Laurie. A few days later, Laurie fired off the following letter:

Kary,

You have fucked up my life again. I asked you to stay away from me. Why couldn't you listen? No, you had to keep coming when you knew I had somebody who I loved dearly. You have made me lose the only person I had and the only person who I knew loved me and was real. I was beginning to feel like everything was going to be OK. I was beginning to feel like I had a reason to live, but now all of that is gone. You lied to the police about me and who knows what else you said about me that I don't know about. Just please stay out of my life. There is no way you can make up for what you've done. No way. You will be pulled off my visiting list tomorrow. I don't want anything else to do with you. What we had—our relationship, our friendship—is all in the past. Face reality and just stay away. Find someone who will love you, I don't. Yes, I did but I will never love anyone ever again. Kim is gone and so is all the love I ever had.

But within a week or so Laurie was apologetic again, as shown in this letter dated August 13:

Kary,

I need you. I still do. If you really want to testify against me, then do it. All I ask is still be my friend. Laurie has been dead for a long time. They took her away when I got arrested. Kim was right about one thing—she told me that you would testify against me in the end. That was one of the main reasons she didn't want me to see you. I didn't believe her. I believed in our friendship. I love you guys. I love Melinda. I always will no matter what happens. The times we had, the things we shared, I'll never forget. You may not need me but I know I will always need you. I swear I was never a devil worshiper, I never had any evil intentions and I think deep down in your heart you know that. Kary, there's one saying I've always went by: where there is genuine love there is understanding. Please don't leave me. You can help Melinda—just don't go away.

By the end of the summer, Kary was confused and despondent. She wrote Laurie the following letter:

Laurie (Mary),

You have got to understand something. I do not want to testify against you. I want out. You and Melinda have really messed me up. My life will never be the same. I don't trust anybody. Not even Larry and Terry. Laurie, I'm very upset with you because you took my feelings and emotions and messed them up. I don't want to live. I just want to die. I really did love you but you pushed me away. Every time I care about someone they leave or die. I can't handle my life anymore. I'm so alone. No one cares anymore. Look what I was going to

do just to be with you. I'm not going to trial. They are
going to have to arrest me. You left me. Why? Over
some stupid bitch who never has or never will care for
you as much as I did or still do. I care for Melinda and
you. Nothing will ever change how I feel about both of
you all. Where is Kim? This letter better not be a joke
to mess with my feelings. I hope it's not because you
will put me in an early grave. This is your last chance.
Push me away again and it's over.

Throughout the summer Laurie had also been corre-
sponding with Mysi Thornton, a friend from Madison. Mysi
ran with the crowd Laurie had hung with before she met
Kary and Melinda. Mysi was also friends with Hope and the
Leatherburys. Laurie had just begun to introduce Mysi to
the mystical world of the occult when she was arrested. She
considered herself the tutor and Mysi her pupil. Her letters
to Mysi indicate just how seriously Laurie had submerged
herself into her unusual beliefs. In a letter sent on August
18, Laurie schooled Mysi in the finer points of communica-
ting with a spirit that Mysi claimed had made contact with
her.

Be careful. I'll tell you why. If you are her from a past
life, she wouldn't be able to communicate with you.
You would be her and vice versa. By the way you
described her she is a spirit. She has been dead a long
time and her spirit is lost. Your spirit is yours and it's
still with you. You and her are two different souls—two
different spirits. Can you understand all what I'm
trying to explain to you? Are you into witchcraft and
becoming a young vampire? Me and Hope talked to a
spirit a while back in a field close to my house and she
warned us about a cliff. Ask Hope. I know she remembers. It's the same spirit that is trying to contact you, I
can feel it. Her husband might come after you—but
not likely—he isn't even alive right now.

At the end of the letter Laurie vented her contempt of
Toni:

176

Toni already made a statement against Hope that will hurt her. Toni is a backstabbing bitch, who can only be in the police's face telling them shit. It just makes me mad to even think about it.

In a letter sent to Mysi three weeks later, Laurie revealed her resentment of Melinda and promised her pupil that good times lay ahead.

Melinda is blaming me and Hope for that little girl's death. Kary said that Melinda hates me but I could care less. Melinda is a bitch. She's proud to know that Shanda is dead and she caused it. She doesn't have one ounce of remorse. And if she regrets doing it at all, she probably only wishes that she'd have done it differently. I don't know why we left Shanda where we did. We were all scared and I guess we were just desperate to have her out of the car. I miss you and the times we had. Just take care of yourself and I promise to find you whenever me and Hope get released and we'll come see you and we'll all party. You'll swear all hell broke loose when we do!!! We'll have fun times again I promise. And I never break a promise. I mean there's nothing we can do to change the past but we create our future. Just remember that, OK.

At the close of the letter, Laurie responded to Mysi's claims that she'd met a vampire:

If you really do know a true-to-god vampire, please tell him that I love vamps and would give my life to be one. Does he have fangs and is he immortal? If so, I'm more serious in what I said than in anything. Be careful in drinking blood. Don't take it from just anyone!!! And I'm talking about AIDS, so please be careful!!!

In a letter sent on September 12, Laurie was once again preoccupied with thoughts of Melinda:

I think I'm going to take psychology here. I think I would be a good one. I hate it here. I hate the people (especially the fucking niggers). They better not give me a lot of time. I can't handle it. All I ever want to do is cry or kill myself or sleep. I don't have a fucking criminal record. Why did this have to happen to me? I hate Melinda so damn much. Killing someone and laughing about it afterward. I mean, what kind of freak is she? And what was the purpose? Shanda was only twelve. God, when I was twelve all I knew was how much I wanted to have a friend. I have to live with this for the rest of my life. I wake up sometimes screaming —having nightmares about that night. Isn't that punishment enough???

If I see Melinda while we're at court this month I'll scream at her and tell her how much of a bitch she is. She doesn't deserve anything but a hot curling iron shoved up her ass. Excuse my language, but I hate her.

One month later, Melinda was moved from the Clark County jail to the Indiana Women's Prison. Now that they were fellow inmates, Laurie's opinion of Melinda changed dramatically, as she wrote in this October 15 letter to Mysi:

Melinda is here now and we are friends again. She saw me out her window and flipped her light on and off about six or seven times and waved and I waved back. She's so cute. I couldn't be mad at her anymore. But the real reason I'm not mad anymore is because I'm as guilty as she is. We were in it together and I can't be mad. I mean, she didn't force me to be there, she just sort of trapped me. At any rate, I won't hate her. I could've stopped it from happening but I didn't. We're all at fault and we're all as guilty. There's not one of us who is more guilty. We're all the same. Do you understand what I'm trying to say?

This letter was sent shortly after Laurie made an appearance at the Madison courthouse, dressed demurely in a flower-print dress. "About my dress last Tuesday," Laurie wrote, "that was merely something of innocence. A dress for the judge. As for my religion. That religion fucked my mind up when I was little and I'll never get back into their fucking fellowship and fire and brimstone bullshit."

After a curious signoff—"Happy exploiting, Love Laurie"—Laurie added an even weirder postscript: "Monkey see, Monkey do, Monkey will destroy you. Bad Monkey, Bad Monkey, Bad Monkey, Bad Monkey. Ahhgh!!!!"

Detective Steve Henry had felt that, of the four girls, Laurie would adapt best to prison life. She was tough enough to handle herself in a fight, and since her home life had been so bleak beforehand, she wouldn't miss her family as much as the other girls. Henry's opinion may prove correct in the long run, but Laurie's first six months in prison were filled with turmoil. In February she cut her wrist and was placed in isolation. In July she lost two weeks of privileges because of disorderly conduct. After she broke up with Kim, her former lover threatened her. In preparation for a conflict, Laurie managed to steal a razor blade and conceal it in her cell. When jailers found it she was given a full year of isolation for possession of a deadly weapon. While there she got into even more trouble when she ripped a sink out of a wall.

In Indiana prisoners have one day taken off the end of their sentence for each day served of good time. After six months, Laurie had accumulated no good time.

15

Jefferson circuit judge Ted Todd, who sat on the bench for the sentencing hearings of Melinda, Laurie, and Toni, would say later that he felt like he was "caught in the eye of a hurricane."

He had presided over two prior murder trials, but neither had been high-profile cases. He'd never been exposed to a media crunch like that surrounding Shanda's murder, with reporters camped outside his office on a daily basis and phone calls coming in from the national press.

Then there were the stacks of paperwork filed by the prosecutor and the lawyers for the girls—dozens of motions, responses, depositions, and reports that threatened constantly to overwhelm his court staff, which already had its hands full with its usual docket of divorces, child-custody cases, and criminal complaints.

"I hope I never have to, or the community never has to, go through anything like that again," Todd said later. "It was taxing to us all."

The balding, fifty-three-year-old Todd, a graduate of Duke University, was a medium-sized man with a slight paunch that he constantly tried to work off by running a few miles each day. He was well educated and was a soft-spoken but engaging conversationalist outside the courtroom. On the bench, however, he was all business, dealing with minor domestic disputes with the same sincere, serious manner as criminal cases.

With a wife and three children of his own, Todd was deeply disturbed by the grisly nature of Shanda's murder, but he was determined not to let his personal feelings sway his decisions. In fact, he admitted afterward that he bent over backward to accommodate the various requests by defense counsel to have the court pay for additional legal help, private investigators, and psychologists.

"I didn't want there to be any chance of a reversal of a decision because of something I didn't give the defense," Todd said.

None of this set well with prosecutor Guy Townsend, who felt that Todd was too cozy with the defense counsels. Todd and Townsend had never been close. Their differences dated back to Townsend's stormy campaign against former prosecutor Merritt Alcorn. Todd knew he'd have to work with whoever won the race, so he stayed out of the political fray and didn't openly support either Townsend or Alcorn. But despite his public neutrality, Todd sensed that Townsend held a grudge against him.

"For some reason Guy has always thought me a part of the Alcorn camp even though I purposely kept a low profile during the campaign," Todd said.

Townsend's disenchantment with Todd came to a head that summer when the judge agreed to let Melinda's attorney, Mike Walro, hire a second counsel with public defender money.

Walro, a solidly built man with a bushy mustache, had the sure, easy manner of an old-time country lawyer, but he knew he was in over his head with this case. Although an able criminal attorney, he had limited experience in murder trials. He remedied that by bringing in Russell Johnson, a young but experienced defense attorney from Franklin, Indiana, a small town just south of Indianapolis.

Johnson worked out of a humble office, but he had Big City Lawyer written all over him. Possessing Robert Redford-like, all-American good looks, he was an impeccable dresser and was always neatly coifed. He spoke in smooth, knowing tones and carried himself with an air of complete self-assurance. Though only thirty-seven, he had a reputation as one of the best murder defense lawyers in the state. His greatest triumph had come the previous summer in the Jack Dobkins death-penalty case. Dobkins had been charged with the torture slaying of a Shelbyville, Indiana, woman who had been found with her nipples bitten off. The state's case hinged on a forensic report that said the teeth prints on the woman's breasts were made by Dobkins. But the case was dismissed before it went to trial when Johnson produced a forensic expert who proved that the teeth marks had not been made by Dobkins.

Despite Townsend's objections, Todd granted Walro's request that Johnson come on as co-counsel at a rate of $60 an hour for 300 hours. But a short time later, in a private meeting attended by Townsend, Walro told Todd that Johnson had turned down the appointment because of the $18,000 pay limit.

Several weeks after that conversation, however, Johnson made his first court appearance as Melinda's counsel. After the hearing, Townsend pulled Walro aside.

"So Russ has decided that he'll work for $18,000 after all," Townsend said.

"Well, let's just say he's on the job," Walro answered.

Townsend later learned that Johnson had changed his mind after Melinda's family had agreed to sell their home to pay excess expenses if Johnson's bill exceeded $18,000.

Angered that Todd had approved the arrangement without first consulting him, Townsend filed a motion asking that Todd be removed as the judge in Melinda's trial. Townsend contended that Judge Todd had violated the judicial code of conduct by having clandestine meetings with Walro and Johnson, in which the defense's strategy was discussed behind Townsend's back.

When Judge Todd held a hearing on the motion on June 5, Johnson testified that he'd sent Todd a letter outlining his arrangement with the Loveless family but had had no other conversations with the judge about it. Walro also denied discussing the matter with Todd.

Townsend wasn't satisfied. "I have a problem with it when a public defender is appointed because someone is declared indigent and then accepts payments from the defendant," he said indignantly.

Obviously upset at being charged with improprieties, Todd remained quiet until Townsend referred to a 1986 U.S. appellate court decision pertaining to out-of-court conversations between judges and counsels.

"You keep citing that case," Todd said. "Can you tell me the facts of that case? Was it a criminal case or a civil case?"

To his embarrassment, Townsend did not know. He told the judge that although he was not familiar with the details of the case, they weren't important to appreciate the court's ruling against out-of-court conversations.

"You've made some very strong accusations against this court," Todd responded harshly, "and I want you to substantiate them. You've cited a case and you don't know what it says. You haven't even read the case."

Townsend bristled at Todd's remarks, then went on the offensive. "Melinda Loveless has the right to a fair trial," he said. "But she does not have a right to a trial in which the deck is stacked against the state. The state also has the right to have this case heard by a judge who will not carry on clandestine conversations with defense counsel, who will not join with the defense in keeping secrets from the state of Indiana, who will not secretly agree to permit defense counsel to receive secret payments for his representation."

Judge Todd was not impressed with Townsend's oratory. "The only communication I've had with Mr. Walro has been in regard to administrative matters. Your motion is without merit, completely unsubstantiated, and has no basis in fact."

Townsend's gambit had failed. He was stuck with Judge Todd on the bench and Russ Johnson in Melinda's corner.

Johnson would say later that he and Townsend "mixed like oil and water. I got the impression he thought I was a bigshot hired to come in to make him look bad."

Having lost that battle, Townsend turned his attention again to the plea agreements. He thought that Laurie, Melinda, and Hope would all be eager to plead to one count of murder—which was still his offer—once Toni Lawrence agreed to testify. But that was not the case.

"The defense counsels kept saying that they wouldn't plead unless I could guarantee them a deal of only forty years for the murder," Townsend said, noting that this meant they could be out in twenty years on good behavior. "I wasn't about to do that. I wanted them to accept a plea that would allow the judge to set the sentence."

Frustrated by the stalemate, Townsend decided to play his trump card: He would file for the death penalty.

"From the very beginning I didn't think there was much possibility that I could get the death penalty," Townsend said. "I was aware of Judge Todd's stance against it."

Townsend also knew that no one under eighteen had received the death penalty in Indiana since the Paula Cooper murder case in 1985. Cooper, a fifteen-year-old from Gary, Indiana, was sentenced to the death penalty after she was found guilty of stabbing Ruth Pelke, a seventy-eight-year-old Bible teacher, thirty-seven times with a butcher knife. But after a worldwide campaign for clemency—including an appeal from Pope John Paul II and a petition signed by a million people delivered to the United Nations—the case was appealed and it was declared unconstitutional to impose the death penalty on someone under the age of sixteen. In 1989 Cooper's sentence was reduced to sixty years in prison. In the interim, the Indiana legislature raised its medieval ten-year-old standard and made sixteen the minimum age for the death penalty.

Although Melinda, sixteen, and Laurie, seventeen, were eligible, therefore, the odds were against their receiving the death penalty. Of the 133 people executed by the state in its history, only three had been under the age of eighteen—each of those had been seventeen at the age of the crime.

In addition, Townsend himself was philosophically opposed to the death penalty.

"I had a personal aversion to the idea of the state killing people but also knew that duty sometimes requires you to do things that you find personally distasteful," Townsend said. "I think the defense counsels were counting on me not having the guts to use it. They had no motivation to plead because they didn't think I was going to use the big stick. I told them that if they wanted to force us to go to trial, then we're going to trial with the stakes as high as I could raise them."

During the second week of June, therefore, Townsend filed for the maximum sentence against Melinda Loveless and Laurie Tackett. He could not do the same for Hope Rippey, because she was under sixteen at the time of the murder.

The filing for the death penalty meant that Mike Walro and Robert Barlow could no longer serve as lead counsels for Melinda and Laurie because neither was death-penalty qualified. State law says the lead counsel in a death-penalty case must have at least five years of criminal trial experience, have tried at least five felony cases, and have been lead counsel or co-counsel on a previous death-penalty case.

Although neither of the original public defenders was death-penalty qualified, Todd elected to keep them both on the case to assure continuity in the girls' defense. Russ Johnson became lead counsel in Melinda's defense. The lead counsel for Laurie would be Wil Goering, the former chief deputy prosecutor who had gained Townsend's enmity during his bitter political campaign against Merritt Alcorn.

Goering, forty, resented the way that Townsend had used the death-penalty filing. "Clearly, the reason he filed for the death penalty was to leverage a guilty plea," he said. "He was saying plead guilty or we're going to kill you."

When Toni Lawrence agreed to testify against the other girls, she'd hoped that the bargain would include her release on bail. It didn't. Spring gave way to summer and she was still locked in her tiny cell, waiting for the legal maneuvering to end, waiting for her day in court. She became increasingly depressed, and frequent visits from her parents did little to raise her spirits. She continued to have nightmares about Shanda's death and would wake up screaming. Her cell was equipped with a video camera, and the constant supervision made her even more paranoid. By August, the pressure of being the state's key witness had worn her down. She dreaded the thought of having to face Melinda and Laurie in court.

On August 17, a Monday afternoon, Toni asked to use the phone. The jailers said later that they didn't know whom she called, but on her way back to her cell she seemed happy and talkative.

Ten minutes later, the jailer monitoring the video camera noticed Toni lying on the floor of her cell. Nothing unusual, as she did that all the time. But something about it didn't seem right. He knocked on her cell door and called to her. No response. Opening the door, he saw there were a couple of pills—prescribed antidepressants that she was supposed to take daily—lying beside her. Unable to shake Toni awake, the jailer called for an ambulance and had her rushed to the Scott County hospital.

Later, Scott County sheriff John Lizenby found an empty soft drink can in the cell. Five more pills were stuck to its bottom.

"She hadn't been taking her medicine, she'd been storing it," Lizenby told reporters. "The pills were supposed to have been crushed, but she'd talked the jailer out of doing so. She must have hoarded a bunch of them."

Toni's condition was so serious that she was flown by helicopter to Kosair's Children Hospital in Louisville, where she lay in a coma for five days.

One month after filing the death-penalty charges, Townsend's case was suddenly thrown into jeopardy.

"There was a point where we didn't know whether she would pull through," Townsend said. "It's always distressing when a child tries to take her own life. Our first concern, of course, was for her safety. But yes, I will admit I worried how it would affect the case. We had an investment in her. It did put us in a bad position. Getting the results would have been more difficult without her."

Toni came out of her coma gradually. Weeks of therapy at LifeSpring Mental Health Services followed. On September 21 she was admitted to Larue Carter Memorial Hospital in Indianapolis for further therapy.

On the date of Toni's discharge, October 8, therapist Esther Schubert wrote a report in which she made the following observations:

> Toni's parents admit that she is a strong-willed child who often got her way by pouting. They usually gave in; however, as she became older, they tended to treat her with grounding when she was disobedient. Nevertheless, there was a significant number of years early in her life when she ran the show and she continues to do that in her relationship with her parents. She appears to have grown up assuming she could also have whatever she wanted.
>
> Toni has a long history of rebellion against her parents. Apparently as early as age ten or eleven she began to sneak out of the house at night and was involved in parties and apparently some drugs and alcohol. She had been smoking cigarettes since she was thirteen, and although her parents do not approve of this they have never had the courage to tell her not to smoke. She did not make good choices in friends. She seems to have some difficulties with her conscience development and her ability to make decisions. In many cases her tendency has been to decide whether to do something on the basis of whether she would be caught, rather than on the rightness or wrongness of the action.

Toni told her therapist that she'd taken the overdose because her parents were going out of town for a while and she was feeling abandoned.

"She states categorically that she did not mean to kill herself," Schubert wrote in her report.

> My impression is that Toni has learned over the years that there are no consequences to her behavior. She was unable to discuss the wrongful behavior in which she participated [Shanda's death] and assumes that because she was not physically striking some of the blows

187

that she therefore was not responsible for anything that happened. She claims that she is not responsible because she was so afraid of these girls, but she had several opportunities before Shanda was killed to call home or leave or call someone for help. The family commented that Toni has vacillated since she has been in jail between feeling remorse that she is in this mess and feeling that she did nothing wrong. There does not seem to be a genuine concern or empathy for the child who was murdered.

The therapist characterized Toni as "a follower" whose intelligence appeared to be "low average." She wrote that Toni considered herself ugly "and always has."

Part of Toni's therapy called for her to give written answers to various questions. To the question "What do you believe in?" Toni wrote: "The things I believe in are God; love at first sight; premarital sex; having babies out of wedlock; and peace."

To the question "What would you change about yourself?" she wrote: "I'd like to change the way I judge and trust because I don't take time to think and I make quick decisions and trust too easy. I'd also like to change my looks. I don't like my glasses and I need a little more meat on my bones. I'd like to be prettier and a couple of inches taller. I'd like to have a healthy life because I don't like being suicidal and depressed and sick all the time."

Asked to say something about her feelings, Toni wrote:

I'm very confused, angry, sad and I feel suicidal. I'm confused because of all the shit that's going on in my life. I'm angry because you're making me do these stupid questions again. I'm sad because I want to go home and be with my family. And I'm suicidal because I think it's the only way to get out of this mess completely. I'm worried because I'm afraid I'm going to succeed in killing myself one of these days and because my ninety-seven-year-old great-granny doesn't know any of what's going on in my life and I'm afraid she'll have a heart attack when she finds out.

In another paper, Toni wrote what she hoped to be doing in ten years:

> I want to have one kid and adopt two. I want to have a well-paying job and I want my husband to have a well-paying job. I want to live in a big house in the country with ten mustangs. I also want a vacation home in the Bahamas. I want to go to France for two years. I studied it [French] for two years. I hope to have gotten all of this mess behind me and be finished with it all. And I want to stay close to all my family.

In closing, Schubert wrote that the staff at Larue Carter "found Toni to be a morally salvageable adolescent provided she be placed in a program that includes education, psychotherapy, and plans for eventual re-entry into the home community after her legal obligations have been satisfied."

With Toni's recovery assured, Townsend put the pressure on the attorneys for Melinda and Laurie by setting a deadline for them to accept his final offer of a plea agreement. Townsend said he would not seek the death penalty and would drop all other charges against the girls if they would plead guilty to murder, arson, and criminal confinement. Townsend also offered to recommend that the sentences on those charges run concurrently, which meant that the sentences the girls received for each individual charge would all run at the same time; the alternative would have been for the sentences to run consecutively, or one after the other. Thus each girl would now be facing a sentence of between thirty and sixty years, which is the sentencing range for murder, the most serious charge. In exchange for the deal, both girls would have to agree to give statements and to testify against the others at their sentencing hearings.

On September 21, the day before the expiration of the deadline, Melinda and Laurie accepted the deal.

"We had to," Russ Johnson said. "We knew we had problems if we went to trial. The extreme priority was to get the death penalty dismissed."

Goering said, "Laurie was not eager to deal and her father

did not want her to deal, but after I got a look at the evidence it was the only way we could go."

Not missing a chance to criticize Townsend, however, Goering continued: "We definitely got a better deal than we would have gotten from an experienced prosecutor, but the case was almost prosecutor proof. Steve Henry had done a thorough job. The evidence was there to convict. Even Townsend would have had a difficult time botching it."

16

On the same day that Laurie Tackett accepted her plea agreement, she was steered into the jury room of the Jefferson County courthouse by Steve Henry and Sheriff Shipley. As part of her plea bargain, Laurie had agreed to tell her side of the story.

Henry had not talked to Laurie since the night of her arrest, and he was full of questions. The picture of Laurie painted by Kary Pope and Larry Leatherbury was almost too bizarre to believe. He wanted to get Laurie's version of her occult practices, but first he had to deal with the matter at hand: What had been her role in Shanda's murder?

With her attorney, Wil Goering, by her side, Laurie launched into the series of events that led to her first meeting with Melinda. As Laurie spoke of Melinda, Henry could detect the resentment in her voice. Whatever their relationship had been at the time of Shanda's murder, Laurie made no secret of the fact that she now blamed Melinda for everything that had happened. It was Melinda's fault, she believed, that she, Hope, and Toni were behind bars.

Laurie told Henry and Shipley that she, Hope, and Toni

had had no idea that Melinda planned to kill Shanda. She said they'd gone along with the ruse to lure Shanda out of the house thinking only that Melinda wanted to beat her up.

Laurie said that Melinda "just went off on" Shanda when they got her out of the car on the dirt road near her home. "Melinda kept beating her up and Shanda wasn't trying to fight back," she said.

Laurie said that after Melinda had beat Shanda senseless, all four girls put Shanda into the trunk, then drove to her house. Laurie claimed that she did Shanda no harm when she went outside alone to quiet her barking dog.

"I opened the trunk and looked in on her," Laurie said. "I said, 'Shanda,' and she looked up at me and her eyes rolled back in her head. It just scared me to death. She was all bloody. There was blood everywhere. I grabbed the red blanket out of the backseat and put it over her because she was shivering."

Laurie claimed it was Melinda who suggested they drive off with Shanda in the trunk and Melinda who thought up several schemes to finish Shanda off and dispose of her body.

"Do you know how Shanda sustained the injuries to her body?" Henry asked.

"No," Laurie said. "But it was Melinda who brought up the idea to burn her. She said her friend Crystal Wathen said that if she was going to kill Shanda the best way to get rid of her body was to burn it. Melinda was the burner. We laid her on the ground. Melinda got the gas and poured it on Shanda."

Henry looked at Shipley. They were both fairly certain by now that Hope had been the first to pour the gas. This is what Melinda had told her attorney, and Toni had confessed that Hope had admitted the same to her. But the lawmen said nothing and let Laurie continue.

"Shanda started crying," Laurie said. "I was bending down over her. I was going to lift up the blanket. I guess I was going to try to talk to her again and then the fire went up in my face and it singed my bangs."

Laurie said they got back in the car but hadn't driven far when Melinda told them to turn around.

"Melinda said she needed to make sure she was on fire all the way," Laurie said. "Melinda got out and poured the rest of the gas on her. Melinda kept saying, 'I'm so happy she's dead. I'm so happy she's out of mine and Amanda's life,' and she was laughing and carrying on. Then we went back to Melinda's house to go to sleep. But I couldn't sleep because I just kept hearing Shanda screaming. Melinda told me to shut up and that's the last thing we said to each other before we were arrested."

Laurie sat back in her chair, assuming she was finished, but Henry and Shipley still had questions.

"You said that Melinda poured the gas but you never said who lit the fire," Sheriff Shipley asked.

"I don't know who lit it," the girl insisted. "The fire just went up in my face all of a sudden. It wasn't me. Hope and Melinda were standing around her and I personally feel that Melinda did it."

"At any time during this did you try to get Melinda to stop?" asked Shipley.

"No," Laurie said meekly. "I was scared."

"Scared of who?"

"Nobody would understand unless they were in a situation like this," Laurie explained. "It didn't have to be us. It could have been the nicest people on the earth with one bad person. I went out under the impression that we were going to scare her and that Melinda was going to beat her up. After Shanda went unconscious and all the blood and everything, we were scared to take her anywhere. If I were to take her to a hospital what would they say to me? They'd ask how she got like this."

"I'm sure they would have," Shipley said sarcastically. "Do you know how Shanda sustained her anal injuries?"

Laurie put on her most sincere face. "I don't know. I don't remember that happening. I feel like she might have gotten them before all of this. I feel that she might have had sex with somebody else that did that. That's the only thing I can think of that would have done that because we sure didn't do anything. We didn't molest her. We didn't do anything to her in any way . . . like molested her or anything. I mean, it wasn't like that."

Henry took over the questioning and asked, "How did she get the injuries in the back of her head?"

"My lawyers have asked me the same question," Laurie said matter-of-factly, as if she were commenting on some mundane detail. "I think she did a lot of banging around in the back of the trunk. She did a lot of banging around. It sounded like she was kicking the back of my car out. I kept wondering to myself how she had that much strength. She was kicking around a lot and there was a big old tire back there too I think. She could have hit her head on the trunk part. She could have done anything by kicking like that."

Henry was tired of fooling around. "Once you left your house, did you at any time stop, open the trunk, and hit her with a tire tool or anything?" he asked bluntly.

"No."

"Did anyone?"

"Not to my knowledge," Laurie said. Then, realizing that this was another opportunity to shift the blame to Melinda, she continued: "Melinda went back to the trunk when I was sitting in the car. She stopped the car and went back to the trunk several times."

Henry pressed Laurie for more details about the long drive with Shanda in the trunk.

"I can only remember parts of what was happening," Laurie said coolly. "It's totally blacked out from the time we were out on the country road to the time we got to my house."

"It seems that there's a lot of things you can't remember," said Henry, showing his frustration.

"Yeah," Laurie said, becoming defensive. "That's because we were out there a long time. It seemed like an eternity. It seemed like we were out there forever."

"Toni indicated in her statement that when you and Melinda came back from your drive that you both had blood on you."

"I don't remember that," Laurie said.

Changing the subject, Henry asked Laurie about her fascination with witchcraft and about Larry Leatherbury's statement that she wanted to watch somebody being burned alive.

Laurie denied ever saying that and claimed that her interest in the occult was minor, although she had tried to channel with spirits.

"Tell me about that," Henry said.

"That was just something I did to make people like me," Laurie said. "I just wanted to be liked by people."

With the interview over, Henry and Shipley drove Laurie back to the Indiana State Women's Prison in Indianapolis. During the drive, Henry asked Laurie about something that had been bothering him for some time. The stories he'd heard about Laurie's battles with her mother over going to church had piqued his curiosity. A teenage girl who refused to identify herself had called him at the police station two or three years earlier. She'd asked if it was a form of child abuse for her parents to make her go to church when she didn't want to go. She had told Henry that her parents strictly disciplined her when she refused to attend services. Henry had told her that her best bet was to call the welfare department in her county, and he hadn't thought any more about it until now. Now he just had to know: Was Laurie the caller?

"Yes," Laurie said. "It was me."

"Well I'll be doggone," Henry said.

The following week, Henry and Shipley drove back to the women's prison to interview Melinda Loveless, hoping they'd learn more from her than they had from Laurie.

"We felt that Laurie was lying about a lot of things," Henry said later. "She seemed to have been living in a fantasy land."

Melinda had been moved to the state prison the previous week, after an eventful incarceration in the Clark County jail. Melinda had created problems for her jailers from the start. She thought of herself as a celebrity and had tried to obtain special privileges. She'd written the head jailers dozens of requests, ranging from demands for more visitation time with her family and friends to a request that she be able to wear a more comfortable jail uniform. She got into several altercations with other female inmates over what programs to watch on television and seemed to constantly be stirring up trouble with her haughty ways.

When some of the other inmates began teasing her about newspaper and television reports that Shanda had been killed out of jealousy over another girl, Melinda insisted that she was not a lesbian. She told them that it had been a matter of jealousy but that it was over a boy named Justin.

One of Melinda's former cellmates, Arlinda Randle, said that Melinda took her celebrity status to extremes, once even giving out autographs.

Randle said that Melinda was always talking about how little time she would have to do for the murder. She felt as if she would be released in a couple of years. Randle said that Melinda had a copy of her Hazelwood yearbook, which she would show off to other prisoners. Over Shanda's picture she'd written "So young. So pretty. Had to die early." Melinda had also hung a picture of herself on the wall and inscribed on it "Most Wanted."

Randle said that Melinda's cruel sense of humor was also used against other inmates.

"One time a girl asked her for a cigarette," Randle said. "While the girl wasn't looking, Melinda stuck the cigarette up her nose and rolled it around and then gave it to her. And on another occasion another girl wanted a cigarette and Melinda stuck it up in her vagina and gave it to the girl afterward. She was always flirting with the guards. A couple of times she flashed them. Raised her skirt up. I told her not to do that. I told her that if she was my daughter that would upset me."

On Sunday night, September 27, Melinda was caught having sex with a male jailer in a command-post room. When another jailer burst in on them, Melinda hiked up her pants and ran back to her cell. The next day Melinda bragged to the other inmates that she'd screwed a jailer that they all thought was cute. The jailer resigned the next day rather than face a dismissal hearing.

Melinda's sexual exploits had already become an item of interest around the Jefferson County courthouse. When she came to court for one of her early hearings and was changing her clothes, one of the jail matrons noticed that she had hickeys all over her body.

Henry would later learn that Melinda had quickly found a lesbian lover at the Indiana State Women's Prison, but on the day he interviewed her she hadn't yet settled into her new surroundings and was noticeably nervous.

With her attorney, Russ Johnson, by her side in the small interview room, Melinda gave a detailed account of her lesbian relationship with Amanda and how it had been wrecked by Shanda's "interference." She admitted that she despised Shanda for coming between her and Amanda, but she claimed that she'd never intended to kill the girl. Her only intention had been to beat her up and "teach her a lesson."

Melinda's version of events differed little from the statements given by Toni and Laurie up to the point where she and Laurie came out of the hardcore show and went to join Toni and Hope in the car. Melinda claimed that the two girls weren't just talking to the two boys in the car.

"Hope and Toni were in there with a black guy and white guy and the windows were steamy," Melinda said. "We beat on the car and finally they let us in. They had to pull up their pants. I guess they were having sex. They said they wanted to finish, so we shut the door and went to a phone booth. I had Tackett call Shanda to make sure she was home but the answering machine was on, so we went back to the car. This time Hope had the other guy. They had switched partners. Finally we got the guys out of the car and we went back to Shanda's house."

Melinda's tale of the abduction and the trip to the Witches' Castle was similar to the stories told by Toni and Laurie, and she admitted that she'd punched and kneed Shanda on the dirt road. From there on, however, her version of what happened was dramatically different from Laurie's. Melinda claimed that she backed off from Shanda and told Laurie it was time to take her home. But Laurie wouldn't listen.

"She just went off," said Melinda, who referred, curiously, to Laurie by her last name throughout the interview. "I walked over by the car and Tackett still had her. Shanda called for me to help her but I didn't do nothing. Tackett had her on the ground and was choking her with a rope. She put it around Shanda's neck and started strangling her. That's when Shanda wasn't moving. I guess she was unconscious because she stopped kicking. I thought she was dead."

Her account of the fight was suddenly interrupted by tears. Russ Johnson handed her his handkerchief, and after a few minutes Melinda picked up where she'd left off.

"Tackett had the knife," she said. "I hate talking about this, but she just started cutting her. She told me to come help her. She just kept saying, 'We need to finish her, Melinda. It's already too late.' She kept saying, 'I think she's dead. Let's just finish her. Help me.' I said, 'No.' At that time she snatched my hand and put it on top of hers with the knife and just started stabbing. I pulled my hand away and went back to the car. I started crying and saying, 'I don't want nothing to do with this.' I was like shocked. I'd never seen anything like that. I just freaked out. I couldn't move. I just wanted to go help her or scream, but I couldn't. I was actually like frozen. I don't know how to explain it."

Melinda's recollection of her and Laurie's drive through the country was much clearer than Laurie's. Melinda claimed she never saw Laurie actually strike Shanda with the tire iron, but she heard it.

"I watched through the rear-view but I couldn't see much," Melinda said. "I heard something thump and there was like a weeping sound. I heard this hit like you would hear when someone hits you in your stomach."

Melinda said that when Laurie returned to the car, she stuck the bloody tire iron under Melinda's nose and told her to smell it. She also claimed that it was Laurie who came up with the plan to burn Shanda and that it was Hope who first poured the gasoline.

"Tackett was standing there with these matches," Melinda said. "She tells Hope to pour the gasoline. At first Hope says 'No' and tries to hand the gas to Tackett, but Tackett says, 'Just hurry up and throw it on her.' So Hope puts some gasoline on her. Soaks her. Tackett lit the match and *poof,* throws it on her. That was when everything just went up."

Melinda was crying again now, but at Henry's urging she continued her story.

"That's when she tells me to get out of the car and to pour the rest of the gasoline on her. Tackett was saying, 'This was your idea, Melinda. You wanted this. You need to finish her. It's only right.' I'm saying no but Hope reached over me, opened the door, and pushed me out. She handed me the bottle and she was crying and screaming at me. 'Just do it. Just do as she says.'"

Melinda said she stepped out of the car with the half-full bottle of gasoline and walked over to Shanda's smoking body.

"I looked at her and I threw the two-liter," Melinda said with a choked voice. "It went beside her and it hit the ground. That's when it started going again. I could see her face. She was burned to a crisp. You couldn't recognize her. Her tongue was sticking out. I remember her feet were up in the air. They were straight up in the air. I could see her panties or a shirt. Something was still on her but it was burned. I mean she was totally crisp black. I ran back to the car. I was sick. . . . I'm sick."

Melinda once again started crying. Whether or not they were genuine tears, Henry couldn't tell. He gave her a moment to compose herself, then asked if she knew how Shanda had gotten her anal injuries.

"No," Melinda said adamantly. "I wasn't even aware that it happened until they told me about the molestation."

"Did Laurie Tackett have the opportunity to inflict that injury?"

"Yeah," Melinda said eagerly. "At two different times. She went back to the trunk when we stopped one time when we were driving around. It took a while and there was screaming on and off. It could have been there or it could have been when we were at her house and she said she was going out to take care of Shanda. She was there for a while."

Still no proof of who sodomized Shanda. Henry switched

off the tape recorder. The interview was over. The next time he'd see Melinda Loveless would be in court.

Judge Todd had decided to hold Melinda's sentencing hearing first because she was the catalyst in the crime. The question of her guilt was already settled. She had killed Shanda, and she admitted it. The facts of the case would be presented in much the same manner as a trial, only there would be no jury. Judge Todd would determine how many years she would serve. The sentencing range was between thirty and sixty years.

Melinda's attorney, Russ Johnson, felt his client had a good chance for a sentence at the lower end of that spectrum. She had a good defense team. In addition to Johnson, there was Mike Walro, who was a former legal colleague of Judge Todd. Even though Walro didn't expect any favors from Todd, it could only help to have someone in his corner who was familiar with the way the judge ran things. The third member of the team was Bob Hammerle, a top-notch Indianapolis criminal attorney with plenty of experience in murder cases.

The defense strategy would be twofold. First, they would try to shift as much of the blame as possible to Laurie Tackett. Second, they'd attempt to build sympathy for Melinda by bringing out the sordid details of her disturbing home life.

When Johnson first began work on the case he suspected that Melinda might have come from an abusive home. He'd done enough reading to know that the vast majority of teenage killers have past histories of childhood abuse. Even so, he was shocked when Melinda's mother, Margie, and two older sisters, Michelle and Melissa, told him about their domestic life.

Margie, forty-six, looked as though she'd aged ten years since Melinda's arrest. Her face was haggard, and she had deep circles under her eyes. Once an attractive woman, she now looked worn, beaten down by the shame Melinda had brought on the family.

Michelle and Melissa Loveless had the same long dark curly hair as their younger sister, but neither had Melinda's striking beauty. Melissa, twenty-two, still lived at home with her mother and her stepfather, Michael Donahue, whom Margie had married a year earlier.

Michelle, twenty-five, who had a bachelor's degree in psychology and worked as an activity director at a home for the elderly, was out on her own now. She was the one who helped Johnson convince Margie that they would have to air all of the family's deep secrets if Melinda was going to have a chance at a reduced sentence.

(The following information came from an interview with Johnson and from court testimony. The allegations against Larry Loveless have not been proved and Loveless has denied the charges.)

Over the course of several meetings with the Loveless women, Johnson was told that Melinda's father, Larry Loveless, had ruled the home with perverse cruelty until he walked out on Margie and his three daughters two and a half years earlier. Larry was an alcoholic Vietnam veteran who'd wandered through a series of jobs—railroad worker, truck driver, postal carrier, small-town cop—but he was out of work as often as not. His short stint as a New Albany police officer ended in scandal in 1973, when he used his billy club to throttle a black man he thought was flirting with Margie. To avoid going to jail, Larry resigned from the police force.

Larry was not imposing physically. About five-foot-six and 150 pounds, he carried a potbelly and wore glasses. Nevertheless, he had delusions of grandeur and thought of himself as one tough hombre.

"My dad had a big fetish with guns," Michelle Loveless said later. "He thought he was Clint Eastwood. He would put on a poncho and would tell us that he wanted to live back in the Old West so he could just walk down the street and blow somebody's head off if they bothered him. My dad would hold a gun to my mom's head and tell her that if she left him he would kill her and us three girls. One day he was showing me his gun and he pointed it at my head and shot, but it missed and hit the wall. I peed on myself."

Melinda's sisters and mother told Johnson that Larry was a loathsome sloth, who would lay around the house for months at a time while Margie, a nurse, worked double shifts at Floyd Memorial Hospital to keep food on the table. They said that Larry would get sopping drunk and explode into violence.

"He beat my mom right in front of us," Michelle said. "He choked her. Threw her down steps. He raped her one time in the bathroom. This all went on in front of Melinda, who would beg him to stop. Sometimes when he punished me he'd lock me in a closet and wouldn't let me out all night.

"There was no privacy in our house," Michelle continued. "Your bedroom wasn't really your bedroom. He would come in and sleep in the bed and he would come into the bathroom when you were in the shower. Sometimes he'd pour cold water on you when you were in the shower or would make you get out. He would watch us from the mirror and look at us in the bathtub, and if you asked him to stop he would say, 'Why would I want to look at you? You're ugly. You have nothing I want to see.' And sometimes when you wanted to use the bathroom he'd make you pee in a dixie cup in front of him. He would wear my clothes. Sometimes I'd come home and he'd have on my underwear. He would wear my running shorts and my shirts. He'd use my makeup and my perfume. I was scared to death to throw my underwear away because he would get them out of the garbage and smell them in front of everyone and tell me they stink. He had a gym bag full of underwear, and he would masturbate in them and put them under the mattresses throughout the house and on the windowsill outside the house."

Michelle and Melissa both said that their father would fondle them and insisted on pulling down their pants to spank them until they were in their midteens and strong enough to fight him off. Although they never saw him touch their younger sister in her private areas, he would often take Melinda, whom he called Lindy Star, with him to bed and close the door. This occurred from the time Melinda was an infant until she was a teenager.

"He'd say, 'Lindy Star, let's go to bed, come up to my bed,'" Michelle recalled. "I would say, 'Dad, please don't take her.'"

Johnson was told that when Melinda was about five, Larry

suddenly embraced religion and announced to the family that he was a born-again Christian. He began to quote zealously from the Scriptures, and he forced Margie and the girls to dress conservatively and to follow several feet behind him when they walked together.

At one point, Michelle said, Larry decided that all his children's toys had been possessed by demons and he burned them in an incinerator. He also became obsessed with the thought that Melinda had been possessed by the Devil and he took her to have an exorcism.

"We drove to this motel and dropped her off with a middle-aged man for several hours," Michelle remembered. "My dad took her in his arms and carried her to the door of this motel room and gave her to this man."

Margie told Johnson that she'd tried suicide on two occasions. On the first, when Melinda was five, the girls found their mother in the basement, passed out from an overdose of sleeping pills, with pictures of her three daughters scattered around her.

The second attempt came on the tumultuous night that Larry left the family. That evening began with Larry taking Melinda, who was then thirteen, and her cousin Lisa, who was twelve, swimming at the indoor pool at the New Albany Holiday Inn. When they came home, Lisa was crying. She said that Larry had been peeking over the shower at her and Melinda and poking their naked bodies with a cane. Margie exploded. She chased Larry out of the house with a kitchen knife and ended up slashing his hand before police arrived and took him away.

Later that night Margie took an overdose of sleeping pills and her daughters had to walk her around the house, keeping her awake until the ambulance arrived.

After Larry left, Melinda became quiet and withdrawn. Despite all the abuse she'd witnessed, Melinda had remained close to her father.

"You see, she always took up for my father and stayed by his side," Michelle said. "They had always had a relationship that was more husband and wife than father and daughter. When he left she didn't really want to talk to any of us."

It was shortly after Larry left that Melinda began her relationship with Amanda. Even though Michelle and Melissa were lesbians themselves, they claimed they discouraged Melinda from getting serious with Amanda.

"We told Melinda she was too young to be involved with anyone, male or female, and she told me that Amanda spoke and acted like my dad," Michelle said. "She thought Amanda looked like my dad."

Even more graphic descriptions of Larry's sexual abuses came from Melinda's cousins, Teddy Lynn Barber and Eddie Rager. In the hope of helping Melinda's defense, the two cousins agreed to talk to Johnson.

Thirty-two-year-old Eddie Rager, who used to babysit the Loveless girls, described her uncle Larry as "a very sick, warped personality."

Rager said that whenever she spent the night at the Loveless house, Larry would get her panties out of her overnight bag and smell them. At other times, Rager claimed, Larry would parade around the house smelling Margie's panties and making rude remarks.

Rager contended that Larry first abused her on a Saturday morning when she was ten years old. She was lying on the living-room carpet of the Loveless home, watching cartoons, when he lay down beside her and started to fondle her breasts. Rager said Larry's hand worked its way down her stomach and into her panties.

Another alleged molestation took place when Rager was sleeping in the same bed as her aunt Margie, and Larry slipped into bed beside his niece.

"I thought I was having a nightmare and I was trying to wake out of it," Rager recalled. "In the nightmare somebody was holding their hand over my mouth. When I did wake up, Larry's hand was over my mouth and his other arm was around me and his penis was in my rectum."

Rager's younger sister, twenty-nine-year-old Teddy Lynn Barber, told Johnson that Larry started abusing her when she was ten. She said it started in a playful manner with him tickling her feet, but he soon started touching her breasts and vagina. Barber claimed that this took place within view of Michelle and Melissa, who were several years younger than she.

"It got to where he would have vaginal, anal, and oral sex with me," Barber later testified in court. "He would pull me in bed and then he would have sex, all different kinds, with me."

Barber told Johnson that some of the abuse also occurred in the Loveless bathroom, where Larry would force her to perform oral sex on him. Although Barber never actually saw Larry molest his daughters, she said he would often take Melinda into the bathroom with him and close the door.

Barber said there were times when she and the Loveless girls witnessed Larry and Margie having sex with other adults who would come to their house. During these orgies "the girls would be there and there were no doors closed to hide anything," Barber said.

Barber claimed that she told her mother about the molestations when she was a teenager and that her mother talked to Margie about it. She said that the incidents were never reported to the police or any social agencies, however, "because you didn't talk about things like that back then."

Luckily for Johnson and the defense he was constructing, some of the details of Larry's abuse of his wife and daughters had been documented. There were police reports of some of his beatings of Margie. In addition, Michelle had sought therapy for depression in April of 1990, shortly after her parents were divorced. At that time she told psychologists at LifeSpring Mental Health Services in Jeffersonville that she and Melissa had been sexually abused by their father and she suspected that Melinda had been abused as well.

In February of 1991, Melinda told a counselor at Hazelwood that her mother disapproved of her lesbian relationship with Amanda. The counselor met with Margie and suggested that they both seek professional therapy. Over the next several months, therefore, Margie and all three of her daughters received counseling at LifeSpring.

In her report on Melinda, Lifespring staff therapist Mina Thevenin wrote: "Melinda exhibits worry and anxiety about her sisters' alleged sexual abuse by their father. She was also recently involved in a same-sex relationship which caused increased conflict between her mother and herself."

Melinda told Thevenin about the time that her father watched her and her cousin in the shower at the Holiday Inn, but she insisted that she had no clear memory of her father ever sexually molesting her.

Still, Thevenin had her suspicions. She wrote in her report: "As patient's father allegedly molested her two older sisters, it is possible that she was also molested. She reports having some nightmares about her father molesting her."

Melinda's sisters and cousins agreed to testify about the abuse. "They were all very brave young women," Johnson would say later. "They were willing to relive those horrible memories in order to help Melinda."

Although Margie had concurred with much of what her daughters told Johnson, he couldn't risk putting her on the stand.

"Margie wanted to be supportive but I soon discovered that she needed emotional support herself," Johnson said. "We'd be in Melinda's jail cell and her mother would come in. Melinda would sit on her lap or vice versa and they would do nothing but hug each other and cry. I also knew that her mother would have to take part of the blame for the abuse Melinda suffered as a child."

Usually there's no better character witness than a defendant's mother. But then most mothers haven't been accused of participating in group sex in front of her daughters. Johnson knew that any prosecutor worth his salt would destroy Margie on the witness stand. Melinda's mother would have to sit this one out.

The same went for Melinda herself.

"Going into the hearing I was 99 percent sure I wasn't going to put her on the stand," Johnson said. "I was afraid she would break down under the pressure. Melinda was having a tough time dealing with everything that had happened. I don't believe she fully comprehended the seriousness of her situation. She was dealing with it as if it was a dream that she was going to wake up out of eventually."

17

No sooner had Shanda's parents fended off the local press than the long-distance calls started.

Donahue, Oprah Winfrey, and Sally Jesse Raphael extended invitations to fly them to New York. The tabloid television shows "Hard Copy," "A Current Affair," and others offered to send film crews to their homes. Movie producers dogged the family for screen rights to Shanda's story.

Behind their interest and concern, Jacque and Steve could imagine the backroom conversations. A bizarre murder in America's heartland had all the ingredients for a boffo movie of the week. Talk about a ratings sweep. Teenage killers. Lesbians. Rumors of witchcraft and blood drinking. The burned corpse of a twelve-year-old. Parents in anguish. Hell, it was too sensational. It might even have to be toned down to get past the censors. "But we'll treat it with proper respect, that we promise you, Mrs. Ott. It will be a fitting tribute to Shanda's memory, Mr. Sharer. You have our word."

"Jacque and I decided early on not to talk to anyone," Steve Sharer said. "We were afraid to do anything that might jeopardize the case against these girls."

Coping with Shanda's death was tough enough without the distractions. Steve was haunted by the thought that his daughter might still be alive if he'd only let Michele Durham spend the night that Friday. If Michele had been there, it's likely that would have discouraged her daughter's kidnappers.

Steve also believed that Shanda hadn't left willingly, that she'd been forced into the car. Even though Toni, Melinda, and Laurie had all given statements that Shanda didn't put up a struggle, Steve didn't buy it. If Shanda had planned on going with the girls, why didn't she take her purse and coat? Then there was the question of why the family dog was outside and limping that morning. Shanda knew that Sparky, the miniature rottweiler, was supposed to stay in the house at night. Even if Shanda had gone with the girls willingly, she wouldn't have left Sparky outdoors.

Steve believed it happened like this: Hope and Laurie told Shanda that Amanda was waiting in the car, so she went out for a quick talk without her coat and purse, with Sparky by her side. When Shanda saw that Amanda wasn't in the car she tried to leave, but the girls forced her inside. Steve thinks that Sparky tried to interfere and was hit or kicked by one of the girls or else the dog gave chase to the car and was somehow struck as it drove away.

"Sparky was limping badly when I found him on the driveway that morning," Steve said. "His left rear hindquarter was so sore he wouldn't put any weight on it."

Steve had returned to his job within a week of Shanda's murder, thinking it best to keep his hands and mind occupied. "It was an escape for me," he said. "If I sat around the house all I would do was think of Shanda."

Still, there were times when the grief seemed to overwhelm Steve, and he took comfort in the counsel of Catholic nuns at the St. Catherine Convent in Louisville.

"I don't know why it worked out that way," Steve said. "But I had to do routine maintenance of the convent's heating and air-conditioning system, and it seemed like every time I went there I was at my lowest point. Sister Mary Amelda, a little, sweet lady, would always end up having a long talk with me."

Steve is a Methodist and Jacque a Catholic. Although neither was a steady churchgoer, they both believe strongly in God and saw to it that Shanda went to church or Sunday school regularly. Not that Shanda needed to be pushed, since she'd always had a fascination with Bible stories.

"Shanda had not been baptized yet," Steve said. "She was always on us to get her baptized but we felt she should wait a few years until she was a little older, then let her decide on her own if she wanted to be a Methodist or a Catholic. But after she died the fact that she wasn't baptized troubled me. I asked Sister Amelda how I would know she was in Heaven if she wasn't baptized. Sister asked me, 'Did she believe in God and did she believe in Jesus?' and I told her yes. Sister Amelda said, 'Well then, don't worry. She is in Heaven already.' That sweet lady helped me get through this. I will always owe her a debt."

Steve's wife, Sharon, tried to console her husband, but she was consumed by her own grief. Sharon and Shanda had become very close during the three and a half years of her marriage to Steve.

"Shanda was not just Steve's daughter," Sharon said. "I thought of her as my daughter too. She was another grandchild for my parents to love, another sister for my children and a niece for my brothers and sisters. They all loved her very much and she loved them in return. Whenever Shanda came into our house she would always hug and kiss everybody. When she called on the phone she never hung up without saying 'I love you' and she meant it. I hurt for my husband because I see his sorrow and pain every day. And I hurt for Jacque too because even though Steve and Jacque are divorced, we're a family and we all care about each other. Shanda loved all of us. They've taken more than her away. They took her love from us. I know she's in Heaven now and that's the thing that helps me through it."

Jacque Ott had also returned to work shortly after Shanda's death, but each day was a struggle to keep herself from breaking down into tears.

Like Steve, Jacque was plagued by what-ifs. On the Friday morning before the murder, as Jacque was taking Shanda to school, her daughter asked if she could stay home that weekend. Shanda knew that Steve would be working on the house and figured he wouldn't have much time for her. Jacque told Shanda that Steve and Sharon would be disappointed if Shanda didn't spend the weekend with them. And Sharon had bought tickets to a Rod Stewart concert in Louisville for Saturday night and had planned to take Shanda.

"When I reminded Shanda about the concert she perked up and said she thought that would be fun," Jacque said. "I keep thinking back on that conversation. If I'd have just told her she could stay home, she would still be here with me."

Jacque became infuriated when she learned from Steve Henry about the letters that Amanda's father had turned over to the Floyd County probation office. One of the letters said that Melinda wanted Shanda dead. And although probation officer Virgil Seay had spoken to Melinda about the letters, he hadn't notified Jacque or Steve of their contents.

"At that point I had no idea that Melinda had threatened Shanda," Jacque said. "Steve and I would have been even more protective, we'd have taken more precautions, if we knew that Melinda was after Shanda. I will never forgive that man for not telling us about those letters."

The questions and regrets weighed heavily on Jacque.

"Every day at three o'clock I'd find myself sitting by my office phone waiting for Shanda to call and tell me that she was home from school, as she always did," she said. "I began to drink a lot. I thought that would help me put it all out of my mind. But I couldn't stop thinking about how much Shanda must have suffered. I could hear her screaming for me. I wanted to die so I could be with her. I started thinking about committing suicide and I realized I needed help."

Jacque checked herself into Jefferson Hospital, a mental-health facility in Jeffersonville.

"Walking through those doors was like admitting defeat," Jacque said. "I had always been strong. I had told myself that I was strong enough to deal with this, but I wasn't. I was at the end of my rope."

At first Jacque didn't respond to private counseling or group therapy. She was reluctant to talk about her feelings. Her emotions had been wound so tight for so long she was afraid they would spin out of control if she let go. Finally, counselor Sandra Graves found the right button to push. Graves told Jacque to imagine that Shanda was sitting in an empty chair she put in front of Jacque and to tell her everything she wanted to say to Shanda. Then she told Jacque to sit in the chair and for her to be Shanda and to say what she believed Shanda would say to her.

"It was very emotional," Jacque said. "Then she told me to be Shanda and she would be me. I talked to her as if I was Shanda and it brought me closer to Shanda. I ended up crying uncontrollably. Everything I had been storing up came pouring out. I have a strong belief in God and Sandra helped me realize that I would see Shanda again and that there was a purpose to my life."

After that day, Jacque began to open up in group sessions. With each day she grew emotionally stronger, although there were occasional setbacks. There were evenings when she would sit alone in the gazebo behind the hospital and stare into space until the memories and the tears overwhelmed her. One evening when Jacque went to the gazebo she found someone else there. The tall bearded man nodded at her, smiled softly, then lit a cigarette and turned his attention the other way.

The man was so quiet Jacque soon forgot he was there. She smoked a cigarette herself and thought about Shanda. She didn't realize she was sobbing until the man touched her on the shoulder and asked if she was all right.

"I just opened up to him," Jacque said. "I told him everything. He sat on the floor next to me and held me while I cried."

Suddenly Doug Vaught's own worries seemed very small. The thirty-nine-year-old ex-Army paratrooper had checked himself into Jefferson Hospital when his marriage failed and he'd begun drinking too much. "What I had gone through was nothing compared to what Jacque was dealing with," said Vaught, a postal worker in Louisville.

Jacque was drawn to Doug's quiet strength and laid-back nature. They began meeting at the gazebo every evening and would take walks around the hospital property.

"I'd been through a lot of relationships and so had Doug," Jacque said. "We were attracted to each other, but we were both scared to get involved because we both knew how vulnerable I was. We decided to just be friends, but after I checked out of the hospital I realized how much I missed him."

Jacque's counselors had told her that she had turned the corner. She had come to grips with her grief, and it was time for her to take the next step. It was time for her to leave. Jacque moved in with her friend Connie Dean. Then one day she got a call from Doug, who had left the hospital on the same day as Jacque.

"When we saw each other again we knew we didn't want to be separated again," Jacque said. "We knew we were in love."

On October 2, less than two weeks after Melinda and Laurie had accepted their plea agreements, Jacque and Doug were married in a quiet civil ceremony. They bought a house in a small village north of New Albany. Jackie gathered together some of Shanda's photographs and keepsakes and had them put under glass in two large shadow boxes. She hung them on her living-room wall. They contained the mementos of an active life. There was the bright red letter jacket she had worn after playing basketball at St. Paul Catholic School, the ribbons she'd won in gymnastics, her softball batting glove, her Girl Scout and 4H merit badges, pictures of her on the cheerleading squad, and a picture of the heart-shaped headstone that marked her grave.

Jacque and Doug had invited Shanda's older half-sister, Paije, to move in with them. Paije, nineteen, had become pregnant that spring and decided to have the child out of wedlock.

"When Paije first told me I was so angry," Jacque said. "She had gotten pregnant just six months after Shanda died. I thought it was a cruel joke. Then I realized that a new life

212

was coming into our family and I realized it was a gift from God."

Paije, a student nurse, had her own difficulties dealing with her little sister's murder. She broke down in the days following the funeral and spent three weeks at Our Lady of Peace, a mental health hospital in Louisville.

After her stay in the hospital, the engaging brunette with the pleasant disposition became the rock of the family, offering a shoulder to lean on for Steve, Sharon, and Jacque.

Paije would say later that although she'd come to terms with Shanda's death, she would never understand why it had happened.

"Because of jealousy, she's now gone," Paije said. "My sister can never come back again. These girls can get out of prison and go on with their lives. My sister can't. I worry about my mother every day. I worry about whether she's going to make it or not. Shanda was Steve's only child. They've taken that away from him. I'll never understand."

Paije said she didn't know how Melinda, Laurie, Hope, and Toni could live with themselves.

"At their age how could they do the things that they did to my sister and look at themselves in the mirror? It's ruined my life. Every time I lay down at night I can hear her crying for help. My sister wasn't a mean person. She loved everybody. She wanted to be friends with everybody. She would never have hurt anybody. She didn't deserve to die."

Shanda's murder had also deeply affected her young friends.

"I didn't believe it for a long time," said Michele Durham. "I guess I was in shock. I don't guess I'll ever get over it."

Shanda's cousin Amanda Edrington said it hurt to think about all the fun times they'd had together.

"I looked up to Shanda a lot," Amanda said. "She kind of mother-henned me. She was just that way. I miss her so much. It scared me to think that someone I loved could be taken from me just like that. It still scares me."

The murder was also troubling to the students at Hazelwood who didn't know Shanda well but were well acquainted with Melinda. While many students at Hazelwood were aware of Melinda's homosexuality and her jealous dominance of Amanda, and many had seen her in a few pushing and shoving matches, few of them had thought her capable of such a violent act.

"It's hard to accept that any of this is true," said Jennifer Risner, a classmate. "It just doesn't seem like Melinda. None of us can believe this happened."

"Melinda was a loner when I met her," said Dennis Smith, fifteen. "That's one of the reasons I liked her. She was different. She helped me out when I was having a tough time getting to know people in the seventh grade. She was a good friend. I still don't think she was involved in killing Shanda. I don't care what the police say."

The students at Madison Consolidated High were equally stunned by the arrest of Toni Lawrence and Hope Rippey. They were not, however, surprised to learn that Laurie Tackett had finally gone over the edge. They'd witnessed Laurie's transformation from a shy, self-conscious, churchgoing nerd into a weird, obnoxious showoff who would boast about her magical powers.

"She said she knew a spell she could put on a teacher and that she could punch the air and he'd feel it," said classmate Mikel Pommerehn. "She told us that when she got mad she could make stuff fly around her room."

Pommerehn said that she and most other students kept their distance from Laurie. Her instability scared them. The bolder among them would tell Laurie exactly what they thought of her: She was nuts. Few expressed any regrets when Laurie stopped coming to school in the fall of 1991. Good riddance.

Even after she left school, Laurie clung to her friendship with Hope, said Hope's father Carl Rippey. "Hope sort of felt sorry for Laurie. She would act sisterly to her. But Laurie wasn't Hope's only friend. She was not a loner. She had lots of friends. She was a happy child who could find humor in just about anything."

Hope had an outgoing personality and a bit of brashness about her that won her the acceptance of the more radical crowd at school, though it put off some of her more refined classmates.

"I didn't like Hope that well," said Kelli Skirvin, sixteen, a good friend of Toni. "She was in a, well, lower class sort of."

"Me and Kelli told Toni a few times that she shouldn't hang around with Hope," said Mikel Pommerehn. Mikel thought that Hope, who smoked, cursed, and had gone through a string of boyfriends, was too wild for Toni.

After Hope's arrest her sister, Tina, told an Associated Press reporter that she believed Hope was innocent, although she didn't sound too convincing. "When she's put on trial for murder, what am I supposed to do, say she's guilty like everyone else? She's my baby sister and I'll stand by her."

It was Toni Lawrence's involvement that shocked students and teachers most. The psychological evaluations performed on Toni after her suicide attempt painted her as a pompous and manipulative child, and Henry would say later that Toni seemed to be disrespectful of her parents. But in the eyes of Toni's friends and teachers, she was no more rebellious than the average teenage girl. Most students knew her as a somewhat shy but pleasant girl who did volunteer work at a nursing home, wrote poetry, participated in Girl Scouts and 4H, played trumpet in the school band, and went out for cross-country track, softball, and the swim team.

"I was shocked and stunned to learn that Toni was messed up in this," said Mary Davee, Toni's English teacher. "I remember Toni telling me she wanted to take fashion design in college. She was sometimes talkative and giggly in class but never disruptive."

Beverly Cook, Toni's French teacher, said, "I think Toni would be the last person I'd have picked to be involved in something like that. You could tell from her appearance that she came from a good home."

Mikel called Toni "a very caring person. She's honest and she's there if you have a problem. Toni's real emotional. A boyfriend broke up with me once and Toni got more upset about it than I did."

"She was just always a nice person," Kelli said. "She was not the type of person to get in a fight because she's so small she knew that people would beat her up."

Most of Toni's friends were surprised to learn that she'd even been along in the same car as Laurie Tackett. "Toni didn't like her," Mikel said. "I still don't know why she went out with her that night."

While those who knew Shanda's assailants strained to understand what had happened, the community was doing the same without the insight of personal knowledge.

Louisville and its surrounding metropolitan area—which included the small cities of New Albany, Jeffersonville, and Clarksville directly across the Ohio River—had a population of about one million. And Louisville, particularly, had seen its share of brutal murders in the past few years. Some—like the sadistic, torture murder of a beautiful young woman, Brenda Sue Schaefer, and the decapitation of Kathleen Strange by her husband, John—had grabbed front-page headlines and been continuing stories on local television stations.

To a certain degree, the community had become desensitized to the growing violence. Once one sensational murder trial was over, it seemed that another had begun. It was something people just put out of their minds as they went about their daily lives. Even though the violence they had always associated with bigger cities had suddenly settled in their backyards, they felt some satisfaction that things were far worse elsewhere. They lived in an area where the highlight of the year was a huge festival centered around the Kentucky Derby. They had their college basketball in the winter and their Triple A baseball club in the summer. Although political leaders constantly talked about what needed to be done to keep pace with faster-growing cities like Indianapolis and Nashville, most folks seemed satisfied to be half a step behind. There was a security here, a feeling that life, though it may be slow, was all right.

Shanda's death seemed to change that overnight. No other murder in memory disturbed so many people so completely, probably because no other murder had crushed so many deeply held beliefs. Suddenly their children didn't seem as safe as they had been. As the circumstances of Shanda's gruesome torture murder and Melinda's jealous motivations—and the even more scarier revelation that Laurie, Hope, and Toni didn't even know the victim personally—were drawn out in increasing detail by the press, the community's disillusionment grew.

Preachers shouted out warnings from the pulpit that parents needed to nurture their children, and neighbors conversed over backyard fences, making pacts to keep their eyes on each other's kids.

A few days after the murder, *Louisville Courier-Journal* columnist Betty Baye wrote under a headline "Cradle of Violence" about the shock and confusion the community was feeling.

> My mind simply can't shake away the imagined sound of Shanda's screaming as she was beaten and finally stuffed half-dead into an automobile trunk, while her assailants calmly filled a two-liter soft drink bottle with gasoline they used to burn her body. What manner of jealousy could provoke such young girls to such hatred?
>
> How well I recall my wise mother constantly warning my sisters and me, reminding us, "Jealousy is a rotten disease." But I see cradles being robbed all too often these days by children so consumed by envy that they can injure and, yes, kill others who have greater material wealth, better looks, brighter personalities, or higher grades.
>
> Shanda Renee Sharer didn't live in a big city. She lived in southern Indiana, where small towns abound, where families know each other by name, and where many teenagers' version of a big night out is going to a movie or hanging out in a shopping mall.
>
> Shanda's murder should remind us that living in a small place doesn't guarantee immunity from violence. It's a reminder that no walls are high enough, no

highways wide enough, no bridges long enough, and no rivers deep enough to separate us from senseless violence.

Four months later, another *Courier-Journal* staffer, Linda Stahl, wrote a lengthy article about the rise in violence among teenage girls in the community.

"In this day and age, there's nothing to be surprised about," said a mother whose daughter was assaulted by a gang of teenage girls. "Too many kids out there are ruling their parents, or they don't know where their parents are. It's no surprise they think my daughter's face is a beanbag they can beat on."

A sixth-grade girl whom Stahl interviewed said she got into fights because "it makes you feel like a sissy if you don't."

"It lets out stress," said another.

A sweet-faced blonde with freckles described a fight she'd had recently: "I hit her real hard. I grabbed her hair from behind and hit her head against the wall. I saw blood."

A police officer quoted in the article said, "Girls don't have that prim and proper conditioning they had before. All they have left to model themselves after is the harshness of reality and the hardness of men."

Stahl's story ended with the director of a mental health center commenting on Shanda's murder: "I'm reminded of *Lord of the Flies.* Socialized kids living by the laws of the jungle. I'm so glad I'm not a girl today. Isn't that awful to say?"

It was a bitter pill for the community to swallow, and it went down even harder in the town of Madison, forty miles upriver.

The flush of publicity over Shanda's murder seemed a terrible irony for the town of Madison. For many years it had cultivated its image as a shining example of small-town America. Now Madison was appearing on regional newscasts every night as the site of the most atrocious murder in anyone's memory.

In 1958 the town was considered so typically American that MGM studios came to town to film *Some Came*

Running, a story based in the heartland and starring Frank Sinatra, Shirley MacLaine, and Dean Martin.

It's still much the same in downtown Madison, with its 150-year-old architecture of Greek Revival, Italianate, and Gothic Revival buildings. Many of the old buildings have been turned into antique shops, gift shops, and restaurants to capitalize on the growing tourism business. And farmers still bring their produce to sell it on the sidewalk outside the old courthouse.

In a *Courier-Journal* feature on the town written shortly after the murder, one resident called it "a real time ghost, a Brigadoon."

"Unlike the Scottish village of Broadway legend, however, old Madison didn't just appear out of the mists," wrote reporter David Goetz. "It was preserved in a sort of museum case formed by the hillsides and the river."

With preservationists discouraging commercial growth downtown, new businesses sprung up along IND-62, a five-lane highway on the hill above town. Here it is a different Madison, with fast-food restaurants, movie theaters, gas stations, shopping centers, bowling alleys. And here is where the teenagers hang out on the weekends, congregating in shopping-center parking lots, sitting on car hoods, and swapping stories.

But there was only one story in town after Shanda's murder, and it was a story that lured reporters hundreds, and in some cases thousands, of miles to the small community that had been branded as the spawning ground for murder.

"The age of innocence here ended about 10:45 A.M. last January 11 on a dirt road fifteen miles out of town," wrote Ron Grossman, a reporter for the *Chicago Tribune.*

"It's like you took the Leopold and Loeb case, recast it for girls, and set it in Main Street, USA," Grossman quoted *Madison Courier* reporter Wayne Engle as saying, recalling the notorious 1924 case of two homosexual college students who killed a fourteen-year-old boy for thrills.

USA Today reporter Andrea Stone found Madison adults eager to make excuses for the murder. "Satanism is connected to this," Carol Fisher, forty-two, told Stone. "I don't

219

think teenage girls are capable of doing what they did on their own. It's basically evil what they did." Court clerk Carolyn Peak said, "People are just amazed and shocked at their age and their being girls. Good golly. People aren't born that mean."

The *USA Today* story quoted Madison Consolidated High principal Roger Gallatin: "This is supposed to be an area protected by the values system. When this happens, where do we have a safe place to raise a family?"

A reporter from the *Los Angeles Times* stopped in at Damon's Restaurant across the street from the courthouse and was told by owner Damon Welch, "I guess we never thought that something like this would happen in our little town. Pretty frightening, isn't it?"

In addition to articles in such newspapers as the *New York Times,* the case attracted attention across the Atlantic.

British journalist Richard Grant visited Madison, searching for a key to unlock the mysteries of the horrible murder. In an article that he wrote for the London *Independent,* he implied that the murder could be blamed in part on the unfocused boredom of Madison teenagers, whom he characterized as wild-spirited louts who got drunk and screwed each other every weekend and skirted the edges of violence.

"There ain't much to do around here but drink and fuck," said one unnamed teenager quoted in Grant's article.

Grant observed that "the problem with Madison is the problem with any small town. There is nothing to do. Life is a constant battle against boredom, in which alcohol and cannabis are the most dependable allies. Otherwise, one can have sex in cars, drive at high speed along winding country back roads, or, for an added thrill, drive while drunk at high speed. Almost without exception, the girls wear heavy makeup, and have permed, teased and frosted hairstyles. Eighty percent of them are fiercely blonde. They marry young and divorce young. They dream about escaping Madison, but seldom make it past Louisville. Beyond that, the world is televised. The boys rev their engines and brag about their latest sexual conquests. The girls sit three or four to a car, chattering about school, television, who slept with who, the guy from out of town in a red Corvette Stingray."

Another teen quoted by Grant and identified only as Susan said she "wants to be there when they 'lectrocute that devil-worshiping bitch" who killed Shanda.

According to Grant, the teens he talked to explained the murder with a "crazy-devil-worshiping-Lesbo-bitches-on-acid" theory.

Grant played loose and free with the facts of the case. For instance, he quoted Madison teens who claimed to have "partied" with Shanda and observed her drinking, smoking pot, and having lesbian sex. Whether any of the kids he quoted really existed is questionable, but one thing is not: Shanda had never been to Madison before the night she was killed.

Grant had begun the article with a quote from Donna Jackson, the clerk at the Madison courthouse. Jackson told him that "if that poor young girl had been killed in New York, instead of Madison, Indiana, none of you fellows would have batted an eyelid. We've got a nice little town here, and it's a shame that it takes something like this to get us noticed."

Jackson would later tell a *Courier-Journal* reporter that her quote appeared to be the only truthful thing in the article, which made its way back to Madison when a resident happened to pick up the magazine while in England.

"Everybody is infuriated by it," Jackson said. "It puts down our kids, and we have a lot of good kids in this town."

Local television and newspapers tried their own cultural analyses, interviewing psychologists and sociologists and focusing attention on the growing trend of teen violence. One television station went so far as to have a handwriting expert analyze Melinda Loveless's handwriting. The expert said that the way Melinda shaped her *F*s and *S*s demonstrated her sexual frustration.

The townspeople preferred to view the whole matter as an aberration.

Said Madison mayor Morris Wooden, "This is the type of freak event you expect to happen somewhere else in the world. Anywhere but Madison."

18

A line of television trucks from Louisville, Cincinnati, and Indianapolis lined the street outside the Jefferson County courthouse in Madison.

It was December 14, 1992, the opening day of the sentencing hearing for Melinda Loveless.

A cutting wind blew outside the stately three-story brick building, and reporters and camera crews turned their coat collars up as they stood in the alley between the courthouse and the jail, waiting for Melinda to make her appearance.

Suddenly there she was, looking nervous but still lovely with her long curls and pretty face. She wore a dark blue blouse, loose beige pants, and handcuffs, and was surrounded by two burly sheriff's deputies and her three attorneys, Russ Johnson, Bob Hammerle, and Mike Walro. The cameras pushed closer and the reporters shouted their questions. She said nothing, her eyes downcast, and in seconds she was inside, taking the stairs to the third-floor courtroom of Judge Ted Todd.

The large courtroom was divided evenly in half by a wooden waist-high partition—the judge and attorneys on one side, the gallery on the other. The twelve-foot walls and ceiling were painted a pale green. Darker green drapes were pulled back, but the blinds were down over the windows. There was room for about 150 people in the two sections of benches divided by a center aisle. Shanda's family and friends were seated in the front rows on the right side of the aisle. Melinda's mother, stepfather, and sisters sat on the other side. Behind both families sat reporters and the curious. The benches were about half full, but the room felt stuffy because of the heat being pumped in by an ancient radiator system.

The soft chatter of the crowd increased when Melinda was led into the room by her lawyers and sat at a table to the left of the judge's bench. Her shackles were off. She looked at her mother and smiled slightly, then cast a quick glance at Shanda's family, where her gaze was met by hard stares. She looked down at the table, folded her hands in front of her as if in prayer, and waited.

The murmuring among the spectators stopped when Judge Ted Todd walked slowly into the courtroom and took his seat behind the bench. He shuffled some paper, then told the state's prosecutor, Guy Townsend, to begin his opening statement.

Although Townsend lacked capital-case experience, he was no novice at weaving a story. His background as a writer served him well as he set the scene, beginning with Shanda's first days at Hazelwood Junior High, her fight with Amanda Heavrin, and then how Shanda and Amanda's friendship enraged Melinda's jealousy. The prosecutor paced slowly back and forth in front of the judge as he told of Melinda's meeting with Laurie Tackett and of the fateful night when Laurie, Hope Rippey, and Toni Lawrence became Melinda's partners in revenge.

In vivid detail, Townsend described Shanda's abduction, the trip to the Witches' Castle, the beating and strangulation of Shanda on the logging road, Shanda's imprisonment in the trunk, and the beatings with the tire iron. As his statement built to its grisly climax, the mesmerized spectators hung on every dramatic word.

Jacque moaned slightly and hung her head as Townsend

described the final scene of the tragedy at the burn site on Lemon Road. With the image of Shanda's smoking body lingering in the air, Townsend paused for effect, before adding, "Then the girls drove to Madison and stopped at McDonald's for a bite to eat."

Melinda showed little emotion at first as Townsend questioned a string of witnesses—Donn Foley, the hunter who found the body, and police officers Randy Spry, Richard Shipley, and Curtis Wells—but when the prosecutor argued for admitting a closeup photograph showing Shanda's bloody scalp, Melinda moaned loudly. All eyes in the courtroom shifted to the defendant as she gasped for air, then put her head on the table and sniffled. Attorney Mike Walro placed a comforting hand on her shoulder.

Judge Todd ignored the outburst and allowed most of the photographs into evidence. But a few minutes later, defense attorney Bob Hammerle was on his feet, objecting to admission of the letters Melinda had sent Amanda Heavrin. Hammerle was a slim man in his early forties. His glasses and neatly trimmed beard gave him a mild-mannered appearance, but he had an agile mind, plenty of courtroom savvy, and a sharp tongue.

Hammerle said the defense would allow the admission of the letter in which Melinda wrote "I want Shanda dead" because it did have bearing on the case. He did, however, object strongly to the other letters.

In an indignant tone, Hammerle said, "Every one of these other letters has been selected because of something that has been hinted here but never said. Every one of them has been selected because of sexual overtones between Melinda Loveless and Amanda Heavrin. They are designed to sensationalize that. They have been carefully picked because of certain comments made by Melinda Loveless to Amanda Heavrin. Quite frankly, it's our position that it injects an element of homophobia into this hearing. They are designed to sensationalize certain issues that have no place in a court of law."

Townsend responded in a voice tinged with emotion: "The relationship between Amanda Heavrin and Melinda Loveless is at the very heart of this. That is why Shanda

Sharer is dead, because Shanda Sharer dared to become friends with Melinda Loveless's girlfriend. These letters are relevant to the motive of this crime. They show premeditation, which is an aggravator."

Townsend continued, his face flushed red with anger: "And I greatly resent the accusation of homophobia being directed at us. The state is not trying to sensationalize or in any other way blow this thing out of proportion. We're trying to do our job."

The subject of Melinda's homosexuality had been broached, and reporters scribbled furiously in their notebooks in hurried attempts to record the exchange between Hammerle and Townsend. The entire scene seemed to agitate Judge Todd, who felt that showboating belonged on the river a few blocks away, not in his courtroom. With a silent nod of admonishment to both counsels, Todd allowed the letters to be admitted as evidence.

The day had grown long, and the heat inside the courtroom was stifling. The courthouse radiator system was operating on high to accommodate all the airy county offices on the floors below, but it had turned the closed courtroom into a hothouse. Beads of sweat dotted Townsend's brow, and he asked Judge Todd for permission to remove his jacket. Todd told him to go ahead; then, looking a bit weary himself, the judge loosened the collar of his robe.

Townsend's last witness of the day was Steve Henry.

Henry settled himself in the witness chair and in his easy, sure-handed manner gave a detailed account of his investigation and the arrest of the four girls.

In the course of preparing for the sentencing hearing, Melinda's lead attorney, Russell Johnson, had developed a deep respect for Steve Henry, and he knew that there were no holes in the case the detective had built against Melinda. He also knew that Henry had put together an equally strong case against Laurie Tackett.

"Did you comment to Sheriff Shipley that Laurie Tackett's statement was a fairy tale or a fantasy land?" asked Johnson in his cross-examination.

Henry leaned forward in his chair to make a point. "I

think those comments dealt mainly with her infatuation with witchcraft and spirits and this type of thing."

"It also had to do with spontaneous combustion of the body, did it not?" Johnson asked. "When she gave a statement to you concerning how the body caught fire, she told you that it just burst into flames, didn't she?"

"Yes sir, that's what she said."

"And you didn't believe that?"

"No sir," Henry answered. "I do not."

On the second day of the hearing, a crowd that had been bolstered by news accounts of the previous day's drama packed the third-floor hallway, waiting patiently in a single-file line as deputy sheriffs checked each one with hand-held metal detectors. Coat-and-tie reporters, flannel-shirted farmers, housewives, retirees, and high-school students on Christmas break filed past the deputies until all the seats were filled, and dozens of people were standing in the back and along both sides of the courtroom.

The spectators' wait was a long one. An hour crept by and there was still no sign of Judge Todd, Guy Townsend, or Melinda and her attorneys. Amid the crowd's murmur, someone cursed the heat and damned the old metal radiator that seemed to be working overtime to make everyone uncomfortable. Every so often, someone would nudge a neighbor and nod toward the front row on the right side of the aisle. "That's Shanda's family," they'd say softly, in a voice full of pity. Others would leer at the left front row, where Melinda's mother and sisters and stepfather sat with their eyes straight ahead, ignoring the looks of disgust all around them.

Inside Judge Todd's chamber, he was hearing arguments from Townsend that Hammerle had interfered with one of his witnesses, Jeffrey Stettenbenz, the boy who claimed to have listened into the phone conversation between Melinda and Amanda on the night of the murder. Stettenbenz's mother had told Townsend that Hammerle called her house the night before, trying to dissuade her son from testifying. While Hammerle acknowledged he spoke to Stettenbenz, he denied trying to dissuade him from testifying. But Todd was not satisfied with the evidence and denied Townsend's motion that Hammerle be held in contempt of court.

When court finally convened, Townsend called Toni Lawrence to the stand.

Toni walked slowly into the courtroom with her head turned away from the table where Melinda sat with her lawyers. Thin to begin with, Toni had not yet regained the weight she'd lost after her suicide attempt. Her sweater and slacks hung loosely on her small, fragile frame. Toni looked briefly at the spectators with lonely, haunted eyes, then sat down in the chair facing Judge Todd.

Toni's whispery responses to Townsend's first questions were nearly inaudible, and Judge Todd asked her to speak up. Sensing Toni's nervousness, Townsend left his seat and walked closer to his key witness, smiling softly as he continued his queries in a reassuring tone.

In a quiet voice that had spectators straining to hear, Toni recounted all the horrible details of Shanda's murder. As she told of Melinda pulling the knife on Shanda, she paused for a second and glanced furtively at Melinda, then quickly looked away. Melinda's face was passive, but her stiffly held shoulders revealed her tension. An occasional gasp would rise from the audience as Toni described the various atrocities. By the time she came to Shanda's fiery death, Toni was in tears.

"Melinda got out and poured more gasoline," Toni said. "When she got back in the car she was happy. She was laughing. She said she was glad Shanda was dead."

During Toni's testimony, Melinda's mother, Margie, sat quietly on the front bench beside her new husband, Mike Donahue, and her daughters, Michelle and Melissa. Margie would occasionally catch Melinda's eye and smile faintly, expressing her support. When Toni finished and a recess was called, Margie left her seat and went to the defense table to comfort her by now sobbing daughter. Melinda slipped into her mother's lap and rocked back and forth, whimpering, "I can't do it." She obviously couldn't bear to listen to any more of Toni's damaging testimony. "I'm so scared," she muttered. "I'm so scared."

When court reconvened, Bob Hammerle left his seat at

the defense table and stood directly in front of Toni, leering at her with all the intimidation that he could muster.

"Miss Lawrence," he began, "on the night that you went to the police, you told Detective Henry that the girls took you home before they burned Shanda. That was a lie, wasn't it?"

"Yes."

"But you're telling the truth today, is that right?" Hammerle asked, his voice oozing with sarcasm.

"Yep," Toni said flatly, eyeing the attorney with suspicion.

"Miss Lawrence." Hammerle moved closer, bearing down on the timid witness. "Who was the first person that evening to mention killing anyone?"

"Laurie."

"Let me ask you something." He moved even closer, so close that he could have reached out and touched her. "Laurie Tackett set Shanda on fire, didn't she?"

"I don't know. I wasn't watching."

Hammerle drew a hand across his beard, then slowly turned his back to the witness. He took a step toward the defense table, then wheeled quickly around. Toni's back stiffened. "You didn't tell police that Hope Rippey poured the gas when you gave your first statement, did you?"

"Nope."

"You lied in that first statement, didn't you?"

"I suppose," Toni said smartly.

Hammerle looked at her with disdain. "Do you suppose you're telling the truth today?"

Toni paused to consider the question, but Hammerle didn't wait for a response and dismissed her.

Townsend's next witness, Laurie Tackett, came into the courtroom wearing a gray suit jacket, jeans, and slip-on shoes. Her lips were tight and her eyes squinted. Melinda looked away and trembled as Laurie passed by her and took a seat in the witness chair. While Toni had shied away from elaborating on the gory details of Shanda's murder, Laurie showed no such aversion.

"I remember Melinda beating her up," Laurie said calmly. "I remember Melinda stepping on a knife, trying to force it through the back of her neck. I remember her having a rope and asking me to help her strangle Shanda. She asked me to hold one end of it while she pulled on the other. I pulled on it for about five minutes. She just went unconscious. I let go of it, then Melinda took over and was holding both ends, pulling on it."

Laurie was in the middle of describing the scene at her house when she went outside to check on Shanda—"I opened the trunk. Shanda was laying in the trunk. She was trying to sit up. Her eyes rolled back in her head"—when her testimony was interrupted by a long, sorrowful moan from Melinda. All eyes in the courtroom quickly shifted to Melinda, who cried loudly, "This is sickening." Melinda dropped her head and began crying and shaking.

Laurie began to speak again, but Judge Todd stopped her. "We are going to take a five-minute recess," he said.

As soon as Todd announced the break, Margie left her courtroom seat and rushed to her daughter's side. She sat in a chair next to the defense table and pulled Melinda's weeping face to her shoulder and caressed her long hair.

In mock sympathy, a man in the rear of the courtroom yelled, "Poor thing."

When court resumed, Townsend asked Tackett to pick up her testimony at the point she'd left off, but the courtroom was filled with the chatter of spectators still excited by Melinda's outburst.

Judge Todd banged his gavel. "Let's have a little silence please in the back of the room."

Laurie started again: "I saw Shanda laying there. I tried to talk to her and she couldn't or she wouldn't. She had blood everywhere. Her eyes were rolled back in her head. She acted like she couldn't sit up. She was shivering. After I tried to talk to her, I put the blanket over her, then I closed the trunk. Not all the way but half way, enough to where it would stay, and I went back in the house."

"Was there a reason for not closing the trunk all the way?" Townsend asked.

For the first time Laurie seemed tentative. She closed her

eyes in deep concentration. Then she shook her head and said matter-of-factly, "I just did it. I just didn't close it all the way."

Johnson scribbled a note to himself as Laurie continued. If the trunk was still open and Shanda was conscious, why didn't she escape? There was obviously something that Laurie didn't want the court to know.

Laurie once again said she remembered little of the long drive she and Melinda made with Shanda in the trunk, never mentioning anything about either of the girls using the tire iron to hit Shanda. When she recounted the scene at the burn site, she admitted that Hope had poured the gas—contradicting an earlier statement she'd made in an attempt to protect Hope.

"Who set her on fire?" Townsend asked.

"I have no idea," Laurie said anxiously. "I was bending over her. I was going to take the blanket away from her face because she was crying. She couldn't say anything. She tried to say things but I couldn't understand what she said. She was screaming, trying to say things. I don't know what she was trying to say." Laurie was talking rapidly now, and she needed no further prompting from Townsend. She was reliving the moment, and her words came out in quick, terse phrases. "While I was bent over her the fire went up in my face and singed my hair. Melinda was running and she told me and Hope to come on. We drove down the road awhile. Melinda told me to turn around. She wanted to make sure Shanda was completely on fire. We turned around and went back. She was burning but her legs weren't on fire. Melinda got out of the car and poured the rest of the gas on her. She stood there awhile before she poured the gas, looking at her. After she poured the gas on her Melinda got back in the car and she was laughing. She said that Shanda's tongue was going in and out of her mouth and she was laughing about it. She said things like 'I'm glad Shanda's gone. I'm glad she's out of me and Amanda's lives.' She told us that if we stuck together everything would be okay. From there we went to McDonald's."

When Laurie abruptly stopped talking, the courtroom's

attention shifted to the front row, where Steve Sharer was hunched forward, his elbows on his knees, his face covered in his hands. Jacque's left arm was draped over her ex-husband's back and her head was resting on his shoulder as she cried. Their spouses, Sharon and Doug, sat on either side, giving Steve and Jacque comforting hugs.

Laurie, cool and collected and ready to continue, seemed a bit disappointed when Townsend dismissed her.

The third day of the hearing began with Russ Johnson's cross-examination of Laurie. Assuming an aggressive, contemptuous manner, Johnson accused Laurie of twisting the facts to harm Melinda, pointing out that she'd originally said that Melinda, not Hope, had first poured the gas. Although Laurie appeared cocky at first, Johnson caught her off balance by asking her how Shanda had gotten her anal injuries.

Laurie hesitated for a moment before finally answering: "I feel like she might have had sex with someone else before we picked her up."

Johnson knew that Laurie was improvising now. He had her where he wanted her. He asked her about when she went outside her house to check on Shanda after she and the others heard Laurie's dog barking. "You testified that you just put the trunk lid down far enough where it would stay down, not that it was locked or closed. Is that correct?"

"Yes." Laurie was pensive, eying Johnson with suspicion.

"It never crossed your mind that if you left this trunk open this young lady could have gotten out and walked away?"

"She probably could have."

"When you went outside she was conscious because she was screaming and banging. Is that right?"

"Yes." Not understanding where Johnson was going with this, Laurie stuck firmly to her story.

"Was she still screaming after you put the blanket over her and left?"

"Yes."

"Let me understand this," Johnson said, playing as much

to the spectators as he was to Laurie. "This little girl was screaming and banging on the trunk, and you leave the trunk open and she just lies there screaming and banging."

Laurie began to realize that she was cornered. She hesitated, then answered tentatively, "She probably didn't know I left the trunk cracked open."

"If someone's banging on the lid of that trunk and it's not shut, I assume that trunk's going to fly open." Johnson stepped closer to Laurie. "She wasn't screaming when you left, was she?"

"Yes she was," Laurie said defensively.

Johnson was looming over her now. "Your specific reason for going out to the automobile was to quiet Shanda Sharer, wasn't it?"

"Yes."

"And isn't it a fact that you did quiet her by hitting her with a tire iron?"

Laurie seemed startled. "No," she stated loudly.

"Didn't you tell Crystal Wathen that when Shanda started screaming, you took a tire iron and hit her over the head?"

Laurie sneered back at the attorney. "No." She was on edge, and Johnson could see it.

"Isn't it a fact that you not only hit her with the tire iron but that you also molested her?"

"I didn't hit her and I didn't molest her."

Johnson switched gears and began asking a series of questions about Laurie's fascination with the occult.

"I was never a devil worshiper," Laurie said defensively. "Never had sacrifices. I'm not into it anymore. I was never into it. I was just interested in it."

"Do you believe in God?"

"Yes."

"Then why did you tell Melinda that you didn't believe in God, that you believed in black magic?"

"It was something I tried to portray myself as so people would leave me alone about my past religion."

Johnson was not about to let Laurie off so easily. He pressed on, asking her why she'd shaved her head and why she so often dressed in black. He asked her about her channeling episodes, in which spirits supposedly talked through her body.

"Channeling doesn't work," Laurie said. "It's fake."

"So were you faking it when this Deanna the Vampire would channel through your body and you would talk like a vampire?"

"I believed it at the time, but it doesn't really exist. Deanna doesn't exist. No one ever came into my body and talked through me."

"Have you ever cut your wrist and drank your own blood?"

The crowd stirred and leaned forward, waiting for the answer. Laurie hesitated, then said, "No, I didn't. I've never done that."

"Kary Pope said you cut your wrist and drank your own blood at a party."

Laurie shook her head. "No. A girlfriend drank my blood at a party."

"Did you ever tell Kary Pope that you would kill her grandmother for her?"

"Jokingly, yes."

"Isn't it a fact that you told Mr. Leatherbury that one of your biggest fascinations was to know what it feels like to see someone burn?"

"The answer is no."

Johnson walked closer to Laurie and said softly, "You know what it feels like now, don't you?"

"Yes," Laurie said meekly.

And with this bizarre portrayal of Laurie Tackett firmly in place, the court adjourned for the day.

During his long tenure as Kentucky's chief medical examiner, Dr. George R. Nichols II had testified at countless murder trials. But never had he spent such a curious hour while waiting to take the witness stand. Seated in the law library that served as the witness lounge for Judge Todd's court, the doctor found himself in the company of several teenagers also waiting to testify. The group included Larry Leatherbury and Kary Pope.

"They talked amongst themselves as if I wasn't there," Nichols would later tell a reporter. "The lone boy among them said he was concerned about his testimony. He hoped people wouldn't think he was homosexual because he was really bisexual. One girl said she herself wouldn't mind being sent to women's prison because she could have all the pussy she could eat. It was the strangest conversation I have ever heard."

It is not surprising that the teenagers paid Nichols no mind. A medium-sized man with unruly black hair and spectacles, Nichols was by appearance unimposing. But his unobtrusiveness vanished once he took the witness stand and began testifying about Shanda Sharer's autopsy in his deep, authoritative voice.

"Would the smoke inhalation indicate that Shanda was alive when she was set on fire?" Townsend asked.

Nichols looked Townsend straight in the eyes. In a booming voice he said, "Absolutely."

The courtroom buzzed with anticipation when Townsend announced Amanda Heavrin as his next witness.

A week before the hearing began, Jacque had reluctantly agreed to give an interview to the Louisville *Courier-Journal*. The newspaper had learned through sources about the letters exchanged between Shanda and Amanda and was ready to run a story that would have touched on their lesbian relationship. In hopes of putting the letters in their proper perspective, Jacque openly discussed all her efforts to get Shanda away from Amanda. When Amanda's father, Jerry Heavrin, was contacted in order to give his daughter's side of the story, he refused to be quoted. But he made it clear that he was furious with Jacque for pointing the finger at his daughter, saying that she had nothing to do with the murder.

Although Amanda was not named in the original newspaper account, her name had been revealed to the public on the first day of the sentencing hearing, and the spectators craned their necks to get a good look at the girl whom Melinda had killed for.

Amanda came to court in baggy black pants, a button-down purple shirt, and tennis shoes. With her flat chest and her brown hair cut short, she looked like a young boy. She gave a quick sideways glance at Melinda and slipped into the witness chair. Her left tennis shoe tapped up and down as she quietly and nervously answered questions about her relationship with Melinda, admitting in little more than a whisper that she and Melinda had been lesbian lovers. Townsend had mentioned Melinda's sexual relationship with Amanda during his opening statement, so it came as no surprise to the packed courtroom. But the spectators strained to hear more.

Townsend repeatedly had to rephrase questions for Amanda because she was not able to understand what he meant when he used words such as "persist," "subsequent," and "discontent." He would apologize for "talking like a lawyer" and simplify it for the none-too-bright youngster. Amanda squirmed in her chair and cried as she described the scene at Melinda's house on the afternoon following Shanda's murder. Once again she claimed that Laurie had bragged about killing Shanda.

It was obvious that Amanda was trying her best not to hurt Melinda, but Townsend pressed her by asking, "Did you ever hear Melinda say she wanted to kill Shanda?"

Amanda knew that police had Melinda's letters, so she answered the best she could for her former lover: "I heard her say she wished she was dead, but I don't think she meant it."

Amanda's appearance had been anticlimactic. The public had been anticipating some fashion of femme fatale, but what they saw was simply a bumbling, frightened little girl.

If Crystal Wathen was nervous she didn't show it as she breezed into the courtroom, flashing a friendly smile at Melinda as she walked by the defense table. The pretty blonde wore jeans and a T-shirt that had a picture of dead rock idol Jim Morrison on the back. Playing with the ends of her long hair, she casually described the scene that took place in Laurie's car the afternoon following the murder.

"Tell the judge what Laurie Tackett did with the tire tool," Hammerle said.

"She was tapping it against the dash," Crystal said. "She was feeling on it and she said she could remember what it felt like when she was hitting Shanda in her head. She said it was taking hunks out of her head. She stuck it in my face and told me to smell it."

Hammerle waited a few seconds to let the grisly image sink in and then, raising his voice to make sure that everyone in the courtroom heard, he asked, "Isn't it a fact that Laurie Tackett told you that she found a piece of Shanda's head in the trunk and threw it out in the yard for the dog to eat?"

There were gasps in the courtroom as Crystal answered coolly, "Yes, she did."

Kary Pope and a small entourage of her friends had spent the week camping out in the hallway outside the courtroom.

They seemed to take enjoyment out of raising the eyebrows of the conservative Madison residents who came to the courthouse to watch the hearing. Kary's friends—all girls, except for the Leatherbury brothers, Larry and Terry—spent much of their time hanging on each other and exchanging kisses.

Larry Leatherbury in particular seemed to revel in his newfound notoriety as the friend of killers. He once spied a television crew stationed outside a courthouse exit, so he ran up to Kary and announced in an excited voice that he was going down the steps to be interviewed.

Kary was no less obtrusive. With her short-cut reddish-brown hair, her baggy jeans, and flannel shirt, she walked up and down the hallways slumping her shoulders back and forth with the cocky assurance of a streetwise rapper.

On Tuesday, the second day of the hearing, Kary hung around a water cooler by the back entrance of the courtroom, waiting for a chance to talk to Melinda. During a recess, while Melinda sat in a chair in a foyer near the water cooler, Kary persuaded a guard to let her have a moment with Melinda. Kary knelt at Melinda's side and gave her friend a long hug. She whispered something in Melinda's ear and Melinda laughed.

As this went on, Shanda's mother, Jacque, stood at one end of the hallway and stared at Kary with disgust.

"I want you to know," she told a reporter, "that none of these kids were friends of Shanda. She didn't know any of them other than Melinda and Amanda. Those aren't the type of kids she associated with. What I want to know is where are their parents. What kind of parents wouldn't come to court with their children if their children had to testify at something like this?"

Kary's braggadocio vanished once she stepped into the courtroom and was outside the sight of her friends. She kept her head down as she passed Melinda's table and didn't raise it again until Townsend started asking about the times she'd heard Melinda threaten to kill Shanda.

"How often did she discuss these killing aspects?" he asked.

Kary was reluctant to answer, until Townsend showed her a transcript of the statement she had given Steve Henry. Then he repeated the question.

Kary swallowed and answered, "About every day."

When Melinda heard those words she shook her head and began to cry. Kary hung her head again, ashamed of what she was being forced to do. She breathed a sign of relief when Bob Hammerle began his cross-examination and shifted the focus to Laurie. Kary was still seething from the smart-ass letter Laurie's "wife" had sent her. Laurie had played with her emotions. If it came down to Melinda or Laurie, there was no question: Melinda was the one she really cared for. As Hammerle asked questions about Laurie's dark personality, Kary seemed more than willing to assassinate the character of her former friend. She told how Laurie once offered to kill her grandmother and how she said it would be fun to get high and burn someone alive. She told of Laurie's channeling, her obsession with vampires and witchcraft, and her penchant for drinking her own blood.

Townsend knew there was a risk in putting Kary on the stand and he'd seen his worst fears come true. Hammerle had cleverly turned the state's witness into a witness for the defense. Kary's most damaging statements had been aimed at Laurie, not Melinda. Now he had to go on the attack himself. He jumped out of his seat and swaggered over to the witness for re-cross-examination.

"Miss Pope, what did you say to Melinda when you gave her that long embrace out at the water cooler?"

"I told her I loved her and she'd always have a place in my heart no matter what happens with this."

"Didn't you tell her something else?" Townsend demanded.

Kary looked him in the eye. "I told her that I hope Laurie fries for this."

Townsend and Melinda's attorneys had been trading snide remarks since the hearing began, but it came to a head this time when Hammerle objected to the way Townsend had been hovering over Kary.

"I object to the prosecutor standing up in front of her with his hands on his hips and to the intimidation and argumentative nature of this approach," Hammerle said.

Townsend responded sharply: "If Mr. Hammerle will tell me how he wishes me to position myself while we await this witness's answer I will gladly accommodate him." His last five words were emphasized as if they were an invitation to an alley fight. A tingle of excitement filled the courtroom as Townsend faced off with Hammerle and said with the pugnaciousness of a schoolboy daring a rival to cross a line in the dirt, "I find nothing wrong with the way I'm standing, Mr. Hammerle."

Judge Todd had seen enough of these shenanigans and ordered both counsels to direct their comments to the bench. Then he turned to the witness and asked, "Do you remember his question?"

"Let's see," Kary began. "Oh yeah. I know Melinda pled guilty to murder, but I think that Laurie had control of her mind. I think Laurie was behind her and pushed her because I've been where Melinda was with her."

Townsend struck the same pose that Hammerle had objected to earlier and forcefully asked, "So you're saying it was Laurie who wanted Shanda Sharer dead, right?"

"It didn't matter who it was," Kary replied.

"Well, who was it who died? Who told you she wanted Shanda Sharer dead?"

Kary answered meekly, "Melinda did."

The state's next witness was no stranger to a courtroom. Tracy Lynn Plaskett, twenty-one, had a long history of run-ins with the law. She had been arrested in Louisiana in 1989 for suspicion of forgery, although the charges were eventually dropped. She was arrested again for forgery in Indiana in 1989 and then in Georgia in 1991 for power-of-attorney revocation. After serving a year for the Indiana forgery charges, Plaskett had recently been released from jail.

Plaskett, a slim, attractive brunette, walked into the courtroom with her head held high and a serious look of importance on her face. In short order, she told how she had spent several months in the Clark County jail with Melinda Loveless.

"What did Melinda have to say about the events that led up to her arrest?" Townsend asked.

"She would be laughing about it." Plaskett looked directly at Melinda as she said this, but Melinda turned her head, not meeting the stare. "Melinda said it started over her boyfriend, whose name was Justin. But we got suspicious when she never got any letters from Justin. They were all from Amanda. Eventually she told us that she goes both ways. She told us about her sexual encounters with people."

Plaskett said that Melinda "would literally burst out laughing when she told us about how Shanda was killed."

Hammerle rose from his chair and circled the courtroom in front of Plaskett like a hawk eying his next meal. He'd made mincemeat of Plaskett's kind before. Nothing is more pleasurable to a criminal attorney than to have a convicted criminal on the witness stand. You can bring up their past crimes, you can probe into what kind of deal they got to testify, you can destroy their credibility with a few choice questions.

With a clipped, terse delivery that showed his disregard

for the witness, Hammerle quickly established that Plaskett had used various aliases, including her own daughter's name, on bogus checks.

In relentless fashion Hammerle hammered home the details of Plaskett's extensive criminal record. At various times Townsend and Don Currie, the deputy prosecutor, shouted objections—so often, in fact, that Hammerle complained to Judge Todd.

"Could we have one prosecutor at a time responding to me, or is that impossible?" Hammerle asked.

For once, however, Judge Todd seemed to be enjoying the furious exchanges. "Everybody's been double-teaming each other now and then," he said. "I will allow that. It's a tag team."

Hammerle began harping once again on Plaskett's soiled record when the interrogation took an unexpected turn.

"My criminal record has nothing to do with this case," Plaskett stated with a sudden show of feistiness. "I spent my time. I paid my dues in jail. I've paid my debt to society and I don't have to be subjected to this."

Hammerle retorted, "Why were you put in lockdown in the Clark County jail for thirty days?"

"For fighting," Plaskett answered back sharply. "She was a prostitute."

"What were you fighting about?"

"Her mouth. I don't like to be bullied around. If somebody bullies me, I will bully back."

"I don't doubt that one bit," Hammerle said derisively.

Plaskett wasn't through. "I will not stand for somebody pushing me around. And this was a big girl. She was five-eleven and three hundred pounds."

Hammerle smirked. "Well, did you beat her up pretty good?"

"No."

Hammerle pointed at Melinda. "She was bigger than that little girl, wasn't she?"

"She was bigger than both of us put together."

The spectators chuckled at the last remark. Plaskett's spunkiness had won them over.

Hammerle seemed to be struggling to retain control. "Let me ask you this: Did you plead guilty to twenty-six counts of forgery?"

"Yes, I did. I've answered that question three times. I mean, it's not like I stole a checkbook and wrote twenty thousand checks. My husband was in the service and restricted to the barracks, for God's sake. We were having marital problems. I was told to pay the bills, so I wrote some bad checks. I got caught and like a stupid idiot I pled guilty."

The spectators giggled again.

Off balance but determined to end on a high note, Hammerle questioned Plaskett about what kind of deal she got in order to testify: "Did you decide to come forward because you suddenly got a revelation to become a good citizen? You were seeking some deal, weren't you?"

"No, I did not. I'm a parent. If you're a parent, you tell me you couldn't go forward and tell what somebody told you on something like this. It's a disgusting crime."

Hammerle couldn't resist a final remark: "I'm a parent, but I don't have three prior felony convictions, ma'am."

Plaskett snapped back, "My prior convictions have nothing to do with murder either."

Townsend could see that Hammerle was still smarting from his skirmish with Plaskett, so he decided to rub salt in the wound when he questioned the witness.

"Ms. Plaskett, did Mr. Hammerle ever talk to you before today?"

"Yes, he did."

"What did he tell you about your testimony?"

"He said that my testimony was not crucial."

Hammerle could see that Townsend was about to accuse him once again of tampering with one of the state's witnesses. He shouted an objection: "I want a hearing on this. What are we going into now? I interviewed her in the hallway." Hammerle pointed at the witness as he sneered, "This little felonious person makes an allegation, and I want a hearing off the record."

Judge Todd seemed puzzled by the outburst. "What is it she said?"

Townsend filled him in. "She said that Mr. Hammerle talked to her about her testimony and told her that her testimony didn't amount to anything and that it wouldn't hurt Melinda Loveless."

"And that was in the hall here?" Todd asked.

"That's absolutely untrue," Hammerle responded. "I interviewed her to find out what she was going to say."

Townsend said, "This is the second lie by Mr. Hammerle. It's quite a coincidence, I would say."

For the second time in two days, Townsend and Hammerle were at one another's throats, and Judge Todd had seen enough. He ordered them both to his chambers and administered a tongue-lashing. He made it clear to Hammerle that he would not stand for any interviews outside the courtroom that could possibly be construed as tampering with a witness. Todd then chastised Townsend for his poor courtroom manners.

"Now let's get out there and conduct ourselves like professionals," said Todd, ever the peacemaker.

Russ Johnson would later say of Todd, "The man had the disposition of a saint to put up with everything that happened in that courtroom."

The four days of the hearing had taken their toll on Steve Sharer. Every morning he and Sharon and other members of their family would make the forty-five-minute drive from Jeffersonville to Madison, traveling the same route that Melinda and the others had taken the night they abducted Shanda.

Each day he'd sit in the front row with his family, listening to the horrors inflicted on his daughter. During court recesses he'd slip off into the stairwell to smoke a cigarette and would do his best to join in the conversation when someone brought up college basketball or some other topic.

Once, when a group of spectators were complaining about the persnickety old radiator in the courtroom, Steve, a heating and cooling technician, pulled the court bailiff aside and gave him some tips on how to correct the problem. During these moments, Steve's buoyant nature would surface and an easy smile would cross his lips. But the sadness never left his eyes, and it would grow deeper every day.

"I don't know how I'm hanging on," he said one day while waiting for court to reconvene. "I really don't. I sit in there and it's like a nightmare that will never end. Every day it gets worse."

Now, sitting in the witness chair, Steve was called upon to tell the court about Shanda's last night at home and the heartwrenching experience of discovering her gone the next morning. With the effort to restrain his emotions obvious, Steve recalled the events of that night and the following day. When that was done, Townsend asked Steve to tell the court about his relationship with Shanda and what her loss meant to him.

Steve closed his eyes tightly for a few seconds and swallowed hard. Then he said, "I feel a great deep hole in my chest. My heart sags sorrowfully. What happened to my daughter goes a lot deeper than what they have done to her. They have just totally ruined our family with the loss of Shanda. It's very hard to go to work when you see the school buses and the little children getting on them. It just rips through me."

Steve began to weep. "Give me a minute here," he said in a choked voice. "I guess my mother said it best. Every morning when she gets up she says, 'Well, I'm just one day closer to Shanda.' I say, 'That's right, Mom, because we know where Shanda is now. Nobody can hurt her and maybe one day we'll get there.'"

Steve's shoulders slumped forward and he wiped the tears from his eyes. With what seemed like great effort, he sluggishly lifted himself from the witness chair and returned to his seat.

Sharon Sharer gave her husband a hug as she passed him on the way to the witness chair, where she talked about her love for Shanda. She ended her emotional testimony by asking Judge Todd to give Melinda the maximum sentence.

When Melinda heard those words she lowered her head to the table and let out a shivering scream. Her long wavy hair concealed her face, but everyone in the packed courtroom could hear her moaning and blubbering. Melinda's attorneys patted her on the back, but she continued to cry softly with her face to the table as Shanda's half-sister, Paije, got up to testify.

Paije was in her seventh month of pregnancy, and the long days in court had caused her physical discomfort. Earlier in the week, a deputy had found her a soft chair and placed it at the end of the front-row bench, placing her closer to Melinda than anyone else in her family. Occasionally during the hearing, Paije would turn to Melinda and stare for long minutes at the girl who had taken her little sister's life. Now as she walked to the witness chair, Paije stared again, and as if by cue Melinda lifted her head at that exact moment. Their eyes met, and Melinda turned eyes away, just as she had time and time before when she had found Paije studying her.

Paije began by looking directly at Melinda, her eyes showing her contempt. "They sit and cry, but they didn't cry when they were doing it to her. Why should they cry now? Because they're in trouble. My sister doesn't have a chance to cry. She didn't have a chance at anything. She didn't have a choice but to die."

As soon as Paije was through, Melinda began to wail again. Long, wild screams shook her body and rocked the table on which she rested her head.

If it was an act, as Shanda's mother had suggested after an earlier outburst, it was a convincing one. Perhaps Melinda was feeling genuine remorse for what she had done to Shanda but, more probably, what she was experiencing was the realization that she was going to pay for her crime. The testimony against her had been damaging, and the hatred that Shanda's family felt toward her was palpable. Whatever she might have seemed to herself, however she might have rationalized Shanda's murder, it was suddenly clear to Melinda that everyone else in the courtroom—with the possible exception of her family—now saw her as a murderer.

Melinda was still moaning when Russell Johnson asked Judge Todd for a recess. After Todd nodded his approval, Johnson slipped an arm around Melinda and hoisted her to her feet. Then, with Johnson and Hammerle holding onto her arms, the quivering young murderess was escorted from the courtroom.

After a twenty-minute recess everyone was back in their seats. Melinda's face was ashen and haggard, her eyes deep-set and red. Townsend had rested his case, and it was now the defense's turn.

Larry Leatherbury flashed a self-confident grin as he strode into the courtroom. The day before he had paraded around the courthouse wearing a pair of black lace gloves with the fingers cut out. The garb he'd chosen for his courtroom appearance was no less showy. He wore black boots, black jeans, and a black T-shirt that was decorated with hundreds of safety pins. He waved at Melinda as he walked past her to the witness chair. Melinda just stared back blankly.

Russell Johnson had met with Leatherbury a month earlier to go over his testimony.

"I never met a cockier young man in my life," Johnson would say later. "He marched into my office, perched his feet up on my desk, and related how thrilled he was to be a witness in a murder trial."

Knowing how volatile Leatherbury could be, Johnson started slowly by asking him about his relationship with Laurie Tackett. Leatherbury related that he'd been friends with Laurie for five or six years and that he'd visited her in prison several times since her arrest.

"Okay," Johnson said, "now I want to direct you to some statements Laurie made to you. Has Laurie Tackett ever told you that she would like to kill someone?"

"On several occasions," Leatherbury answered nonchalantly. "Oh, I'd say about ten or twenty."

Judge Todd studied the witness as if he were a specimen under glass. He wasn't quite sure what to make of the young man's cavalier attitude. Was he telling the truth or just boasting?

"Has she talked to you about a dream that you two shared in common?" Johnson continued.

"Yes, she has spoken about that dream."

"And what was that dream?"

"It consisted of charred, mutilated bodies of young babies burned hanging from trees."

Over the course of the week, the spectators had become hardened by what they'd heard from the witness stand, and they were no longer easily shocked. But the image of charred babies stirred some gasps and murmurs. None of this was lost on Leatherbury, who was getting a kick out of shocking his audience. In short order, he reported that Laurie didn't believe in God and that he'd observed her drinking her own blood.

"Have you ever been involved with her doing artwork that would cause her to use blood?"

"Yes."

"Describe that to the court."

"Well, it was a trio, I'd say, a trio effort," Leatherbury said, sounding pleased that he could elaborate on his artwork. "There was me, Danielle, and Laurie. We cut ourselves. It was for release of stress, and then we got a towel and we dabbed the blood all over it and deemed it blood art and signed it."

"While in the women's prison, did Laurie Tackett discuss the death of Shanda Sharer?" Johnson asked.

"She said that she was kind of glad she did it and she said that it was exhilarating. She said she remembered the feeling of the skull giving way to the tire iron."

"Did Laurie Tackett talk to you about any fascinations that she had?"

"She did speak of the fascination of wanting to burn someone."

Johnson was satisfied. "That's all I have."

Townsend smiled benignly as he approached the witness. "Mr. Leatherbury, have you and I met before?"

"Yes, we have, Mr. Townsend."

"Were you sitting over there?" Townsend pointed toward the defense table, and Leatherbury nodded in acknowledgment. "Would you remind His Honor why it was that you were sitting over there?"

Johnson sprung to his feet. "I object to this unless a foundation is laid. I assume he's trying to impeach this witness, but I haven't been given any criminal history of this witness."

Judge Todd's curiosity had been tweaked. He allowed Townsend to continue.

"Were you not in this courtroom last year?"

"I would not go as far as to say it was last year," Leatherbury said with an air of superiority. "More than a year ago."

"Tell the court about your altercation at school with another student."

Leatherbury seemed to be growing bored with the whole scene. In a haughty tone he said, "Being that I wasn't really in the norm at school . . ."

"What do you mean by that?" Townsend interrupted.

"Well, I was so outstandingly different in every aspect. I had been ridiculed for many years for being so different. Ridiculed."

Johnson slumped back in his chair. His fears about calling Leatherbury as a witness were being realized. The kid was just too damn cocky for his own good.

"And so," Leatherbury continued, "I went to school and I intended to intimidate someone."

"How did you intend to do that?"

"I intended to intimidate them with a knife." Leatherbury was coolly confident and reveling in his ability to shock others. "I intended to intimidate the person by applying an element of fear."

"And how did you apply an element of fear, Mr. Leatherbury?"

"With a blade," Leatherbury explained. "I must stress that it was an accidental injury to the person."

"Where was the blade when the injury occurred?"

Leatherbury considered the question for a long time, rubbing his chin in the process. "I would say it was to the left side of the neck."

Through his own admissions, Leatherbury had almost literally cut his own throat as a witness against Laurie. Even in her worst moments on the stand, Laurie had not seemed as casually cruel as her former friend. With no more questions to answer, Leatherbury, looking a bit disappointed that the fun was over, sauntered past Melinda, waving to her as he exited.

On the fifth day of the hearing, Melinda's attorneys put their attacks on Laurie on hold and focused on another villain: Melinda's father, Larry Loveless.

Johnson had tried to get Larry Loveless to testify on his daughter's behalf, but Loveless, who now lived in Florida, did not respond to Johnson's inquiries. His absence made him fair game, and Melinda's sisters, Michelle and Melissa, and cousins Teddy Lynn Barber and Eddie Rager didn't hold back, repeating their tales of sexual abuse at the hands of Melinda's father.

Barber's testimony was the most explicit. She related an incident in which Larry Loveless allegedly raped Barber and his three daughters.

"There was one time when he took me and the three girls into the garage and stripped us from our night clothes and laid us on the concrete floor and used some type of chain to bind us together," Barber testified. "He worked his way down the line. We were all close together. Melinda was three or four."

Townsend and his chief deputy, Don Currie, raised some questions about the validity of the tales of abuse, particularly those of Barber and Rager. Rager testified that she told her mother about the sexual abuse when she was thirteen and her sister, Barber, was ten. If that was true, why had their mother allowed Barber to babysit at the Loveless home for another six years?

Townsend also pointed out that neither of the Loveless sisters had confirmed Barber's claim that they were raped in the garage.

Russ Johnson's next witness was Dr. Richard Lawlor, the first of two clinical psychologists who had been hired to testify on Melinda's behalf.

Lawlor said that Melinda suffered from, among other things, a borderline personality disorder, a condition characterized by sudden mood swings, an inability to take the middle ground on any issue, and a lack of self-esteem.

"Borderlines totally love or totally hate," Lawlor said. "They fail to see aspects of gray. Everything is black or white. You never know if you're going to meet the happy or the depressed one. One minute they can tell you they love you, the next they are spewing venom and hatred. They yell, they scream, but to be physically violent against another person is not typical."

Even though Melinda denied that her father sexually molested her, Lawlor said, "Our feeling is that something bad did happen and it was blocked out. I think her environment was abusive to the extreme. There were no clear memories of molestation, but there were memories of something that occurred at an early age that involved being bathed by her father. There are indications that Larry Loveless used Melinda to make his wife jealous. There was a sexualization of the relationship between her and her father, and when she desired a relationship with another girl, it was with a girl who she felt resembled her father."

Under cross-examination by Deputy Prosecutor Don Currie, Lawlor said that Melinda was someone who was constantly aware of her seductiveness.

"One of the hallmarks of the borderline is sexual provocativeness," Lawlor said. "They send out messages that they themselves aren't even aware of that can entice people. She sits in ways that at times are provocative. She tends to lean forward in ways that move into personal distance and space. She has a way of looking at you. Even in a jail uniform there was a cleavage so that when she would lean forward one could see that. I think that there's many things like that that she displayed that I think is second nature with the way she interacts."

With Currie pressing him, Lawlor acknowledged that Melinda was someone who always wanted her way. "She is very narcissistic, very egocentric," Lawlor said.

"Is rage a common factor when she doesn't get her way?" Currie asked.

"She will become angry, yes," Lawlor said.

The defense's final witness, Dr. Elgan L. Baker, concurred with Lawlor's diagnosis and said that Melinda functioned emotionally as a three- or four-year-old rather than a teenager.

After a lengthy discussion about Melinda's mental state, Johnson asked Baker, who had also studied psychological reports on Laurie Tackett, to compare the two.

Baker said the reports from Laurie's psychologists concluded that Laurie was a sociopath, and "that impression of her as a psychopath is consistent with my own view. I see her as an individual who is probably of above-average intelligence, somewhat oppositional and easily prone to violence. I would say that she is an antisocial personality."

As far as comparing Melinda and Laurie, "I wouldn't say one was sicker than the other," Baker said. "I think they both have significant emotional problems, but I think Melinda's largely have to do with what's going on inside her in terms of her ability to think and deal with her emotions and depression. Miss Tackett's have more to do with her involvement in the world, her impulsivity, her acting out, her capacity for violence."

Johnson asked, "In your professional opinion, do you consider Melinda Loveless a violent person?"

"Absolutely not."

"What about Laurie Tackett?"

"I think the risk of violence with her is very high."

After those last two answers, Townsend was rocking back and forth in his chair, eagerly awaiting his chance at Baker. He would say later that he considered the hired psychologists as nothing more than "high-priced whores. Pay them enough and they'll give you anything you want."

"Dr. Baker," he asked sternly, "do you consider murder a violent act?"

"Yes, I do."

Reminding Baker that Melinda had pleaded guilty to murder, Townsend asked what conclusions he would draw about her capacity for violent acts.

"Clearly, she has been capable of that behavior in the past."

"Now, Doctor," Townsend said smugly. "How many times, Doctor, have you seen and talked to Melinda Loveless?"

"I met with her on one occasion."

"For how long?"

"About an hour."

Townsend paused a few seconds to let Baker's answer linger.

"Doctor, have you had the opportunity to interview Laurie Tackett?

"No, I have not met her."

With a satisfied smile, Townsend dismissed the witness.

In Indiana murder cases, the courts appoint one member of the victim's family to serve as the victim's representative and allow them to speak after all the evidence has been presented.

Jacque Vaught walked slowly toward the judge's bench, her lips held tight, her face hardened with determination. She knew this was her only opportunity to affect the future of the girl who'd masterminded her daughter's murder.

She began by showing Judge Todd the two large shadow boxes containing Shanda's mementos, then asked the court to view a videotape of photographs and film of Shanda. Melinda whimpered and moaned as pictures of Shanda were shown. The screen was turned away from the spectators, but they listened intently as Jacque described scenes from Shanda's short life.

"This is her as a baby. Her first Christmas. This is her and her grandmother. She was always with her grandmother because she spoiled her rotten. This is her grandmother serving her breakfast in bed. Shanda was never camera shy." Jacque smiled faintly. "As you can see, she enjoyed life."

Jacque asked the judge to listen to Shanda's laughter. "One thing Sharon always says is how much she misses Shanda's laughter. She laughed all the time. Her laughter was something we cherished." Jacque turned to Melinda. "She took that away from us."

The confrontation was too much for Melinda. She began crying and moaned loudly, "Oh God." Attorney Mike Walro threw an arm around her shoulder and settled her down again.

Jacque ignored the outburst. "Although Steve and I are

divorced, Shanda lived in a very structured environment, and she was very loved by myself, her father, and other family members. Shanda was very compassionate and she could not stand to see anyone hurt. If Shanda had been in the position these girls were the night that they murdered her, and if they were trying to harm someone, I know my daughter would have done something to save the child from harm. I don't think there's anything worse than burying your own child. All my life I loved my mother so much that I used to pray that I would die before her because I couldn't stand to lose her. Now I know that was a selfish prayer because I know that burying your own daughter is not a natural thing to go through."

At Shanda's funeral, Jacque said, her family was unable to "properly say goodbye" because the casket was closed. "She was so mutilated you couldn't tell she was a human being. She had no face. We couldn't put clothes on her, so we covered her with a blanket of roses."

Directing a steely gaze at Melinda, Jacque said, "I want you to think of the person you love the most and I want you to imagine that person being burned and mutilated. Maybe then you could feel a small portion of the pain our family feels. The proper punishment for Melinda would be to place her in a cell with pictures of Shanda's burned body and force her to continuously listen to a tape of my daughter screaming like she did that night. I know the law will only allow sixty years. To give anything less would be an atrocity equal to my daughter's death. Anyone capable of such a horrendous crime should not be allowed on our streets."

Allowing herself to cry for the first time, Jacque ended her testimony by turning to Melinda and saying, "I hope and pray you remember these words for the rest of your life. May you rot in hell."

As soon as Jacque had finished her statement, the courtroom erupted into applause. Judge Todd banged his gavel. "Quiet. Quiet," he shouted. Melinda dropped her head to the table and wept. Jacque stumbled back toward her family in the front row, seemingly exhausted after having held her emotions in check for so long. She hugged her mother and said, "I love you, Mom," then received hugs and kisses from other family members as she made her way to her seat alongside Doug Vaught, Steve, and Sharon.

After a minute or so of silence, Russ Johnson stood up and announced that Melinda had a statement to make to Shanda's family.

Standing on trembling legs, Melinda looked directly at Jacque and Steve and the other members of Shanda's family, then said in a choked voice, "I know I can't take away your pain and I can't bring Shanda back, but I do feel your pain.

"I'm so sorry. If I could trade places with Shanda I would. I'm so sorry." Crying and moaning, Melinda swooned into the arms of defense attorneys Walro and Johnson.

Throughout the hearing, Steve Sharer couldn't shake the feeling that he knew the man who sat next to Melinda's mother each day in court: Mike Donahue, Melinda's stepfather.

Finally it came to him: Donahue worked for a parts store that Steve frequented. The next time they passed each other in the courthouse stairwell, Steve pulled him aside. Donahue quickly acknowledged that he had also recognized Steve.

"He told me that he didn't know what to say to me," Steve recalled. "He said he'd married Melinda's mother a year or so earlier and felt like he was living a nightmare. I kind of felt sorry for the poor guy."

Townsend began his closing statement by sarcastically complimenting Melinda's attorneys for diverting the blame away from their client. "They would have you think that Larry Loveless is responsible for this murder," he said. "And Shanda did not die because Laurie Tackett hated her or because Laurie Tackett was jealous of her. She died because Melinda Loveless wanted her dead. Shanda lived a short life, but in one sense it was very long indeed. Can anyone doubt that the hours between eleven o'clock on the night of January 10, 1992, and nine o'clock on the morning of January 11 took an eternity to pass for Shanda Sharer? The hours locked in the trunk punctuated only by brief episodes of being beaten and tortured and sodomized must have gone on forever for her. But that night did finally end for Shanda Renee Sharer. It ended in a flash of fire and smoke, which lasted only for a few minutes of your time and my time, of our time. But how long did that flash of fire and smoke last for Shanda? Surely it was another eternity before her life was choked out by the smoke and fire of her burning body. Forever. That's how long that moment lasted for Shanda Sharer. Forever.

"The heinousness of the crime speaks for itself. For eight hours, unspeakable acts of torture were performed on a young girl. Melinda participated willingly and even gleefully. She could not contain her joy when Shanda was burned. Laughter burst out of her mouth and she said the words, 'I'm glad she's dead.'"

In Melinda's defense, Russ Johnson argued that she should only get forty years, the standard sentence for murder by arson, since it was never proven that she did more than hit Shanda with her fist and knee and pour gasoline on her already-burning body.

Johnson said the court shouldn't believe Laurie's version of the events. "I find Laurie Tackett totally unbelievable and I think she is a young woman who has immense dangerous propensities. She came in here and admitted that she lied. Did she lie about some minor thing? No. She lied about who poured the gas on this poor little girl. The prosecutor wants us to believe the testimony of Laurie Tackett. That is probably the most absurd thing I've seen."

Johnson pointed to his client. "The truthful intent of this girl when the evening started was to commit a battery. It was to fight and intimidate this girl. There's no question about that, but I do not believe there was any intent to murder. This crime would not have occurred without the dominating influence of a sociopath named Laurie Tackett."

At the conclusion of Johnson's closing argument, Judge Todd announced that he would wait until after Laurie Tackett's sentencing hearing, which would begin December 28, to pronounce both girls' sentences.

* * *

LITTLE LOST ANGEL

In a few days, southern Indiana would be treated to its first white Christmas in seven years, but as Shanda's relatives made their way out of the courthouse, they were greeted only by a cold rain.

"This should be the happiest time of the year for a family," Jacque said, getting into her car. "But we have nothing but sadness."

19

There was no jury box in Judge Todd's court. The fourteen juror chairs—two reserved for jury alternates—sat facing the judge's bench directly in front of a three-foot-high wooden partition that separated the spectators from the judge, attorney, and defendants.

From this vantage point, Wil Goering watched the Melinda Loveless hearing. He kept a legal notebook on his lap and a pen in his hand, ready to jot down observations that might better his chances of pleading Laurie Tackett's case.

As he watched Melinda's attorneys work their objections against Guy Townsend, Goering had to work hard to suppress a smile. "They're stealing my act," he thought.

Goering's disdain for Townsend knew no bounds. The two had butted heads during Townsend's campaign for office three years earlier, and the only thing they had in common now was their animosity toward each other.

To an unbiased observer it seemed as though Townsend had done an adequate and at times admirable job of presenting the state's case against Melinda Loveless. But Goering didn't see it that way. He felt that Townsend had let

Melinda off easy in order to build the case against Laurie. Had he been in Townsend's shoes, Goering said later, he would never have allowed Russell Johnson to get in so much testimony about Laurie's occult practices and her fascination with death.

"Townsend completely failed to counter the Melinda strategy of blaming Laurie," Goering said. "Time and time again when Melinda's attorneys would object and be overruled, Townsend would change directions completely. They were extremely successful in diverting his attention, and I know Melinda's attorneys made a conscious effort to do that."

Goering felt that Townsend had bungled the Toni Lawrence plea bargain—"He sold the farm to get her to testify"—and that he'd given Melinda and Laurie a better plea arrangement than they could ever have wished for.

"In the end it was probably in his best interest because I'm not sure he would have tried the case without a fundamental mistake that could get it reversed," Goering said. "The cases against Melinda and Laurie were almost prosecutor-proof because Steve Henry had done such a thorough job."

Goering went into Laurie's hearing with high hopes, therefore. Although the evidence was stacked against his client, he was confident that on his worst day he could dance circles around Townsend in a courtroom.

He knew that his worst handicap was Laurie herself.

To Goering's way of thinking, Melinda had pulled off a masterful acting job. She had the look of innocence down pat and had broken down into tears at all the right times. His client, however, had long lost contact with any semblance of innocence. There were no little-girl qualities left in Laurie. She'd been hardened by life, and its hardness was etched in her face and in her movements.

A couple of weeks before Melinda's hearing, Laurie gave an interview to a Cincinnati television station. It was the first and last interview any of the girls would give the press. Laurie had styled her short hair and wore a modest, flower-print dress. But her attempt at evoking earnestness and honesty didn't play particularly well. She claimed unconvincingly that Shanda had hugged her and begged her to stop Melinda.

"She asked me not to let Melinda do it," Laurie said, staring sadly into the camera. "She was crying. There wasn't anything I could do."

During this TV appearance, Laurie blamed everything on Melinda, saying, "She wanted to teach Shanda a lesson. I didn't think she was going to go that far."

Bad reviews of her performance must have gotten back to her, because it would be one of Laurie's last attempts to portray herself with little-girl innocence. Despite Goering's efforts to coach Laurie on how to carry herself in court, she seemed content in her sullenness and was reluctant to put on any airs in her subsequent court appearances.

"She is what she is," Goering said later. "That blank look of hers is her true nature. She was someone who was incapable of feeling emotional pain. She'd shut that off years ago. She was a difficult person to establish a repartee with. She had many psychological problems and had a hard time trusting anybody."

Although Laurie never opened up enough to let Goering get close to her, there were times when he could sense that she had tied all her hopes to him.

"She was looking for a white knight to rescue her," Goering said. "I believe she thought that was me."

"White knight" might be the last phrase Guy Townsend would ever use to describe Goering. The prosecutor had never forgiven Goering for what he believed was underhanded tactics during the election campaign, and they'd lived an uneasy co-existence in the courthouse ever since. But while Goering thought little of Townsend's courtroom ability, that was the one venue in which Townsend afforded Goering respect.

"For whatever else I think about Wil Goering, I will concede that he knows his way around a courtroom," Townsend said prior to the hearing.

And that as much as anything kept Townsend working at a fevered pitch during the Christmas break. He came to court on the crisp Monday morning of December 28, his arms loaded with law books, his mind tired but determined, his purpose set: sixty years for Laurie Tackett, nothing less.

The strategy of Goering and his co-counsels, Ellen O'Connor and Robert Barlow, differed little from that of Melinda's attorneys. They would try to shift as much of the blame as possible from their client and build sympathy for her. That meant portraying Melinda as the ringleader and Laurie as simply an obliging accomplice.

Like Melinda's attorneys, Laurie's had a lot to work with. She too had grown up in an abusive home. The difference was that the ogre of Melinda's childhood, Larry Loveless, was an easy target. He wasn't around to defend himself against charges of sexual molestation and violence. The problem facing Laurie's attorneys was how far they could go in destroying the reputation of Laurie's mother, Peggy Tackett.

Peggy Tackett had refused to have anything to do with her daughter after her arrest, not once visiting Laurie in the state prison. Putting her on the stand was out of the question, since Laurie's defense hinged on making her mother look as bad as possible. Goering had no assurances that Laurie's father or brother would substantiate Laurie's attacks on her mother, so they too were ruled out as witnesses. That left Laurie herself.

"For what we wanted to do, we had to have Laurie testify in her own behalf," Goering said.

As far as other witnesses, the pickings were slim. Goering struggled to find any classmates who had anything favorable to say about Laurie. After interviewing her teachers, he decided that none of them had anything to offer in her defense. Defense counsel Ellen O'Connor, an Indianapolis attorney with death-penalty experience, brought that out in her opening remarks at Laurie's hearing.

"When Laurie told us that none of her teachers ever liked her we didn't think that could be true," O'Connor said. "But we couldn't find one of her teachers who would testify in her behalf. Laurie was an outsider. People considered her weird. Laurie had a desperate need to be accepted but no one accepted her. Peer pressure is tough under normal circumstances, but Laurie didn't grow up under normal circumstances."

O'Connor said that evidence would show that Laurie had been sexually abused as a child and tormented by her zealously religious mother for not sharing her beliefs.

"Laurie is someone who has been a victim all her life," O'Connor said. "She's not the evil demon that took over" and coerced the others to kill Shanda. "She wasn't the leader. She wasn't the planner. Laurie was a chameleon who would do anything to get people to like her."

O'Connor closed by saying, "Clearly these are not normal children that were involved with this crime. They come from dysfunctional homes. People say that's not an excuse. Well, it's not. It's an explanation."

After Steve Henry and Toni Lawrence gave testimonies nearly identical to those they'd given at Melinda's hearing, Melinda herself was called to the stand. Dressed in a long-sleeved shirt and jeans, Melinda scooted quickly across the courtroom and settled into the witness chair without even a glance at the table where Laurie sat with her lawyers.

For two hours, Melinda calmly answered Townsend's questions about the abduction and murder of Shanda. Melinda's testimony was almost identical in its particulars to the statement she'd given Steve Henry a month earlier.

"Tackett didn't cry the whole night," Melinda said. "I've never seen her cry. She just laughed and said it was so neat and so cool."

O'Connor began her cross-examination by grilling Melinda about her relationship with Amanda Heavrin and her jealousy of Shanda. Melinda handled herself well, and it was only when O'Connor brought out photographs of Shanda's dead body that she succeeded in placing Melinda off balance.

"Do I have to look at these?" Melinda whined.

O'Connor shoved the photos within inches of Melinda's face. "Can you show me the places where you saw Laurie make the slash marks?"

"Oh, God!" Melinda shrieked, covering her eyes with her hands, and gasping for breath.

Jacque Vaught was offended by Melinda's histrionics. She muttered something under her breath and abruptly marched out of the courtroom. Standing in the stairwell, she lit a cigarette, her eyes livid with anger. "They're all liars. Melinda is just better at it than the others. All this crying. I bet she wasn't crying when she killed my Shanda."

Back in the courtroom, Melinda continued to sob softly between answers, stopping every once in a while to dab her teary eyes with a crumpled tissue.

"You're getting me confused," Melinda moaned as O'Connor trapped her in a minor inconsistency about the chronology of events surrounding the murder and repeatedly badgered her. After three hours of questioning, it appeared as if Melinda was finally tiring. She was becoming irritated. Her answers no longer rang with careful sincerity. She was becoming defensive. Through sheer endurance, O'Connor had worn her down.

"Why didn't you tell Laurie's mother what was happening when you had the chance?"

"I never thought of it." Melinda's answer was quick and snippy.

"Why didn't you call the police?"

"I was scared," Melinda said sharply, as if that explained it all. "I was scared of the whole situation. I felt like we were going through a nightmare."

O'Connor closed the distance between them with a few quick steps. She hovered over the shaken witness. "You went to Shanda's house with a knife that night, didn't you?"

"Yes," Melinda answered. "But I just wanted to fight her. It got out of hand."

O'Connor stepped even closer, moving in for the kill. "You took a knife to a fistfight, right?"

Melinda's body shrunk down in the chair and she tugged at the sleeves of her shirt until they covered her hands. She studied the ends of the sleeves for a second, then answered, "Yes, but I just wanted to scare her."

Laurie's lawyers began their defense with Sarah Lee Gaylord, a pleasant-faced young woman in her late teens who had once gone to church with Laurie and her mother.

"At one point a girl got up and started dancing around the church and when some of us looked at the minister kind of strange he said she was just in ecstasy and told us to ignore her," Gaylord said. "There was a laying on of hands of one woman. You could hear some of the ladies wailing and quite a bit of shouting. There was a lot of gibberish and speaking in tongues."

Gaylord, who came across as credible, said that Peggy Tackett was a demanding and oppressive mother. "There were a few times when I saw Laurie's mother really get on her for things that didn't really make any sense to yell or scream about," she said. "One time Laurie had gotten a glass of water and hadn't rinsed out the glass, and her mother started yelling at her that she was a devil's child just because she hadn't rinsed out this glass after she drank out of it."

Laurie's stoicism lifted briefly during Gaylord's testimony, and she gave the friendly witness a smile as she left.

Jan Singer, a middle-aged woman who'd lived down the street from the Tacketts, testified next. Singer recalled that several years earlier, Laurie appeared at her door one afternoon, begging to come inside. Laurie was screaming that her mother had gotten her down on the bed and tried to strangle her. There were marks on Laurie's neck, and Singer had reported the incident to the welfare department. Shortly after that, social workers forbade Peggy Tackett from physically disciplining Laurie.

Singer said Laurie was always different from the other youths in the neighborhood. "She wasn't really cute like the other girls," she said. "She had no self-confidence. She was picked on, and my son was as guilty as the other kids."

After Singer had stepped down, Wil Goering nudged his client gently. "Your honor, the defense calls Laurie Tackett."

Laurie rose slowly from her seat as if in a daze. Her eyes were downcast and her arms hung stiffly by her sides as she walked around the table and took the witness seat facing Judge Todd.

For the first time during Laurie's hearing, her father, George Tackett, was not in the courtroom. Tackett, a short, stocky, balding man with powerful arms, waited in the hallway as Laurie testified. Laurie's attorneys wanted it this way. Her testimony was going to heap blame on her mother, Peggy Tackett, who had not even visited Laurie since her arrest. It would be better if George Tackett didn't hear this.

With Goering encouraging her, Laurie denied threatening Shanda at the Witches' Castle, denied beating Shanda with the tire iron, and denied setting her on fire. She launched another protracted assault against Melinda, then went into great detail about her allegedly abusive home life, claiming that her mother first beat her at the age of nine when she resisted going to church.

"She would hit me and get me down on the floor and strangle me or at least try to."

"How often did this happen?" Goering asked.

"At least four times a week, from the time that I was nine until the welfare office stepped in when I was thirteen."

Goering gently prodded Laurie into talking about the times she'd been sexually molested. Laurie said an older cousin had forced her to touch his penis when she was six and that a man in the neighborhood had accosted her by fondling her breasts and trying to kiss her when she was nine. At the age of sixteen, Laurie said, a boy got her high by making her inhale gasoline fumes and then raped her.

"What's the best thing that ever happened to you?" Goering asked.

"Going to prison."

"What's the worst thing that ever happened to you?"

"Being born." Laurie had delivered the last two responses patly, as if they'd been rehearsed.

"How do you feel about what happened?"

Laurie began to cry. Choking back tears, she said, "I don't feel human. I can't believe it happened. I know how terrible it must be to lose somebody. I'll live with that night for the rest of my life. I think about it every day. It's just . . . I just don't know."

Guy Townsend was unimpressed by Laurie's sudden show

of emotion, but he let her have a moment to compose herself before starting in with his own questions.

"You told Mr. Goering that your mother strangled you four times a week, is that right?"

"Well . . ." Laurie paused as if in deep thought. "She hit me four times a week. The strangling she didn't do as often."

Townsend left his chair and walked to the center of the courtroom. "So she would hit you four times a week and maybe strangle you once a week. Why did she do these things to you? Would you do anything to provoke her actions?"

"I can't remember anything particular except not wanting to go to church," Laurie muttered.

"You resented being told what to do?"

"I resent it now. I hated her for making me go."

Townsend grilled Laurie about her claim of being sexually molested at the age of six. "Didn't you tell one of your prison psychiatrists that you didn't have any recollections of anything before the age of nine?"

Laurie stared grimly at Townsend. "All the recollections I have of my childhood are bad memories. I don't have any memories of sunny days. All my memories are black like night."

Unimpressed with Laurie's turgid prose, Townsend pressed her to reveal the name of the cousin who'd allegedly molested her.

Laurie stuttered, then said, "I'm not going to say it to the court."

But Townsend turned the screws, persuading Judge Todd to instruct Laurie to write the cousin's name on a piece of paper. Asking for particulars about each of the molestations, Townsend soon had Laurie befuddled and contradicting herself. Whatever hopes the defense had for building sympathy over the molestations was sinking fast.

Townsend seemed to notice for the first time that Laurie, who usually dressed in jeans and dark shirts, was wearing a flower-print dress. Remembering her earlier testimony about how she hated her mother for making her wear long dresses, Townsend asked, "Did your mother make you wear that long dress today?"

"No, my mother did not."

"When your mother made you wear long dresses to school, you didn't like that, did you?"

Laurie snapped back, "Would you want to wear a long dress?"

"No," Townsend said, only momentarily startled by the sharp remark. "I look funny enough without a long dress on."

Judge Todd cracked a smile and said, "I think we'll recess for the day on that one."

The next morning, Laurie showed up wearing her customary dark jeans and shirt. But there were no more questions about clothing. Townsend kept her off balance by quizzing her about the claims she'd made to her prison doctors that she had multiple personalities.

"Who is Sissy?"

"That is who I . . ." Laurie stopped in midsentence, then answered, "No."

"Who is Sarah?"

"I don't know."

"Who is Darlene?"

"I don't know."

"Who is Geno?"

"I don't know."

"Now don't you know who Sissy, Sarah, Darlene, and Geno are?"

Laurie responded angrily, "I know who I said they were, but they're not real."

"So you lied," Townsend trumpeted, lifting his arms in mock astonishment. "Are you aware that the autopsy report indicates that Shanda had an object shoved three and a half inches up her anus?" he asked.

"I don't remember that taking place," came the pat answer.

Townsend had grown frustrated in his attempts to find out about the sodomy, and he let his emotions show. "That's just as true as all the other testimony you've given today."

Goering objected to the prosecutor's statement, and Judge Todd sustained, but Townsend shrugged it off. He was almost through with Laurie now, but he had one more trick up his sleeve—or, rather, in his shirt pocket.

"You had some matches, didn't you? Was it a book of matches or a box of matches?"

"Just a book of them. They were in my pocket."

"How did the gasoline get on her?"

"Hope got out of the car and poured it on her."

Townsend moved closer to the witness. "You knew at that point certainly that Shanda was going to die, didn't you?"

"Yes."

"So you bent down and were going to talk to her, weren't you?"

Townsend took another step closer, and Laurie recoiled slightly. "I was going to try to get her to talk to me."

"Isn't it true, Laurie, that you went up to Shanda's body after Hope had soaked it with gasoline and took that book of matches out of your pocket?" At that point Townsend reached into his shirt pocket and pulled out a book of matches. "You took one of those matches," he said, pulling a match from the book and striking it. He held the flame out toward Laurie. "You were going to show that match to Shanda Sharer before you set her on fire?"

"No," said Laurie anxiously.

"Oh, that's right. Somehow she just spontaneously combusted. Is that right?"

"I'm not saying that. I don't know how the fire started."

"But you were there beside her, weren't you? You were so close to her that you were getting ready to talk to her."

"I wasn't . . . I had just bent down when the fire went up in my face."

"Where did you bend down? Right beside her?"

"Yes."

Townsend dropped to one knee, still holding out the flaming match. "Okay, you're kneeling down beside Shanda's still living body, and you want to say something to her?"

"I wasn't kneeling like that," Laurie protested.

"Like this?" Townsend lowered his other knee to the floor and leaned over an imaginary body.

"Yes," Laurie said.

The flame was beginning to burn Townsend's fingers but he wasn't about to fan it out. Not yet. "You're getting ready to talk to Shanda Sharer, and all of a sudden in the subfreezing temperature her body combusts."

"The fire just went up."

The flame was too hot finally and Townsend blew it out. He gazed into Laurie's eyes. "What were you going to say to her? What do you say to someone you're about to burn to death?"

"I . . . I don't know what I was going to say," Laurie stammered. "I was just going to try to get her to talk to me."

Townsend stood up and glowered down at the witness. "Some famous last words. Is that what you wanted?"

O'Connor shouted an objection, but it came too late. Everyone in the crowded room had already been mesmerized by the death-scene re-creation. Townsend, the inexperienced prosecutor whom Goering had expected to dance circles around, had pulled off his bold theatrics with a panache that left even the defense team dumbfounded.

Steve, Jacque, Sharon, and Jacque's husband, Doug, were in the courtroom stairwell, smoking cigarettes during a court recess, when they heard several teenage boys yell to them from the floor below.

"Rot in hell," they screamed, mimicking the phrase Jacque had used in court during Melinda's hearing. Doug bolted down the steps after the teens and chased them across the courtyard, closing the distance with bounding strides and finally grabbing one of the boys by the scruff of the neck and swinging him around.

Although a gentle-spirited man, Doug had an intimidating look even when calm. When angry, as he was now, it was enough to cause the lad to whimper an apology. It was only then that the boy realized his error. He had mistaken Shanda's family for relatives of Laurie.

"Listen, mister, you've got to believe me," the boy pleaded. "We thought you was Laurie's kin. I swear to God."

Doug could see that the boy was telling the truth, and he let him go.

In the realm of hired courtroom psychologists, Dr. Eric S. Engum was considered a Top Gun. With degrees in law and clinical psychology, he had testified in sixty murder cases. Well practiced in the art of courtroom oratory, Engum needed only a few rudimentary questions from Goering to expound at great length about Laurie's mental state.

"Miss Tackett has not developed a well-formed personality structure," Engum said. "I've seen the term chameleon-like used, but a better way of describing it would be someone who obtains her identity from those around her. She's never really developed a sense of self. She is somebody who literally enmeshes and intertwines her personality with somebody else."

Engum accepted Laurie's claims of numerous sexual molestations and said they'd had a devastating effect on her personality. These unpleasant childhood memories caused Laurie to have hallucinations and vivid nightmares. Engum said that Laurie's mother had told her that these experiences were normal and that she was simply seeing visions of the Holy Spirit.

"This clouded Laurie's ability to differentiate between what is real and what is not real and explains to some degree her belief in some of the more occult kinds of things," Engum said.

Following Goering's promptings, the doctor said, "There is no way that this is a woman who takes a dominant and directive role in a social situation with her peers. She simply is incapable of doing that. You have to be able to put people under your spell. I'm not saying she didn't participate. She certainly participated. But as far as being the ringleader, the person who exerted peer pressure, there is nothing to suggest that is within her personality structure."

Goering asked, "Can a group be more violent than an individual?"

"Oh, yes," Engum said. "The research shows that over and over again. It's almost like one person feeds off the other. It's a bad example, but it's kind of a shark-eating frenzy. One shark can be fairly destructive, but when you get a pack of them they feed off each other. It's almost like they sense the increased tension in the air and they feed off that."

The doctor said that Laurie had never developed a conscience. "The way I like to describe this is having a little angel on your shoulder telling you that you are doing good or bad. She never learned at even a very basic level what was right or wrong at an early age. There was no opportunity to develop a sense of moral obligation to other people, a sense of assertiveness to inject yourself into a situation and do something. Her emotions have been blunted, dulled flat. You must recognize that this is a girl who literally takes razor blades to herself and cuts herself because she's so dulled to the pain it's virtually meaningless to her. It's almost a pleasurable release for her because it's the only way to deal with all that pain. If you can't relate to your own pain, how do you relate to someone else's pain? If you wanted to create a blueprint for someone who could do something this horrible, this is it."

The hearing was over except for one final rebuttable witness for the state. Townsend had tracked down Grant Pearson, the young man who Laurie claimed had raped her two summers ago.

Pearson, a gangly sixteen-year-old with long brown hair, seemed fit to bust as he hurried into the courtroom and leered menacingly at Laurie, who wouldn't meet his angry gaze.

Pearson told how he and another boy and Laurie and another girl had spent a day together in August of 1991. They ended up at the other boy's house, where they got high by inhaling gasoline fumes from the tank of Pearson's motorcycle. It was called "huffing," Pearson explained. Each of them would take turns placing their mouth over the open gas tank and inhaling deep breaths. After several huffs of gas, Pearson said, he and Laurie had sex in the cab of his friend's truck.

"At no time did she say no or ask me to stop," Pearson said venomously. "There was no way on earth I ever raped her."

Under cross-examination, Robert Barlow argued that Pearson had gotten Laurie intoxicated, then forced her to have sex against her will.

"How do you feel when you huff gas?" Barlow asked.

"You feel pretty weird," Pearson answered with a grin.

"Do you feel promiscuous?"

"I didn't feel like I wanted to go out and rape a girl, if that's what you mean," Pearson grunted.

"Is it a tingling feeling?" Barlow asked.

Pearson looked at Barlow like he was a real square. "You get a buzz on," he said flippantly. "Know what a buzz is, man?"

The spectators laughed and the interrogation was over.

The following Monday morning, newspaper photographers and television cameramen huddled around the rear entrance of the courthouse, waiting for Laurie to be escorted by deputies from the county jail on the other side of the alley. The previous afternoon, after Laurie had testified about her mother, some of her own cousins had heckled her for besmirching her mother's reputation. This morning the crowd of spectators was even larger. This would be their last chance to see Laurie and Melinda, both of whom would be sentenced following the closing arguments.

As Laurie emerged from the jail door flanked by deputies and her attorneys, the news reporters pushed closer, shouting questions and hoping for a response. "How many years do you think you'll get?" one reporter yelled, pushing his microphone as close as possible. Laurie said nothing, although a young man in the crowd shouted, "They should kill her just like she killed that little girl."

Once inside the courthouse doors, the deputies led Laurie up the two flights of stairs to Judge Todd's packed courtroom. The room bristled with excitement and didn't fall quiet until Judge Todd had taken his seat at the bench.

In a smooth, sure voice, Townsend began: "Melinda Loveless wanted somebody killed, and Laurie Tackett wanted to kill somebody. They each had a need, which was met by the other. Melinda got rid of her rival for Amanda Heavrin's affections, and Laurie Tackett finally got the experience of taking another person's life, of burning another human being alive. The loser in all this was twelve-year-old Shanda Sharer, who had the misfortune of gaining the enmity of Melinda Loveless. But Melinda Loveless's hatred alone did not lead to the death of Shanda Sharer. It wasn't until Melinda Loveless's hatred combined with Laurie Tackett's bloodlust that Shanda Sharer's fate was sealed. That Laurie Tackett was willing to take the life of a complete stranger is a far greater horror than the fact that Melinda Loveless was willing to take the life of someone she hated. Jealousy at least explains the fact that Melinda Loveless is a murderer although it does not in any way excuse it. But there is no such explanation for why Laurie Tackett is a murderer. The fact is, Laurie Tackett is a murderer precisely because she holds the lives of other people in such low regard that she is willing to snuff out the life of a twelve-year-old stranger to see how it feels to burn someone alive. Laurie Tackett murders not for vengeance but for pleasure, and the identity of her victim does not matter to her. It is enough for Laurie Tackett that her victim have blood that she can shed, have a skull that she can beat, and, ultimately, have a body that she can burn. For Laurie Tackett it matters not who she kills, but only that she kills."

Goering began his closing argument by saying that the system had failed Laurie, pointing out that after she'd cut herself with her knife, his client had been placed in a mental institution less than a year before the murder.

"Laurie's diagnosis months before this incident was one of self-mutilation, low self-esteem, poor social skills, a rigid family structure, possible family secrets, and a pervasive feeling of hopelessness. No one answered her cry for help."

Goering once again shifted the blame to Melinda.

"If not for Melinda Loveless's jealousy, her rage, her obsession for Amanda Heavrin, there would be no murder. Laurie Tackett is an impaired, dysfunctional person, a weapon used by Melinda Loveless. Who's more responsible for the tiger in the house and the damage that it does, the tiger or the person who places the tiger in the house? Melinda Loveless used Laurie as her weapon. In our society we don't tie a mad dog to a tree and beat it. That's vindictive

271

justice. Instead we have compassion and treatment for those who are in need. Laurie Tackett is the product of a horrible life. Laurie Tackett is a weapon, intentionally selected and chosen by Melinda Loveless and manipulated by Melinda Loveless for Melinda Loveless's purposes. Laurie Tackett is an emotionally and psychologically damaged person. I ask the court to demonstrate the empathy which she cannot feel. I ask the court to demonstrate the mercy that she cannot understand and provide her with the hope that she'd never had. I ask the court for a fair sentence. Thank you, Your Honor."

In a sentencing hearing, the state is allowed to have the last word, and Townsend made the most of it in a short but moving speech.

His voice oozing with sarcasm, Townsend repeated one of Laurie's statements: "'The worst thing that ever happened to me was being born.' If ever there was a self-pitying statement, that was it. But she's not entirely wrong, because Laurie Tackett being born was the worst thing that ever happened to somebody. Laurie Tackett being born was the worst thing to ever happen to Shanda Sharer. There are times when juries are swayed not by the evidence in the case but by the artful arguments of counsel. But this is not a trial and there is no jury, and I do not believe this court is going to base its decision on anything said in closing arguments. I could be as inarticulate as a doorknob, and still the facts in evidence would speak so loudly and so eloquently that my silence would not be noticed. Sixty years, Your Honor. Laurie Tackett deserves not one day less than sixty years."

After a short recess, Melinda was brought into the courtroom for her sentencing. She slipped into the wooden chair and cast her wildly frightened eyes at Judge Todd. Her mother, stepfather, and sisters sat in the front row, literally on the edge of their bench, each leaning forward with their hands clenched, seemingly in prayer.

Judge Todd cleared his throat, then read from the sheet of paper he held before him. As he cited a long list of aggravating factors, including the "gruesome nature" of the murder and the victim's age, Shanda's parents joined hands, anticipating their victory. At last the words came: Todd levied the maximum sentence allowed under the plea agreements, sixty years in prison. Under Indiana law, Melinda would have to serve at least thirty years before being eligible for parole.

"You still have the power to turn yourself around and do something good and useful with your life after prison," Todd said to a weeping Melinda. "Shanda Sharer does not. I hope you take advantage of that opportunity."

Todd banged his gavel and asked for silence when Shanda's parents and about two dozen relatives and friends applauded his announcement of the sentence. Jacque smiled broadly, then broke into tears. Steve hugged his wife, Sharon. Less than ten feet away, Melinda's mother leaned her head on her husband's chest, while her sisters stared into space in disbelief.

Melinda continued sobbing as a deputy led her from the courtroom. A minute later, Laurie stepped through the same door through which Melinda had departed. Her countenance was grim, her jaw set, and she didn't flinch an inch when Judge Todd gave her the same sentence as Melinda.

Heeding Judge Todd's prior warning against celebration, Jacque and Steve quietly hugged family members as Laurie was led away. Laurie's father, George Tackett, turned from his seat and walked with head down to the hallway, where he waited, hoping for a chance to speak to his daughter before she was sent back to prison. Reporters pushed up next to Tackett and asked him to comment on Laurie's sentence. He turned away from his questioners and leaned his forehead against the hallway wall, saying nothing.

Within a year George Tackett would die of cancer. Townspeople said he refused treatment.

20

Shanda Sharer's name remained in the news during the four weeks leading up to the sentencing hearing of Toni Lawrence.

On January 6, Shanda's parents filed suit against the four girls charged in their daughter's murder in order to block them from selling their stories for publication or broadcast. The suit was spurred by a Louisville television station's report that Laurie was negotiating to sell her story to television and movie producers and that Melinda was also considering offers.

Horrified that their daughter's killers might profit from their crime, Jacque and Steve enlisted their private attorney, Bob Donald, to seek $1 billion in damages from the girls. The billion-dollar figure was set to discourage the four girls from trying to cut lucrative deals with publishers and broadcasters.

"Obviously we'll never collect that money," Donald told the Louisville *Courier-Journal*. "But when considering the value of Shanda's life to her family, why should they consider anything less?"

"It's appalling to think that they could profit from killing

Shanda," Jacque said. "But I can't say that I was shocked to hear about their plans. I know the horrible things these girls are capable of."

Steve found it ironic that Laurie should be shopping her story around. "During her testimony she couldn't remember a thing that happened. Now all of a sudden she remembers enough to sell her story. It's a slap in our faces."

Clark County circuit judge Daniel Donahue thought so too. He immediately issued a temporary injunction blocking the girls from making any such deals.

While this was going on, another news story involving the murder was being played out. Based on the testimonies of Melinda's sisters and cousins, Floyd County prosecutor Stan Faith filed charges against Melinda's father, Larry Loveless, accusing him of rape, sodomy, and sexual battery against children.

Faith was pressing the charges rather than Guy Townsend because the molestations allegedly occurred at the Loveless's New Albany home. Larry Loveless was arrested at his home in Florida and extradited back to New Albany to stand trial. After Loveless pleaded not guilty to the charges, his attorney, Michael McDaniel, the pre-eminent criminal lawyer in southern Indiana, said he could make a solid case that the molestations did not occur and were simply trumped up as a scheme to lighten Melinda's sentence. (Loveless's trial encountered numerous delays and was not expected to begin before January 1995.)

Against this background, Toni Lawrence's attorney, twenty-eight-year-old Paul Baugh, put together the final pieces of his defense. He'd closely followed the two previous hearings and intended to call on Melinda and Laurie to retell their stories, since both murderers had testified that Toni did little to help them kill Shanda.

There was no hired psychologist to offer excuses for Toni's role in Shanda's death, and there would be no testimony claiming that Toni's abusive home life had warped her personality. Baugh had been dealt a different hand than the other attorneys. The murder charges against Toni had been dropped when she pleaded guilty of criminal confinement and agreed to be the state's key witness. Under the agreement, Toni faced a sentence of between six and twenty years, and Baugh felt he had a good chance at the lower range. He knew that the public viewed Toni in a different light than they did Melinda, Laurie, and even Hope, now that it had become clear that Hope had been the first one to pour the gasoline on Shanda's body. Toni had already been the subject of several articles and television reports in which the question was asked, What would other teenagers have done if they had been in Toni's place?

Obviously, Toni should have done something to prevent the murder, and Baugh knew that would be Guy Townsend's strongest argument for a lengthy sentence. It was Baugh's duty to offer convincing reasons why Toni had failed to act.

"I had two things on my mind going into the hearing," Baugh said later. "To establish that Toni was too scared of the others to try to stop them and to show that she was not like the other three girls."

Working in Baugh's favor was the fact that Toni went to police after the murder and gave them the information that led to the quick arrest of Melinda and Laurie. Baugh intended to show that Toni was an average but timid teenager from a good home with loving parents, who'd made the fatal mistake of choosing the wrong friends.

The hearing began with a brief opening statement by Baugh: "I've heard some of the attorneys for the other defendants state that Toni received the plea of the century when she pled guilty to criminal confinement. Well, that's absurd. The only crime which Toni is guilty of is the crime to which she pled. The state would never dismiss the murder charge against Toni Lawrence if she was guilty of murder. I hope the judge understands how frightened the events leading up to Shanda's death were to Toni and the fear that she experienced for her own life. Finally, I hope that you realize the deep remorse that Toni has for what happened to Shanda Sharer and that if there was any way she could turn around the events of that night she would."

As Townsend presented the state's case, he seemed to lack the enthusiasm that had driven him during the previous hearings. That was understandable, since he was coming off two big victories. He had succeeded in getting maximum sentences for Melinda and Laurie, and although he would never admit it publicly, he was sympathetic toward Toni. Without her it would have been much harder to prove Melinda and Laurie's guilt. That's not to say there were serious flaws in Townsend's case against Toni. He covered the proper bases, calling as witnesses Steve Henry, Crystal Wathen, Amanda Heavrin, Kary Pope, and Melinda and Laurie. But his examination of those witnesses wasn't as vigorous as it had been at the two previous hearings. Still, Townsend had little trouble in showing that while Toni may not have participated in the violence against Shanda, she did nothing to prevent it and never took advantage of her numerous opportunities to summon help.

Baugh managed to solicit the testimony he wanted from Steve Henry, Melinda, and Laurie. Henry acknowledged that Toni's statement led directly to the arrest of both Melinda and Laurie and that her subsequent plea agreement was the key element in persuading Melinda and Laurie to admit their guilt. Under questioning from Baugh, Melinda and Laurie acknowledged that Toni took no part in beating or killing Shanda. But it was also clear from their testimony that Toni never insisted that they stop. Melinda and Laurie both said that Toni seemed in shock throughout the incident and that she cried and screamed on several occasions.

Laurie admitted that while she was a close friend of Hope Rippey's, she wasn't very close to Toni, explaining that it was because Toni was "a preppy. I didn't want to be a preppy."

Melinda related how Toni spent much of the morning of the murder in silence and biting her knuckles: "She was there but in her mind she didn't want to be there. She was scared."

Before he dismissed Melinda, Baugh wanted to clear up one matter: "You testified at Laurie Tackett's sentencing hearing that when you and Laurie went to the car, that Toni and Hope were in the car with two boys and the boys had to pull their pants up. You also testified that when you came back to the car later, that Toni and Hope had switched partners, didn't you?"

"Yes," Melinda answered quietly.

"You're a homosexual, aren't you?"

"Yes."

"You don't like seeing other girls with boys, do you?"

"It doesn't bother me."

"Isn't it true that when you see girls with boys you conjure up bad notions about them?"

"No. I just think it's based on sex. That's what I think, but it's probably not."

"But that's what you think?" Baugh asked.

"Yeah," Melinda said. "That's what I think of men, I mean."

Baugh began his defense by calling on three of Toni's teachers, all of whom said she was a quiet, good student who had never been in serious trouble before.

"I think Toni would be the last person I'd have picked to be involved in something like that," said Beverly Cook, the girl's French teacher. "You could tell from her appearance that she came from a good home. I thought that Toni was probably going to continue her education in college."

A number of Toni's friends testified that she did not normally hang around with Laurie Tackett or Hope Rippey. The teenage girls who testified on Toni's behalf were much different in appearance than were the troubled youths who had testified at Melinda's and Laurie's hearings. Mikel Pommerehn, a pretty brunette who looked like she might have stepped off the pages of a modeling magazine, came to court wearing a stylish pants suit. In a voice filled with regret, Pommerehn explained how she'd agreed to help Toni trick her parents into thinking that Toni was spending the night with her on the night of the murder. Pommerehn said there was no doubt in her mind that Toni had been coerced into helping the other girls.

"Toni wasn't the type of person to do something like this," she said. "She was in the wrong place at the wrong time."

Toni's father, Clifton Lawrence, fifty-two, a small but wiry man with a black-and-gray speckled beard, and his tiny wife, Glenda, had sat near the back of the courtroom during Melinda's and Laurie's hearings, ignoring the occasional disparaging glances from Shanda's family. Now Clifton was called on to speak in his daughter's defense.

Much of his testimony dealt with the night that he learned of the murder and took Toni to the police, but he also talked about his daughter's rape the year before and how she was discouraged by the police's meager response.

"It's your testimony that Toni reported a serious crime to the police in the past?" Baugh asked, hoping to establish Toni's distrust of police as an explanation of why she didn't call them the night Shanda was killed.

"Yes."

"And the police didn't believe her?"

"They didn't believe her enough to do anything about it."

Toni took the witness stand for the third time in as many hearings and once again claimed that she didn't help Shanda because she feared that Laurie and Melinda would turn on her and kill her too.

Townsend's heart didn't seem to be in the cross-examination. After getting Toni to admit that she'd not taken advantage of numerous opportunities to get help, he dismissed her.

A few minutes later, Toni was on her feet, standing timidly beside her attorney and reading from a written statement. "Mrs. Vaught, Mr. Sharer," she said softly. "I'm so sorry about your little girl. I know that you can never forgive me for being with those girls on January 10 and 11, but I would like to explain some things to you. I do feel very much remorse for your daughter. I've been locked up for ten months and that time has been a living hell. I've had nightmares where I woke up screaming and can't stop and think for a second without seeing Shanda's burned body or hearing her screams. I tried to help Shanda. After I gave her a hug and said I was sorry, I asked Melinda to please take her home but Melinda told me to shut up so I did. I was terrified of Melinda and Laurie. Melinda had a knife and was going to kill Shanda. I know I should be punished, but in my heart, seeing Shanda tortured and burned was punishment in itself. I didn't get help because I was scared they would kill me too. That night and morning will live visibly in my mind for the rest of my life. Mrs. Vaught, Mr. Sharer, I know you have the right to hate me. I wish there was something I could do for you, but all I can say is how very sorry I am."

Toni was sniffling as she finished, but her words seemed to have no effect on Shanda's parents. After a brief pause, Jacque, as the victim's advocate, was once again allowed to vent her anger.

"First off I'd like to say that I do not accept your apology. I've heard a lot of sympathy for Toni. I heard a teacher testify that she worried about Toni being in prison because the people there would have a bad influence on her. It would seem to me that it is a little late to worry about her being around bad influences. I have sat through three hearings and had to listen to attorneys try to convince everyone that these girls were all victims. Yes, there are many victims to this crime, but none of them sat to the left side of me during these hearings. The victims are Shanda Sharer and her family and friends. Toni could have saved my daughter's life that night at any given time. She chose not to. She chose to go along with the other girls and she continued to go along to the bitter end. I beg the court to impose the maximum sentence of twenty years. Her disregard for human life in allowing my daughter to be murdered is a crime that cannot be taken lightly. If this court does not sentence Toni Lawrence to twenty years it will send a message to the world that it's okay to stand by and watch while another human being is being tortured and murdered. We must protect and love our fellow human beings and abide by the law or suffer the consequences set out by the law, regardless of age."

Townsend's closing argument focused on Toni's involvement in Shanda's abduction and the many opportunities she'd had to summon help.

"She claims that she was afraid to stop things because she was scared that what happened to Shanda might happen to her. She could have stopped it when she talked to the boys at the concert in Louisville, or when she talked to the boys at the service station, or when she called her friend while at the service station. There were attendants at the service stations they stopped at during the night and the next morning. She could have put herself in the protective custody of these people and not only saved herself from any injury from Laurie Tackett but also terminated the events that led ultimately to Shanda Sharer's death. She did not do that. And that I believe is Toni Lawrence's abiding failure in the events that led to Shanda's murder."

In countering, Baugh gestured toward Toni as he said, "There has been no testimony that Toni played a role in physically harming Shanda. Toni's only crime is failing to step up and tell the other girls to stop, or failing to get help for Shanda. Yes, Toni recognizes that if she had done something Shanda may still be alive today. She also realizes that if she had done something, she too may have been killed. It's easy for adults to say she should have done this or she should have done that. The reality is that Toni was only fifteen at the time. She was extremely intimidated by these other girls. Without putting ourselves into Toni's position and experiencing the rage of Melinda and Laurie that night, there's no way we can say what each of us would have done in Toni's position. But I'm sure of one thing. Once we viewed that rage we wouldn't want it turned on us. Sure it's easy to say that Toni could have reported it to someone. Toni dealt with this traumatic event by withdrawing from it. Melinda said that Toni was there physically but not mentally. All of us who have children know that at some point in time our children are going to be hanging around with the wrong people. Unfortunately for Toni Lawrence, she was with Hope Rippey, Melinda Loveless, and Laurie Tackett on the night of January 10 and the morning of January 11. Toni was simply in the wrong place at the wrong time with the wrong people."

When court reconvened the next morning, Judge Todd delivered his verdict. "Miss Lawrence," he said, "after considering all the evidence and your personal statement, I believe you have the ability to make something of your life in the future. You can still lead a good and useful life in the future. As you well know, Shanda does not have that chance."

Although Todd cited some mitigating circumstances—Toni's age and her previously clean record—he said he would sentence her to the maximum of twenty years because "this is a crime of a particularly gruesome nature that resulted in the torture, beating, and death of the victim. You knew before the murder that the other girls' actions could lead to Shanda's death. Anything less than the maximum sentence would depreciate the seriousness of the crime committed."

Toni began crying as deputies led her to a court anteroom, where she met with her parents, sisters, and other relatives. As her parents consoled her, Toni let out a wail and began shaking nervously. The Lawrences ignored questions from reporters and quickly left the courthouse while their daughter was escorted to jail.

Judge Todd said later that Toni's sentence was the hardest of the three to determine. "I lost a lot of sleep over Toni's case," he said. "I gave a lot of consideration to giving her less than the maximum. The thing that kept me from it was the phone call she'd made from the first gas station. She had a golden opportunity there to tell the boy she talked to what was going on. At that point she knew that Shanda was in dire danger, yet she made a conscious decision not to take that step to help her. In my eyes, that was unforgivable."

Shanda's parents were relieved and mildly surprised by the sentence.

"We all wanted the maximum and were very pleased with the judge," Steve said. "I think he's right that Toni is an intelligent girl who can still have a good life after her time in jail. I felt it was justice for her. I know that if Shanda's and Toni's positions had been reversed, my daughter would have done something to stop it. I think that most kids would."

Jacque said, "I think he did the right thing. I think he sent a message to people that society is not going to tolerate this."

Hope Rippey's sentencing hearing was moved from Madison to South Bend, Indiana, at the request of her attorney,

Darryl Auxier, who hoped to distance his client from the media pressure he felt was influencing the sentencings.

"Hope had already been tried and found guilty by the local press," Auxier said later.

Hope had pleaded guilty to the same charges as Melinda and Laurie and faced the same sentence—between thirty and sixty years in prison—but Auxier felt he could persuade the new judge, Jeanne Jourdan, to set punishment at the lower end of that range.

When the hearing began on June 1 in St. Joseph's Superior Court in South Bend, Jacque Vaught was on edge and volatile. She burned with anger as she saw Steve Henry exchange friendly remarks with Hope during a court recess the first day of the hearing. Jacque later confronted Henry in the hallway and derided him for being cozy with Shanda's murderer. Henry walked away, saying that he didn't need to take such abuse. Later, after Steve, Doug, and Sharon had chided Jacque, she apologized to the detective who had worked so hard on the investigation. As was his nature, Henry genially shrugged it off and told Jacque to forget about it. "No offense taken," he said.

The easygoing Henry couldn't hold a grudge against Jacque any more than he could work up any hatred for Toni, Hope, or even Melinda and Laurie. It was his job to put Shanda's killers behind bars, and he devoted himself to that purpose. But he felt no malice toward the girls, only sorrow for their fate.

"When I go to the mall anymore I end up looking at all the teenagers and thinking this is where those four girls ought to be," Henry said later. "I tried to be straight up with each one of them. I told them it was nothing personal. It was just my job. I ended up getting along with all of them, even Laurie."

Henry was determined to see something good come out of Shanda's horrific murder, and he'd had long talks with Kary Pope, Larry Leatherbury, and other teens he'd met during his investigation.

"I told them up front that I didn't care about their sexuality," Henry said. "I talked to them like I would talk to my own kids. I told them that they had a second chance at life. Any one of them could have come along with the other four girls in the car that night. I hope that they learned something from all this. Kary Pope calls me every once in a while and tells me how she's doing. She's got a job now and I think she's on the right track."

Henry's deepest regret was that he never learned what was going through the girls' minds during those hours when Shanda's life hung in the balance.

"I asked every one of them to tell me what they were thinking about that night," he said, "but none of them ever truly opened up the way I wished they had."

Hope hadn't testified at the other hearings.

Townsend had decided it would be pointless to put Hope on the stand. Since she was charged with the murder, she could refuse to answer questions on the grounds that it could incriminate her. "The only way that she was going to talk was if I granted her immunity and obviously I wasn't going to do that," he said.

Shortly before her hearing, Hope gave her only statement on the murders. Auxier, who had not forgotten Townsend's damaging cross-examination of Laurie, thought it best that Hope not testify in her own defense.

"Hope's statement was like all the others," Henry said. "We were able to get what we needed but not all we wanted. It was like pulling teeth with Hope, just like it was with the others. She wasn't very forthcoming."

Hope had admitted her most horrendous act: pouring the gasoline the first time. She also told Henry about Melinda's reluctance to help at the burn site.

"She was disgusted with Melinda for helping to lift Shanda out of the trunk," Henry said. "The only thing she denied was spraying the Windex on Shanda. She claimed she'd just sprayed it on a sweater to try to get it to ignite."

The change of venue seemed to have recharged Townsend's batteries. He had bounce in his step and a determined look on his face as he came into the courtroom for the first day of Hope's hearing.

The strategy of Auxier and his co-counsel, Charles Asher, was to show that Hope had acted under the domination of

Melinda and Laurie. Their key witness was psychologist Michael Sheehan, who began by saying he was impressed with Hope's "honesty and forthrightness. I found that she was somewhat immature for her age but that she was basically a healthy individual. I was stunned. I have evaluated a number of murderers and Hope was not like any of them."

Sheehan said that Hope was a timid type who learned at an early age to avoid confrontation. "When verbal violence did happen in her home, she coped by avoidance," he said.

Throughout his testimony, Sheehan praised Hope. "She was willing to accept responsibility for her actions. She never whined about any unfairness. I saw a sixteen-year-old with a lot of potential character. In her own heart she knows she's not a murderer. She did not participate in the cruelty, the tormenting. She puts on a tough act but inside she is real tender."

Sheehan said his interviews with Hope convinced him that she was "a reluctant participant" who was coerced into helping kill Shanda by "the dominant personalities of Melinda and Laurie." Hope had adopted Laurie as a "surrogate big sister," he said. "She went along with Laurie because she didn't want Laurie to be mad at her. You had one girl [Laurie] who wanted to kill someone, one girl [Melinda] who wanted someone killed, and you had two chumps [Hope and Toni]."

Townsend's first witness, Steve Henry, recounted Hope's involvement throughout Shanda's abduction and murder, stressing that she had chosen the spot to burn Shanda and had been the first to pour the gas. On cross-examination, Auxier asked Henry if he had an opinion on who had sodomized Shanda.

"Yes, I do," Henry said. "Melinda and Laurie pointed fingers at each other in every other aspect of the murder. But when we asked them about the anal injury they both claimed ignorance. It's just my opinion, but that leads me to believe they both did it."

Hope showed up for the second day of the hearing wearing her jail uniform and with her long brown hair pulled back in a ponytail. She sniffled as Steve Sharer took the stand.

"My stomach turns and knots up when I hear what was done to my Shanda and how she must have felt," Steve said. "To me torture is the meanest, most horrible thing to do to any living creature on this earth."

The next person to testify, Jacque, related once again how Shanda's death had torn apart the lives of the family she'd left behind. Jacque asked Hope to close her eyes and think of how she would feel if a young niece she particularly loved were burned alive.

"Imagine how you would feel if someone did to your niece what you did to our child," Jacque said as Hope lowered her head and began to cry. "You cannot know the pain we've felt. There is no greater pain than losing your child."

In closing, Townsend scoffed at the testimony of Dr. Sheehan, calling it "a wonder land. I thought the Mad Hatter and the White Rabbit would run through this courtroom while the good doctor was testifying. Dr. Sheehan said the optimal feature of Hope's personality is that she cares. I'd hate to think of the horrors she might have inflicted if she didn't care. In one sense, Hope was guilty of pouring gasoline on two occasions. The first was when she asked incendiary questions of Shanda's friendship with Amanda that were virually guaranteed to rile the heated passions of Melinda Loveless, who was hiding in the back-seat, armed and dangerous. Hope Rippey was the only one of the four that did have an opportunity to act outside the group dynamic. When she was alone with Shanda at the door, she could have derailed the whole course of events with the word of warning that Melinda was waiting in the car."

Auxier argued for a sentence of thirty-five years with fifteen years of probation for his client because Hope had "acted under strong provocation from the aggressive, hostile personalities of Tackett and Loveless."

Co-defense attorney Charles Asher said that much of Townsend's case against Hope was based on the testimony of "two liars"—Melinda and Laurie—and that during earlier sentencing hearings Townsend had placed most of the blame on Melinda and Laurie. "You can't have it both ways," he said. "The state would have you believe that if you're in for a penny, you're in for a pound. It's not that easy."

Judge Jourdan had a few words to say herself before she passed sentence: "Hope Rippey lacked mercy. She thinks of herself as tough on the outside and tender on the inside. Neither is true. If mercy requires tender courage, and I think it does, Hope showed no courage and felt no tenderness. As Melinda and Laurie improvised each hideous step of the way, Toni sat silent, strong enough to avoid action, too weak to take the action needed to help. Hope had choices. There were avenues of escape, ways to help herself, ways to help Shanda. She decided to help Laurie, even though she knew it would hurt Shanda. She poured the gasoline so no one would get caught, even though she knew it would kill Shanda. Her lack of mercy, of tender courage, is a horrifying lesson to us all.

"Children need nurturing, protection, guidance, and good examples from all adults. The judicial world is not able to make the world safe for children. Kids grow up outside of courtrooms. Television, other kids, the adults in each child's life—these are the things that provide the lessons by which kids learn to grow. The prosecutor, the defense lawyer, and the judge act after the harm has been done. It is too late to spare Shanda the harm that was done her. I cannot make it right. It is beyond this court's power to reverse the harm. But it is not beyond our power to touch the people in our lives. I encourage us all to learn a lesson from this. And that lesson is to nurture our children."

Judge Jourdan looked directly at Hope as she said, "I sentence you to sixty years with ten years suspended and ten years of probation."

Hope was in tears as a deputy shackled her with handcuffs and led her from the room. The fifty-year direct sentence meant that she would have to spend at least twenty-five years in prison, and after that she would still be on probation for another ten years.

"This chapter is over," Steve told a group of reporters outside the courtroom. "I know Shanda is in Heaven, so I don't worry so much about that. But I'm always thinking about her friends and cousins because it's hard for them. They come up to me and give me a hug and a kiss and say they don't understand."

Jacque said, "I'm glad it's over, but in some ways I'm having a hard time with this being the end. As long as this was going on, people had to listen and hopefully learn something from how horrible it was. I'm just afraid that now everyone is going to forget about Shanda, and I don't want that to happen."

21

According to an article in *Scholastic Update*, the typical sixteen-year-old has witnessed an estimated 200,000 acts of violence, including 33,000 murders on television. Inevitably, contend some experts, some young people will imitate the brutalities in real life. All that violence is numbing, and it signals that violence is normal.

Worth noting here is southern Indiana police officer Gary Hall's observation that two days before Shanda's murder, a television tabloid show aired a lengthy report on the 1985 California murder of seventeen-year-old Missy Avila by two of her female classmates. The motive, as in Shanda's case, was jealousy. There was never any evidence that Melinda or Laurie had watched that program, but Hall thought the similarities between the crimes—both girls were lured to their death and killed in the country—were, at the very least, sadly ironic.

While sociologists debate the causes, youth violence continues to grow. Attorney-General Janet Reno said in 1993 that violence by young people was "the greatest single crime problem in America today."

Between 1987 and 1991, the last year for which statistics are available, the number of teenagers arrested for murder around the country increased by 85 percent, according to the Department of Justice. In 1991, ten- to seventeen-year-olds accounted for 17 percent of all violent crimes, and there's every indication that percentage is growing.

Judge Jeanne Jourdan cut to the heart of Shanda's tragic death when she noted Hope Rippey's "lack of mercy, of tender courage." And who could dispute Jourdan's warning that parents need to nurture their children.

But there were still many unanswered questions beyond who sodomized Shanda. Perplexing questions—not about the details of the murder, but around its very occurrence.

Prosecutor Guy Townsend's theory that Melinda Loveless wanted someone killed and Laurie Tackett wanted to kill someone was generally accepted as a bare-boned but logical explanation of the murder. But Townsend readily admitted that his courtroom comments were fashioned for a clear purpose: to put the guilty parties behind bars.

"Obviously, the motivations at work here reach deeper than that," Townsend said. "Who's to say how these girls ever got to that point where murder came so easy? That's for the sociologists to debate."

When not on the job, Townsend is probably as liberal and open-minded a thinker as you will find in Madison and not one for quick judgments. But he had a hard time swallowing the defense's arguments concerning the psychological damage done to Melinda and Laurie by their parents.

"The defense made a lot of hay out of Melinda's and Laurie's supposedly horrid home lives," he said. "But I was never convinced that their home lives were as horrible as the defense attorneys and their paid psychologists claimed. They were hired to put on a show, and they did. As for Melinda's sisters and cousins, they obviously had an interest in making Melinda—not Shanda—seem like the victim."

Melinda's co-counsel Mike Walro, however, thought that his client's background had a tremendous effect on her psyche.

"When I first met Melinda I was struck by the vulnerability of this girl," Walro said. "I couldn't figure out how a girl so nice, so normal, so genuine, so concerned for other people, could be involved in the things she said she did."

Walro said all his questions were answered when he learned of the conditions she had grown up under.

"Melinda is a handicapped person in the sense that she comes from a home where the normal was not what we consider normal," he said. "She and her sisters grew up where crotch grabbing, finger sniffing, and underwear smelling were the norm, where they saw their mother physically abused, mentally abused, and emotionally abused and where the same thing happened to them."

But Dr. Nancy Moore, a Louisville clinical psychologist who followed the case through the news, said the testimonies of psychologists for Melinda and Laurie "should be taken with a grain of salt. Clearly, coming up with sympathetic opinions was what they were paid to do."

While Moore agreed that victims of abuse are more likely to abuse others than those who haven't been abused, she was quick to add that most abuse victims learn to deal with their painful pasts without turning to violence.

Dr. Rodney Young, another Louisville clinical psychologist, said, "I have talked with child sexual abuse victims about this case, and they were horrified that someone could do this to someone else. And these were girls who had gone through as much or worse than what supposedly happened to Loveless or Tackett."

The fact remains, however, that many killers were abused as children. A study by researcher Dorothy Lewis published by the American Academy of Child and Adolescent Psychiatry in 1988 found that twelve of fourteen juveniles on death row in four states had long histories of severe beatings and sexual abuse.

Another Lewis study, quoted in a July 1993 *Newsweek* article on teen violence, found that maltreatment increased children's inclination to act impulsively, predisposed them to lash out, and often caused children to lose their ability to feel empathy for others. All of which is an echo of Laurie's defense.

A similar article published in the January 17, 1994 issue

of *U.S. News & World Report*—an issue that featured a photo of Laurie Tackett—quoted Terence P. Thornberry, a psychologist at the State University of New York in Albany, as saying, "Violence does not drop out of the sky at fifteen. It is part of a long developmental process that begins in early childhood." Thornberry said that kids who grow up in families where there is a history of violent behavior learn early on to act out physically when they are frustrated or upset.

Most experts agree, however, that child abuse is just a piece of the puzzle and that the epidemic of youth violence in our society can also be blamed on the general breakdown of families, schools, and other community institutions. Then there are those who point to the dehumanizing effect of television and movies, from *A Clockwork Orange* to *Menace II Society*, that feed children a steady diet of glorified violence.

Not only is youth violence more widespread, it has taken on a more vicious, remorseless nature. Police report increasing instances of youths killing for kicks and then bragging of their exploits.

Court testimony showed that Laurie Tackett had wanted to murder someone for all the publicity. Similar sentiments were expressed last year by seventeen-year-old Raul Omar Villareal, one of six teenage boys arrested in the brutal rape and strangulation of two Houston girls. "Hey great, we hit the big time," said Villareal, who added, "Human life means nothing." And Melinda's glee following Shanda's murder was echoed last year when one of three teenage boys arrested for fatally stabbing another teen in Dartmouth, Massachusetts, reportedly laughed about the killing afterward.

"We're seeing a new breed of young people who are very reckless, very carefree, and who have thrown off the inhibitions that typically constrained adolescent behavior," Victor Herbert, the executive director of New York City's public high schools, told *Scholastic Update*. "They take the attitude, 'Why not do almost anything, why not knock someone over if they are in the way.'"

Colonel Leonard Supenski of the Baltimore County police department told *Fortune* magazine in 1992, "There are a whole lot of disaffected, alienated youth out there who use violence, and use it with no remorse."

Dr. Richard Johnson, a clinical psychologist in Louisville, felt that Laurie Tackett's fascination with the occult just compounded those nihilistic feelings. The occult is enticing to some teenagers because it "places no limits sexually or physically on pleasing yourself," Johnson said. "If you want to hurt someone, go for it. That appears to be the kind of behavior displayed here."

The *U.S. News & World Report* article said, "Behind the rash of violence is a startling shift in adolescent attitudes. Suddenly—chillingly—respect for life has ebbed sharply among teenagers."

Just as chillingly, Shanda's murder, with all its peculiarities, seems to fit neatly into one of the typical scenarios for teen violence, that of group participation. Unlike adult criminals, who usually act alone, violent teens normally move in a pack. In the *Newsweek* article University of Pennsylvania criminologist Marvin Wolfgang said that research has shown that about 85 percent of juvenile offenses are committed by groups of two or more. In a gang the conscience that would normally stop a healthy person from committing a crime is damaged or missing altogether. That's when gruesome acts can happen. The victim becomes dehumanized in the attackers' minds, said Richard Pesikoff, a Baylor College of Medicine psychiatrist for children and adolescents. "Then they are treated as things."

Dr. Eric Engum, the psychologist who testified on Laurie's behalf, described this as "sharks in a feeding frenzy," where one person's actions spur others to do things they wouldn't have considered on their own. "As horrible as the violence is, everyone goes along with the crowd rather than go it alone."

"I think that makes sense here," Dr. Nancy Moore said. "We've all seen how adolescents behave in a group, how they lose their sense of what's normal. What these girls did to Shanda Sharer is that taken to the extreme."

Wayne Engle, who covered Shanda's murder for the *Madison Courier,* also believes that was the case here.

"There was a synergism between Melinda and Laurie," Engle said. "Although Melinda said she wanted to kill Shanda, I don't think she was strong enough to do it until she met Laurie. Their personalities meshed into someone or something that was capable."

Dr. Charles Patrick Ewing, a professor of criminology at the State University of New York in Buffalo and author of the book *Kids Who Kill,* said that when murders are committed by more than one person "a group mentality comes into play, a kind of one-upmanship that may start harmlessly but escalates to violence as one says to the other, 'You did that; well, I'll do this.'"

When juveniles kill, "they tend to overkill," said Ewing, who was familiar with the details of Shanda's murder. "The violence they inflict is extreme, much more than is necessary to accomplish the murder. Boys are twenty times more likely to kill than girls, but when girls do kill, they tend to have an accomplice, as in this case."

Girls more than boys seek group acceptance for their anger, said Judith Lambeth, executive director of Maryhurst, a home for emotionally troubled teenagers in Louisville.

"If boys are angry they tend to explode and it's over," Lambeth said. "Girls carry it on and talk about it until they work themselves into a frenzy. It's altogether possible that Loveless said she wanted to kill her, but she never really believed that she would, and it was like a snowballing effect, with none of these kids being strong enough to stop or say no. I think Tackett was the colder one and that Melinda was the emotional one. What was Tackett's motive? Her payoff was the evil of it."

A number of studies have shown that girls are committing violent crimes with increasing frequency. In 1987, 15 percent of the crimes that girls were convicted of committing were violent offenses. By 1991, that number had soared to 38 percent.

Deborah Grisham Blair, a Louisville clinical psychologist, said, "I see girls acting out violently. I didn't used to see girls like this. I really didn't. They are more aggressive. Are we raising a generation of paranoid kids who are overly responsive to possible threats? Or are we socializing our kids less and neglecting them more and letting them raise themselves?"

Arlene Taylor, a bus driver in the Louisville school system, sees fighting escalating among girls. "Girls did not fight like that a few years ago. Girls now really inflict pain when they fight. They scratch, pull hair, claw, and bite. They carry knives for protection. When I ask them why they say, 'You don't know what it's like out there.'"

"I've been amazed by the brutality of the beatings of girls by other girls," Dr. Naftali Berrill, director of the New York Forensic Mental Health Group, told *Newsweek* magazine, which cited the rise in girls committing violent acts as a sign that "the plague of teen violence is now an equal-opportunity scourge."

Louisville psychologists who followed the Sharer case had various opinions about why Toni Lawrence apparently stood by and watched the beatings and murder but didn't directly participate.

"She might have feared for her own safety," Dr. Nancy Moore said. "Once you get a picture of that rage, you don't want that rage turned on you."

Judith Lambeth suspects Lawrence was in shock. "Sometimes when viewing a traumatic event, it becomes like an out-of-body experience," she said. "You are there, but you are not there. You disassociate so that you don't have to deal with it."

Richard Coomer, a psychiatric social worker in Louisville, believes that each girl crossed a personal line that night from which there was no turning back.

"For one it might have been the kidnapping," he said. "For another the beating. But there was a point where each of them should have said: 'Oops, I messed up. I made a mistake in getting involved. This is enough.' But they didn't, and once they crossed that line, they felt they were in too much trouble. They were out on a limb and there was no turning back."

Detective Steve Henry, who knows more about the case than anyone, had his own opinion of why it happened. Henry said that when Melinda lost Amanda to Shanda, it wasn't at all like a typical junior-high girl losing her boy-friend to another girl. If Melinda had been older it would have been easier for her to find another gay companion. At that age, where life revolves around your school, there wasn't much likelihood of finding another classmate who would return her affections.

"That's why Amanda was so special to Melinda," Henry said. "The normal jealousy that a girl would feel by being jilted was heightened to a dangerous level."

Even so, Henry believes that Melinda probably did not intend to kill Shanda when she lured her to the car that night and that her purpose was always to just hurt her.

"I think Melinda was ready to stop at the logging road and that's where Laurie just took over," Henry said. "Laurie had all this frustration building up inside her for years and this was her chance to let it out."

Laurie's own attorney had referred to her in animalistic terms, such as "tiger" and "mad dog," but of the four girls, she was clearly the intellectual superior. Melinda was a sixteen-year-old eighth-grader who made poor grades. And nothing in Hope's or Toni's background suggested that they were anything but average thinkers. Laurie's problems with school stemmed from her radical behavior, not her learning ability. Unfortunately, Laurie's mind had always sought escape rather than enlightenment, embracing the unsettling universe of the occult rather than finding a way through the hard reality of the world around her. Laurie's life was a long, lonely progression from one delusion to another.

"I can't say for sure why this was the night, why the conditions were right, for Laurie's anger to explode," Henry said. "Kary Pope said it didn't matter to Laurie who she killed, and I think that's true to an extent. As for that moment in time, I believe Laurie was trying to prove herself to Melinda, trying to play the man's role in their relation-ship. Once Laurie had hurt Shanda badly, once she was past the point where they could take her home and not get in serious trouble, Melinda was in all the way. She saw killing Shanda as her only way out."

Henry believes that Hope Rippey made the same choice, although hers came later that night.

"Hope was playing it both ways all night," Henry said. "Whenever she was alone with Toni she'd be saying things like 'Oh God, what are they doing,' but when she was with Laurie she was a willing partner. Hope was the only one of the girls who had a chance to act outside the view of all the others that night and that came when she was alone with Shanda at the door. At that point she could have warned her that a trap was being set and the whole thing could have ended there, without the other girls even suspecting that she said something. She could have come back to the car and lied that Shanda's father got up and wouldn't let her leave. No, Hope went along with the plan because Laurie had left her at the door and she didn't want to let Laurie down."

Although it was never clear whether Hope was trying to help Shanda or Melinda and Laurie in the scuffle on the logging road, after that she returned to the car with Toni and did what Toni did—simply watched. She tried to distance herself from what was going on once again when she stayed with Toni at the house while Laurie and Melinda drove off with Shanda.

Testimony during Hope's sentencing hearing showed that she willingly took part and even enjoyed the early stages of tormenting Shanda. Shanda, with her good looks and prim manner, was representative of all the preppy girls at Madison High who had looked down on Hope. But Hope didn't really choose her direction until Melinda and Laurie returned to the house with Shanda in the trunk and Hope saw her bloody body. At that point Hope seemed to make a conscious decision, some might argue a practical decision, to get it over with, to finish her off, to dispose of the body and try to cover their tracks. She apparently sprayed Shanda with the Windex, thinking it might be an accelerant; she told Melinda how to find Shanda's heart when Melinda wanted to stab her; she directed them to the burn site; she helped lift Shanda from the trunk and she poured the gasoline.

Although Hope's actions were inexcusable, they weren't inconsistent with the elements of group violence. In gang situations there are leaders and there are willing accomplices. Hope was one of the latter, the type who likes to hang with a rough crowd and who, with the proper push, will do her part. Jails are filled with Hope's type, those who enjoy the thrill of acting tough.

"Hope made a conscious decision to help kill Shanda after the girls got back to the house," Henry said. "And that's why she got fifty years and Toni only got twenty."

There was a degree of public sympathy for Toni Lawrence, the only one of the girls whose actions, or lack of actions, seemed the least bit understandable, although not at all acceptable. *Courier-Journal* columnist Dale Moss expressed the feelings of many when he wrote after Toni's sentencing hearing: "Toni Lawrence was gutless for not stopping her friends from murdering Shanda Sharer. But the hemorrhaging from this horrific chapter should end. Lawrence's maximum twenty-year term only serves as understandable vengeance for Shanda's loved ones. Lawrence clearly was far from ideal. At fifteen, she also was far from maturity. She apparently didn't harm Shanda and she alerted police to the murder. She isn't a lost cause, or, it would seem, a public threat. The longer she wastes her young-adult years in prison, the more likely she could be. Instead, after a more reasonable stretch, take Lawrence to high schools. Make her explain to every mealy-mouthed teenager with punks for friends the difference between being a hero and being a felon."

Jacque Vaught was angered by Moss's column. She had said many times that each of the girls was as guilty as the others. That Toni seemed to have more moral character than the others, but not the strength to exert it, earned her no sympathy from Jacque, who felt that Toni was the only possible hope that Shanda had that night and Toni was too weak, too selfish, to take that one step that would have saved Shanda—a phone call to police.

Dr. George Nichols, who performed Shanda's autopsy, told Jacque and Steve that Shanda could probably have survived her injuries had she not been set on fire. The fact that Shanda's life could have been saved during any of the seven or eight hours that Toni sat idly by was unforgivable to Jacque.

"Toni was convicted for doing nothing," Jacque said.

"And it was due justice because if she would have done something, Shanda would not have died."

The actions of Toni's father, Clifton Lawrence, who insisted that Toni confess to the police, seem to demonstrate that Toni had been brought up by parents who knew the difference between right and wrong, who knew about social responsibility. What is also apparent is that whatever moral courage Toni learned from her parents was absent that night and morning in January 1992.

Of all the stories written about the murder, articles in the *Chicago Tribune,* the *Los Angeles Times,* the *Advocate* (California's gay and lesbian voice), the *Baltimore Sun,* and many others, the most insightful may have been written by Louisville *Courier-Journal* columnist Jim Adams:

Do you know what people are thinking every time these teenage terrorists appear on the television screen being led from courthouse to jail? They think, "But these girls look so normal."

There is the one whose hair could have been painted by Botticelli, whose wardrobe is the sort compiled only through serious mall time. We're repelled by the horrible crime, and then we're confused by the young and immaculate murderess. And that name—not even a bad novelist would call a heartless villain Melinda Loveless.

Two others cross our living rooms, appearing well treated by life. Laurie Tackett, on the other hand, is the possible exception to the conflict between manner and deed. Her TV face is hard, and old beyond her years.

The teen years as I knew them twenty and twenty-five years ago are long dead. The level of parental control we knew is gone. Twenty-five years ago, I'd never heard of four girls in their midteens who ever actually stayed out all night; even the wildest girls in school had curfews, and no one ever heard them talk the next day about murdering any small children while they were out on the town.

Even the standard of normalcy has changed beyond recognition. As just one sickened newspaper reader, I can barely stand to face one more story about what kids are doing to each other.

Creatures such as Loveless and Tackett aren't made by freak chance, and they aren't made in healthy, loving homes.

What is frightening, therefore, is just how close to normal they may actually be.

Epilogue

~~~~~~~

As the *Courier-Journal* reporter who covered Shanda's murder, I knew all too well what my colleague Jim Adams was feeling. As I researched this book, seeking the answer to the question "Why?" I pored through a labyrinth of interviews, court transcripts, depositions, letters, psychological reports, magazine articles, and books. I never found a satisfying solution to the question, but I did come across two clues that linger with me and may one day help me understand. One was a stream-of-consciousness essay Laurie Tackett wrote while in prison:

PLEASE HEAR WHAT I'M NOT SAYING

Don't be fooled by me. Don't be fooled by the face I wear. For I wear a mask, a thousand masks. Masks that I'm afraid to take off and none of them is me. Pretending is an art that's second nature to me. But don't be fooled. For God's sake don't be fooled. I give you the impression that confidence is my name and coolness my game. That the water's calm and I'm in command and that I need no one. But don't believe me. My surface may seem smooth, but my surface is my mask, ever-varying and ever-concealing. Beneath lies no com-

placence. Beneath lies confusion and fear and alone-
ness. But I hide this. I panic at the thought of my
weakness and fear being exposed. That's why I franti-
cally create a mask to hide behind, a nonchalant,
sophisticated facade to help me pretend, to protect me
from the glance that knows. But such a glance is
precisely my salvation. My only hope and I know it.
That is, if followed by love. It's the only thing that can
liberate me from myself, from my own self-built prison
walls, from the barriers I so painstakingly erect. It's the
only thing that will assure me of what I can't assure
myself. So, I play my game—a mask without, and a
trembling child within. The empty parade of masks. I
tell you everything that's really nothing and nothing of
what's everything, of what's crying within me. Only
you can wipe away from my eyes the blank stare of the
breathing dead. Who am I, you may wonder. I am
someone you know very well. Yourself.

The other piece that puzzles my mind is an essay taken
from the book *Diary*, written by Andrew O'Hagan, an
assistant editor of the *London Review of Books*. Reacting to
the 1992 abduction and murder of a two-year-old boy from
Liverpool, allegedly by two ten-year-old boys, O'Hagan
reminisced about his own childhood endeavors into violence:

The kids who were targeted were thought deviant in
some way—maybe they were serious, bright, quiet,
keeping to themselves. When I was nine, there was a
particular boy who lived two squares up. For years, I'd
listened to boys telling of how they'd love to do him in.
I sort of liked him, but I joined in the chase when we
pursued him in and out of housing projects and across
fields.
    If all this sounds uncommonly horrific, then I can
only say that it did not seem so then. There was no
steady regression toward the juvenile barbarism fa-
mously depicted in the *Lord of the Flies*. We lived two
lives at once. We all made our First Communion, did

our homework and became altar boys. We didn't stop to think, nor did our parents, that something dire might result from the darker of our extracurricular activities. Except when that murky side took over and our bad-bastardness became obvious to everyone. It was scary and competitive, and it brought out the very worst in anybody who had anything to do with it.

It's not that any of us were evil but now and then we got out of hand. The boys I hung with were always losing their heads. What started out as a game of crazy golf would end up as a game of clubbing the neighbor's cat to death. A night of camping could usually be turned into an opportunity for the wrecking of vegetable gardens, or killing frogs and people's pet rabbits. Mindless stuff. Yet now and again people would get into things that you sensed were about to go over the edge or were already over it. Something happened when we were all together. We were competitive, deluded, and full of our own small powers. As only dependents can be, we were full of our own independence. The approval that really mattered was that of the wee pals we ran around with. There are times when I'm sure we could've led one another into just about anything.

The essay ended with O'Hagan's recollection of David, a three-year-old boy from his neighborhood. O'Hagan admitted that he and others would often take sport in roughing up the lad, once beating his legs with a coiled strap. One day David disappeared after being last seen playing on a construction site frequented by O'Hagan and his young cohorts. The boy was never found, and adults assumed that he'd either fallen into a pipe trench and been covered or that he'd been abducted.

"Yet in silent, instinctive ways we understood something of David's other possible end, the one that wasn't an accident," O'Hagan wrote. "We knew something of children's fearful cruelty to children. None of us believed that David was playing alone at that building site that day. As many of us grew older, we came to think it not inconceivable that David had come to grief at the hands of boys not a lot older than himself."

Melinda Loveless, Laurie Tackett, and Hope Rippey are now serving their murder sentences at the Indiana State Women's Prison in Indianapolis. Toni Lawrence, who didn't have the resolve to stop them and who passed up numerous opportunities to summon help or simply just walk away, once again finds herself in the company of killers, for she too is confined at the Indianapolis prison, doing time for her role in confining Shanda.

Each girl has filed an appeal in hopes of having her sentence reduced, but if there are no reductions Toni will walk out of prison in 2002, when she is twenty-five; Hope in 2117, when she is forty; and Melinda and Laurie in 2022. At that time, Melinda will be forty-six, Laurie will be forty-seven.

In February 1994, the last time I saw Steve Sharer, he and his wife, Sharon, were relaxing in their living room—the same room in which they'd last seen Shanda.

Photographs of Shanda hung on the walls, daily reminders of what once was, frozen moments of a securer, happier time.

The passage of months had eased the tension from Steve's face; the iron look of determination he'd worn in the courtroom was gone. Although it was still difficult for him to discuss his daughter's death without breaking into tears, he seemed to finally be at peace with it in his mind.

"I know she's waiting for me in Heaven, so I have to make sure I lead a good life so I can see her again," Steve said.

After Shanda's death Steve and Sharon received dozens of phone calls and letters from parents and youngsters asking for advice for problems they were having, most concerning the peer pressure children face in today's world.

They diligently responded to each inquiry, opening up their hearts with advice that might possibly prevent a reoccurrence of the pain they feel.

"I tell them all the same thing," Steve said. "I tell parents to listen to their children and children to listen to their parents. It's a simple message, but sometimes we forget it."

Forgetting is not something that Steve and Sharon have the luxury to do anymore.

"I have a little ritual I go through every morning when I leave for work," Steve said. "I look at the picture of Shanda that I keep on my dashboard. I kiss my fingertips, then touch her face and tell her that I love her."

My last visit with Jacque Vaught was around the same time. In the months after Shanda's death, Jacque, who had spoken so eloquently during the sentencing hearings, received numerous invitations to speak to parents and students at local schools.

After seeing the effect her words had on adults and youngsters, the speaking engagements became her passion, her way of dealing with Shanda's death. She and Sandra Graves, the grief counselor who helped her recover from depression after the murder, formed an organization called "No Silence About Violence," in hopes that it will one day have the same sort of widespread effect that Mothers Against Drunk Drivers has had in raising awareness of the destruction done by intoxicated motorists.

By early 1994, Jacque had spoken at dozens of area schools and expanded her horizons, accepting invitations to speak in cities around the country, most recently in St. Louis and Seattle.

She begins each speaking engagement by relating the events that led to Shanda's abduction and grimly leads her audience down the dark path that ends with Shanda's fiery death, sparing no grisly details. Jacque then looks parents straight in the eyes and tells them that they shouldn't try to be their children's friends.

"They have enough friends," she says. "You be a parent. You watch who they run around with. And you, with no uncertainty, step in when you think they are running with the wrong crowd."

To children she says, "Remember what happened to Shanda. Don't you ever forget it. It could happen to you or to your friends. Shanda's friends never thought it could happen. Neither did Shanda. Neither did I."

The effect on listeners is palpable. Parents cry and children come up afterward and hug Jacque.

"I know some people question why I'm doing this and why I don't put my daughter to rest," Jacque said. "Maybe most people would react that way, try to put what happened out of their mind. But I could never do that. If the lesson of Shanda's death can save one other life, it's been worth it."

As Jacque talked, her eleven-month-old granddaughter, Aspin, grabbed the edge of the living-room couch and shakily pulled herself to her feet. Jacque leaned over and asked Aspin, "Where's Shanda, where's Aunt Shanda?"

The toddler turned and pointed toward the shadow boxes that hung on the wall, the glass cases filled with photographs and mementos of Shanda's life.

"I can't tell whether she's pointing to Shanda's picture or to Heaven," Jacque said, pulling Aspin onto her lap and hugging the infant closer to her chest.